BLOOD OVER WATER

DAVID LIVINGSTON studied for a BA in Biological Sciences at Christ Church, Oxford, and then stayed for a further year to complete an MSc in Management Research at the Saïd Business School. Since leaving university he has represented Great Britain at rowing on a number of occasions. He currently works as an investment analyst at a private wealth management firm.

JAMES LIVINGSTON went to Cambridge to read Natural Sciences, after which he completed a one-year management course. He has rowed at a number of World Championships at senior and under-23 level and attended the Athens Olympics as part of Team GB. He now lives in London and works in venture capital, investing in rapidly growing technology companies.

BLOOD OVER WATER
David and James Livingston

B L O O M S B U R Y
LONDON • NEW DELHI • NEW YORK • SYDNEY

First published in Great Britain 2009

This paperback edition published 2010

Copyright © by David and James Livingston 2009

Map and diagram © John Gilkes

Bloomsbury Publishing Plc
50 Bedford Square
London WC1B 3DP

www.bloomsbury.com

Bloomsbury Publishing, London, New Delhi, New York and Sydney

A CIP catalogue record for this book is available from the British Library

ISBN 978 1 4088 0119 2

10 9 8 7 6 5 4 3

Typeset by Hewer Text UK Ltd, Edinburgh
Printed and bound in Great Britain by CPI (UK) Ltd, Croydon CR0 4YY

For Mum and Dad

Contents

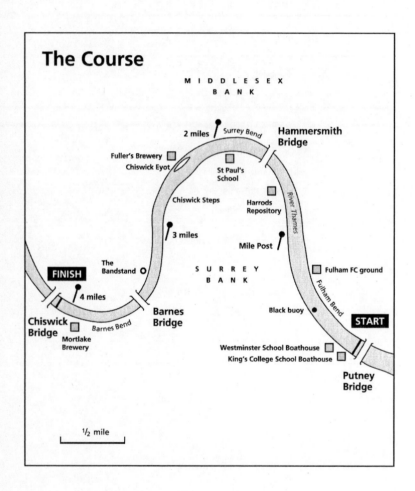

The Course

MIDDLESEX
BANK

2 miles Surrey Bend

**Hammersmith
Bridge**

Fuller's Brewery
Chiswick Eyot

St Paul's
School

Chiswick Steps

Harrods
Repository

River Thames

3 miles

Mile Post

The
Bandstand

SURREY
BANK

Fulham FC ground

FINISH

4 miles

**Chiswick
Bridge**

Barnes Bend

Mortlake
Brewery

**Barnes
Bridge**

Black buoy

Fulham Bend

START

Westminster School Boathouse
King's College School Boathouse

**Putney
Bridge**

½ mile

Introduction

It is an annual four-and-a-quarter-mile rowing race from Putney to Mortlake on the river Thames between two of the most prestigious universities in the world, Oxford and Cambridge. The competitors train twice a day, six days a week, striving to achieve their goal of representing their universities. Everything else in their lives becomes secondary. It is not done for money but for honour and the hope of victory. There is no second place, as second is last. They call it simply The Boat Race.

Prologue

James:

'Come on, Dave, we'll miss it!'

Cycling through Richmond Park, my rangy, blond fifteen-year-old brother, riding a hand-me-down bike that is patently too small for his long legs, puts on a spurt of effort to catch up with me and our friends Matt and Ben.

Two sets of brothers, we whizz out of the park, down Roehampton Lane and across the green into Putney, regularly checking our watches. It's a glorious sunny day in the school holidays and we're excited. Squeezing on to the embankment through packed crowds, about half a mile up from Putney Bridge, we peer expectantly downriver. Our heroes are lining up. A helicopter passes overhead, following our line of sight.

'What time do you make it, Smithy?' I ask.

Matt checks his watch again. 'They should be starting any minute now.'

On cue a roar goes up, rising like high-pitched thunder. We've got to get to the front. We push through the crowd until the front wheels of our bikes are almost hanging over the river, craning our necks to see upstream.

'Here they come!' shouts Matt, as two boats edge into view around the curve in the river. They close rapidly on our position, borne by the tide and the efforts of the oarsmen. Our part of the bank erupts.

'Come on, Cambridge!' I shout.

'Go, Oxford!' screams Matt.

'Cambridge!' shouts Dave.

The crews draw level with us. We pull our bikes away from the river's edge and start to cycle manically along the bank, weaving through the packed crowd.

'Coming through!'

'Watch out!'

Cycling at breakneck pace, we almost keep up with the crews, our eyes snapping back and forth from the people on the bank ahead of us to the combatants. Oxford are beginning to struggle and their fear and growing desperation are evident, even to us on bikes a hundred feet away. Cambridge look invincible and their strokeman, who we know is a massive German called Tim Wooge, appears magically unconcerned by the competition.

'Cambridge!' we Livingstons yell happily.

'Oxford!' Matt shouts stubbornly, even though, despite their best efforts, the crew is continuing to fall behind. Ben is happy just to watch. We are all in awe of those on the water, so perfectly synchronised, keeping up such an impossible tempo.

At Hammersmith Bridge, when the thickness of the crowd becomes impossible, we pull our bikes to a halt and watch until the boats move out of sight, Cambridge comfortably in the lead.

We turn to each other, laugh at the madness of a race so long, and begin the ride home.

Part I

'It is not the critic who counts . . . The credit belongs to the man who is actually in the arena, whose face is marred by dust and sweat and blood . . . If he fails, at least he fails while daring greatly; so that his place shall never be with those cold and timid souls who know neither victory nor defeat.'

Theodore Roosevelt, 'Citizenship in a Republic'
Paris, 23 April 1910

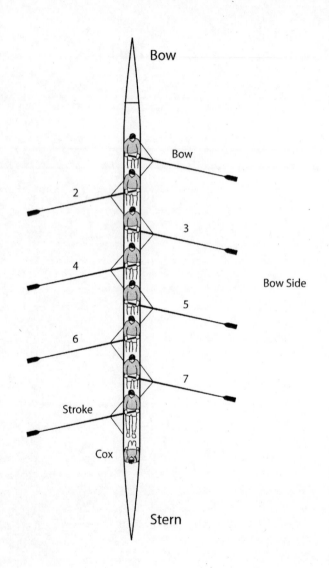

Bow

Bow

2

3

Stroke Side

4

Bow Side

5

6

7

Stroke

Cox

Stern

Chapter 1
Tears and Joy

James:
Saturday 30 March 16:03, Putney Bridge

The murky water of the Thames swirls quickly under the boat, the rising tide curling into eddies and ripples around our hull and oars. Closing my eyes, I can feel my heart thumping against my ribcage, almost keeping time with the 'thunk, thunk, thunk, thunk' of the blades of the helicopter hovering above us. The chopper seems dark and oppressive, a malevolent presence; its down draught pressing upon us, its cameras locked on.

God, don't fuck this up.

'Get straight, both crews.' The umpire's loudhailer breaks my trance.

Ellie's voice comes through the boat's speaker system, strong, clear and full of nervous energy.

'Hold it, Sam!'

Sam, the American rowing international sitting behind me, squares his oar face into the water and the resistance against the tide slews the boat violently round to the right.

'Too much, Sam. Tom, take us back,' Ellie demands, her voice ratcheting upwards a notch, straining to compete with that of the umpire, who is issuing increasingly fraught instructions in the effort to get the two boats aligned. We're already several minutes past race time. The TV slot is ticking away, the sponsors restless.

In the bow seat, Tom, our president, squares up his oar and we swing back to my left. The tide keeps hurrying past us, rushing to fulfil its promise as the highest tide of spring.

I look up at Seb's square back and reach out and grasp his shoulder. 'Let's go for it, mate. With you all the way.'

He turns, grasps my forearm in a grip which betrays his iron strength and nods to me, slowly, almost reverently, before turning back.

He's already competed in two Olympic Games with the German team and is renowned for his machine-like nature in competition. What am I doing here? I haven't been to one Olympics, let alone two!

Don't mess this up.

I'm mortally afraid of losing and even worse, being singled out as the reason for the defeat. My overactive brain trips to a text message of support I received a few days ago from a good friend at college: 'What is our aim? Victory at all costs, victory in spite of terror. Victory, however long and hard the road may be, for without victory there is no survival. You the man.'

Eyes open again, looking above Seb's head; another few feet away is the shaggy hair of Josh, the tallest man ever to row in the Boat Race, another World Championship medallist, for Great Britain this time. Six foot ten.

What am I doing here?

Sixty feet further on is Putney Bridge, packed deep with people waving flags, holding light and dark blue balloons and shouting.

'In the Surrey stakeboat, let them out about a foot,' comes the tense voice from the loudhailer again. The umpire must have been told that the boats are not quite level. I curse under my breath as the Oxford hull slips up past us a little. Every inch is going to be an agonising battle and I develop an instant and irrational hatred of the umpire. He's meant to be a Cambridge man too. Traitor.

I glance to my oar, out to the left of the boat. Looks fine. Beyond the boats, on the Fulham bank, stands the University Stone, the official start line for the race since it moved from Westminster to what was then the quiet country town of Putney in 1845, sixteen years after the inaugural race at Henley. Around the stone are more people, against the backdrop of a vast TV wall, twenty-five feet high. It's showing live BBC coverage of the race. The cameraman is panning along our Cambridge line-up.

Jesus, there I am.

I snap my eyes away, over to the right, and there are Oxford. In their stern, at stroke next to their cox, sits Matt. I could pick his back out a mile off, having had a similar view for years in the school eight. He was one of my best friends. We'd gone through bad haircuts together; discovered girls together, sometimes the same ones (although not at the same time); started rowing together; won and lost together; and grown from boys to young men alongside one another. We'd even played in a rock band together. We were awful. Matt was perhaps the worst bass player ever to hold the instrument and I was no better on the guitar, not that it mattered.

All that history should make it weird, to see one of your best friends lining up to race against you, like watching a friend defect and turn on you in a time of war. But I don't feel anything apart from my heart pounding in my chest. We are not close friends any more. He's gone one way and I've gone another.

Now I could shut him out. He is there to be beaten like the rest of them. The opponent, Oxford.

'The boats are level. Get yourselves straight,' demands the umpire, desperate to get the show on the road.

'My hand is up!' shouts Ellie urgently as her right arm shoots up ramrod straight, the signal to the umpire that we are not yet ready to go. 'Tom, tap it now!' The boat slews again to my left, across the tide, twisting the boat off balance.

Suddenly the umpire's red flag shoots upwards. Shit! We're not ready.

'Attention!' bellows the umpire, as our boat swings around. Can't he see we're not ready? My stomach cramps with apprehension. He can't do this to us. 'GO!'

Ear-splitting screams from the bank rise to deafen us. We dig our oars in against the pull of the current and every muscle strains with the load. The momentum of the boat's swing tilts the hull down to the left and, as our bowside oars pull deeper and deeper, for a horrifying microsecond I think we're going to capsize. The boat lurches to the side, the strokeside oars skimming the surface of the water, firing spray everywhere. While we are stuck in slow motion Oxford launch themselves away with tight, small strokes that feel like jabs to the midsection.

After a fraction of a second that seems like an age, we pull our bowside oars clean of the water and manage to level the boat. Collecting ourselves with tentative strokes, finally we put our foot to the floor in chase. Rick, our World Champion strokeman, takes us up to over fifty strokes a minute, but our wheels are spinning and Oxford are keeping up their high tempo, their cox screaming in elation as they pull ahead.

After 45 seconds we push down into the rhythm that will last us the four-mile course, but almost immediately Tom, at bow, shouts, 'Two-man move!' Lukas, sitting at six in front of Josh, passes the call breathlessly down to Ellie. This is our code phrase to signal that the Oxford cox, in the stern of their boat, is level with our man in the two-seat, sitting nearly at the front of our boat. We must push now or they'll break clear and the race will be over.

'Two-man move on our bend in five,' screams Ellie, struggling to make herself heard over the deafening crowd. We reach the Fulham Bend and the river turns away but Ellie doesn't follow the turn, instead holding her line and pushing Oxford further over to the outside of the bend.

This manoeuvre gets the umpire agitated. He furiously waves his flag, 'Cambridge to Middlesex, Cambridge to Middlesex!'

Ellie ignores him for a few strokes before she flicks the rudder to the right towards Fulham Football Club. 'In two, in one. NOW!'

I steel myself to launch the twenty biggest strokes of my life and from the first stroke I can feel the surge of power as all of us commit our full strength. In front of me, Seb's frame is shaking with the immense force he is sending down. The boat rises like a hydrofoil and takes off. My heart lifts as we pull level with Oxford, who we have forced to take the bend late. We're still in this race!

David:
Saturday 30 March 16:05, Chiswick Bridge

The yells of joy from my Isis crewmates echo back from the stone arches of Chiswick Bridge. The defeated Cambridge reserve team, Goldie, drifts under the arch silently behind us, slumped over their oars. The hulking light-blue torsos of Ben Clare and Alex McGarel-Groves hang over the side of their boat; how had a scrawny fresher like me beaten older, muscle-men like them?

'Three cheers for Goldie!' calls our cox Acer, his voice hoarse from bellowing instructions and pushes during the race. 'Hip, hip . . .'

'Hooray!' we shout back with the gusto of victory.

Each 'Hooray' hits those in the Goldie boat with the hammer blow of failure. It's not meant to be that way. It is meant as a mark of respect for their competition in a great and very close reserve University Boat Race.

In Goldie, those who aren't vomiting or passed out, return a mournful three cheers.

The race between Isis (the Oxford University second eight) and Goldie (the Cambridge University second eight) takes place half an hour before the main race and is made up of those who've narrowly missed out on a prestigious full Blue. For those involved it's every bit as important as the main race; we wear Oxford's dark blue, undergo the same training and the pride and pain of taking part burn just as hard.

The umpire raises his white flag, signalling a fair race. Our victory is officially sealed. I clench my right fist in joy and punch the air. Despite having missed out on a place in the first boat, the taste of victory is just as sweet as I'd imagined it would be.

'Bow four, ready, row.' Under Acer's command our boat slips slowly towards the stony shore of the Mortlake Boat Club, listing from side to side as the wash from the following launches moves beneath us. The banks are lined with thousands of people, here to watch the main race. I can pretend.

Reevo, our bowman, launches himself into the bracing water, impatient to get to the shore and begin the celebrations. I rip my feet out of the shoes and immerse them in the grey Thames water, stumbling awkwardly up the bank. 'Well done, mate,' I muster between breaths, giving John Adams a sweaty and tired hug. A beaming smile illuminates his ghostly white face, his blood still pumping around his heart and muscles. The ecstasy of victory is hard to hide and the physical pain endured is almost forgotten.

I'd imagined this scene all year: the euphoria of a win against Cambridge – mission accomplished! After striving every day for tiny, incremental improvements the feeling of contentment is a new one. Hutchy grabs me. 'Yeah, Livingston. Great job!' he screams, his gleaming-white, all-American smile on full display.

'We did it, we bloody did it,' I reply, dazed, patting my friend on the back. The adrenalin begins to trickle away and I realise that I've barely enough power in my legs to remain standing.

Acer, the only one with energy to spare, jumps at me and I catch him, scooping him easily clear of the ground, his bare feet dangling in the air. 'Yeah, Dave, we did it! We fucking did it!' he screams jubilantly, his wide eyes telling the tale of how much he'd wanted this win. He'd performed perfectly today, his calls clear and decisive.

'Wahheeeyy.' A cork flies over my head, arcing towards the river and spraying sticky fizz over our joyous group. Wiping the stinging champagne from my eyes, I see Nick, one of our coaches, carrying a foaming Nebuchadnezzar of Veuve Clicquot.

'Well done, Dave! Great job,' says Nick in his gruff voice while shaking my hand. 'Now get some of this down you,' he says, handing me the huge fifteen-litre bottle. Using both hands, I raise it to my parched lips and as I do so I feel it tipped up from the other end. I have no choice but to gulp down the liquid.

When I can drink no more and it's cascading down my face, I lower the neck. 'We couldn't have done it without you and Jonny, thank you, Nick.'

'Henry, now it's your turn,' says Nick, referring to my schooldays' rowing rival but now close friend. I plonk the hefty bottle into Henry's arms. No doubt his extensive female fan base will be eager to see the good-looking charmer tonight.

The triumphant scene continues with more champagne drinking, embraces and smiles, and ends with the crew throwing Acer into the river. Lost in our little celebration at the finish line, at first we don't hear Nick shouting, 'The Boat Race has already started, boys!'

We rush up the concrete stairs of the boathouse and squeeze into the already crowded bar. Hundreds of eyes are fixed on the tiny television set mounted in the corner of the room. Matt Pinsent's voice booms out of the straining speakers, 'Oxford were in a great position two minutes ago, three quarters of a boat length up. Now that advantage has gone. What is still in their favour is the Surrey Bend but it looks pretty ominous for the Oxford crew. Cambridge seem to be holding their speed out in front.'

The light blues of Cambridge have a slight lead as they come up to the Harrods Repository; the added confidence of their lead seems to be pushing them on. The camera zooms in on the Oxford boat. Matt, at stroke, is gritting his teeth and getting in more strokes than his Cambridge opposition; he knows he's going to have to work incredibly hard to benefit from Oxford's approaching advantage of the inside of the Surrey Bend.

'Come on, Cambridge!' a supporter shouts from behind me, 'OXXF-FOORRDDD!' my Isis crewmates chant back and I join in with the end of the shout. I've trained all year with the men in the Blue Boat and I'd hate to see them lose; the Oxford University rowers are my closest friends. I know they'll hold on for grim death. Then the BBC cuts to the side-on perspective and I can see James rowing powerfully, mouth agape, searching for breath like a goldfish. He sits behind the invincible Sebastian Mayer, who looks as though he's putting down some strong strokes. If James wins I'll be happy for him, despite a likely onset of feverish jealousy.

The race continues to unfold but I can barely watch the screen. I'm excited for my brother yet I wear the dark blue of Oxford. Who should I support? I can't bear to see either lose. The light blue Cambridge crew flies under the Hammersmith Bridge, half a boat length ahead on the outside of the long meandering Surrey Bend. Oxford will have the advantage of the inside for the next few minutes. I swell with pride for my brother; he's rowing excellently.

'Come on, James,' I say under my breath, not loud enough for my crewmates to hear.

James:

Saturday 30 March 16:16, The Bandstand

I'm feeling invincible. I think we can win this. We have just held Oxford on the huge Surrey Bend; everything they have thrown at us we have pushed back. We are half a boat length ahead. In my seat towards the Cambridge bows, I am well clear of their boat and can sense them beginning to struggle as they run out of river.

The astonishing agony which had built over the previous ten minutes is subsiding a little as we bide our time, letting Oxford spend themselves, like waves striking a rocky shore. We wait for the final bend to turn in our favour so we can deliver the killer blow.

Passing the Bandstand to our left, another marker on the Boat Race course, I revel in each stroke that brings us closer to the finish. Seb has been pulling his heart out, stroke after stroke, and I'm even more in awe of him now than I was when I started the race: he's a hero. His head is beginning to drop a little, but we are all exhausted and there are just a few minutes left.

'Head up, Seb,' I reassure him breathlessly. 'We can do this, mate. Head up. Breathe.'

The boats shoot together under the dark metallic arch of Barnes

Bridge. Oxford are not going to make this easy for us, as expected, but I can feel a growing confidence in our crew. We know the bend is with us and that Rick, our strokeman, had led his Great Britain four to gold at the World Championships for the last two years with a phenomenal final sprint. No one is coming past us.

But a few more strokes on and Seb's head begins to drop further upon his chest and I see his oar flail a little wildly.

'Seb, breathe! We have this.' My confidence starts to slip away. He doesn't even register my calls. To my horror I realise he is beyond the comprehension of speech.

Numbed, I hear Ellie call for the final sprint. This is what we've been waiting for, the moment to finally crush Oxford. We launch ourselves at it but as the men in the stern try to lift the tempo for the final push, it feels as though we have got the handbrake on. Somehow Seb is pushing harder and harder, but his head is dropping further and further.

God, no, please!

'Seb! Please, breathe. Breathe!' I plead. He keeps pushing himself. He is on the verge of passing out. His brain is shutting his body down to let it get enough oxygen. I can see the end of his blade waving uncontrolled and uncoordinated in the air, going in late every stroke to little effect.

Two hundred yards to go and Oxford can smell blood. Their cox can see the disaster unfolding in our boat and soon they are on us like ravenous dogs. They pull level with us. This can't be happening.

'This is it, Cambridge! Twenty strokes. Everything!' Ellie screams but it is too late. Seb crumples in front of me. He has blacked out and all but stops moving. My heart freezes; I know what this means and I feel gut-wrenchingly sick. Now he isn't rowing in sync my oar slams into his back each time I come forward to take a desperate stroke. My oar handle rams into his kidneys again and again and I shout at him, beg him, but he is unconscious. We are rowing with seven and a dead weight.

The rest of my crew realise something has gone horribly, disastrously wrong. I can't row effectively with Seb passed out at my feet and, perversely, I begin to catch my breath when I'd most dearly love to be spending it.

When I see big Josh turn his head round to the left, desperate for the relief of the finishing post, rather than to the right to see where Oxford are, I know all is lost.

David:

Saturday 30 March 16:19, Mortlake, Anglian and Alpha Boathouse, Chiswick Bridge

'Oxford are going to win this,' says the TV commentator, as the crews sprint for the finishing line. The race is so close that the bar is hushed in disbelief.

Zoning out from our collective trance, we rush out of the bar and on to the crowded balcony to get a glimpse of the final strokes to the finish line beyond the arches of Chiswick Bridge. As the crews near, the banks erupt with a wave of noisy excitement.

Oxford come through the line first, and throw their arms up, punching the air in victory, hollering and splashing just like us half an hour ago. Cambridge are slumped forward, exhausted and disappointed with their efforts. Oxford have done it! We rush down the stairs and on to the shore to cheer our boys in and start the celebrations. Both races won, such a great day for Oxford University!

'Yeah, Oxford!' screams the bear-like Hutch, as the Blues row slowly towards us, still letting out whoops of joy. It feels surreal; the fleeting moments our team have prepared for all year have just passed. Seeing my teammates' victory strengthens my resolve to come back next year: I want to be in that boat. Then, beyond the victorious Oxford crew, Cambridge drift into view. The contrast is stark. They are sullen, dejected and shattered. There is James slumped over his oar, Sebastian Mayer lies back in his lap. The brutality of this race shakes me. But that is what makes it what it is. Poor James will be inconsolable. He has committed himself for three years to win this race. It's been his dream and now it's over.

I hear splashing and turn back to see my crewmates running into the water to congratulate the Blue Boat as they come ashore. I run to join them. We have forged great friendships over the past nine months, training day in and day out with each other. We are a close team, almost brothers.

'You did it, mate, you did it!' I tell a stunned-looking Matt, sitting at stroke. The party begins in earnest on the shore with the two Oxford crews, coaches, family and support staff.

A few minutes later I break away from the celebrations as I notice Cambridge paddle into the bank silently. The desolation is almost too painful to watch. James stumbles out of the boat and takes a few uneasy steps up the bank before his legs give out beneath him and he falls to the ground. Sitting up on the gravel, he turns to face the river, and places his head in his hands.

After giving him a few moments to gather his thoughts, I approach to console him. Crouching behind him, I gently place my right hand on his back. Seeing me, he manages to stand but keeps looking at the ground. The tears stream down his face. He embraces me tightly and cries on my shoulder.

'At least one Livingston won today,' he gets out between tears. All the training and effort has been for nothing. The race is black and white, winners and losers, first and last, and James has lost his final chance of victory. I have never seen my brother this upset; I don't know if he will ever recover.

In the no man's land between the jubilation of Oxford and the desolation of Cambridge we stand, James and I, one in light blue, the other in dark blue. Over James's shoulder I see his crewmate Seb being carried away, arms over the shoulders of the Cambridge coaches, his feet dragging. They are taking him to the ambulance.

Part II

'During their college years the oarsmen put in terribly long hours, often showing up at the boathouse at 6:00am for pre-class practices. Both physically and psychologically, they were separated from their class-mates. Events that seemed earth-shattering to them – for example, who was demoted from the varsity to the junior varsity – went almost unnoticed by the rest of the students. In many ways they were like combat veterans coming back from a small, bitter and distant war, able to talk only to other veterans.'

From *The Amateurs* by David Halberstam

Chapter 2
A Vow to Return

2002

James:

Thursday 9 May 19:47, St Catharine's College library, Cambridge

Silence blankets the library. The desk I've monopolised with my girlfriend Sam for the last few weeks is awash with papers, notes, books and pens. An inch-high plasticine man stands next to an inexpertly made plasticine penis on the desk corner. It looks like he might be swept away by a torrent of literature. Post-it notes climb the partition in front of me like square yellow ivy. My copies of *Behavioural Ecology* and *The Open Ocean*, the latter by the appropriately named Professor Herring, nestle along with Sam's thick, leather-bound legal books. Every time I see her lifting one of the tomes to research a particular case I think to myself, 'It could be worse. I could have done law.' She seems far too beautiful for such a dry subject.

I start to gaze round the library again, unable to focus. In the far corner a slim, dark-haired student lifts his ruler to underline something in his notes before taking a controlled swig from his water bottle. Known to the rest of us as 'The Machine', he hasn't been seen out of the library for weeks. No matter how early you arrive or how late you crawl to bed after a night's Red-Bull-fuelled cramming, The Machine is there, reading, writing and ticking things off his lists with infuriating care.

Only nineteen days to my final exams at Cambridge, the last of my three years. Unlike many other universities, at Cambridge it is only your final year's grade that counts. As long as you don't fail and get 'sent down', you can do more or less what you like in your first two years. That was great news to start with but now we're reaching the business end of the third year the nerves are starting to mount. With no marks in the bank at all, there is an awful lot staked on one week in June. If I don't get that 2:1 then it's likely the management consultancy firm I have a contract with will not take me on and I'll have to spend months back home struggling to find another job. More importantly I'll have wasted the priceless opportunity of studying at one of the world's greatest academic institutions.

Since the race I've thrown myself into catching up on my academic studies. It has been a huge uphill battle. No matter how much I read, note and photocopy, I still can't begin to answer many of the previous year's exam questions. It was only after one particular in-depth discussion with my classmate Hannah, who has been the saviour of my degree over the last three years, that I discovered I've missed an entire lecture course on physiological adaptation. It took place on Tuesday afternoons, when I was away rowing. Cue more frantic photocopying of notes and speed reading.

Despite the frustrations and the building pressure, I'm actually enjoying my time in the library. I am seeing much more of Sam, my wonderful girlfriend, who's been so supportive after the defeat, and also more of my other college friends. It's great to be with them again. I'm glad I turned down the invitation to race at the Great Britain under-23 trials. Academically it would have been impossible and it's good to have time for people again.

The library also allows me plenty of peace to reflect and daydream about the race. The initial shock of losing the biggest race of my life in such a cruel manner quickly turned to anger at the unfairness of it all, followed by a long period of self-doubt, before settling into the dull ache of chronic disappointment. Some members of the crew had initially blamed Seb for the defeat but I found myself so impressed by his mental strength – a mind so strong it could drive his superbly trained Olympian body to blackout – that I admired him more now than before the race. Anyhow, it was hard to criticise a man who had so clearly pushed himself harder than anyone. It cemented just how physically challenging the Boat Race is; it isn't the normal 2,000 metre distance raced at the Olympics, but four and a quarter miles, over three times as long. Whether he'd been ill, hadn't paced it right or simply pushed too hard, it didn't matter now.

Still, the unfairness of the defeat kept biting and the more it bit, the more I thought about coming back for a final, ultimate roll of the dice. The issue being that I had only weeks left of my degree. I needed to find another course. One thing was for sure, it wasn't going to be further work in biological sciences. The beauty and completeness of Darwin's great idea was clear and my curiosity satiated. Besides, I'm terrible at lab work and lack the necessary patience for lengthy research.

I'd spoken to a few college friends who had decided to follow their third year with a one-year management studies degree. It is possible to undertake this as a fourth year and remain an undergraduate, thereby avoiding the painful graduate fees. I'd always enjoyed economics at school and as I'd decided to start my career in strategy consulting it seemed a perfect match. It also had the bonus of being rowing-friendly, not involving hours of lab work in the afternoons.

I imagine finally lifting the trophy. Three years already spent in its pursuit. In forty years, would I regret another chance, another year at university? I doubt it.

Yes, I'm decided. I will put my life and career on hold and come back for a final year in a last desperate attempt at a Boat Race victory.

A few days later, as I submit my application, it strikes me that Dave will still be at Oxford. He will undoubtedly be striving for his place in their Blue Boat. If Dave makes it, I cannot let him stand in my way.

David:
Friday 17 May 19:25, Christ Church, Oxford

Maria and I sit on the window bench in the corner of my college room, absorbed in the view over the small quad below. Enclosing the squares of perfectly kept grass are neat sandstone walls bearing chalk inscriptions of college sporting accolades. The sun is just beginning to disappear behind the college ramparts. A student rushes out of one of the staircases and beetles across the quad at speed. Probably late for a tutorial; the weekly one-on-one academic meeting with the college tutor.

Noticing the fading light, I glance down at my watch. 'Shit! Is that the time? Maria, I'm so sorry. I'm already over an hour late, I was meant to be there at six. I've got to go,' I lean in and kiss her before hurriedly rushing over to my wardrobe and burrowing through the contents.

'I'm sure they won't mind,' she replies, unhurriedly.

'Yeah, right. There are penalty drinks for lateness. One pint downed for every fifteen minutes past the allotted time of arrival.' I drag off my

T-shirt and grab my Oxford University Boat Club bowling shirt from its hanger and pull it on, one of the more random pieces of 'stash' we've been given by the boat club during the season and mandatory wear for our drinks tonight. More drinking fines would result without it.

'And besides, I haven't seen the guys much recently. I've been stuck in the library.'

Maria gives me a look of annoyance mixed with disbelief; she knows I've spent hour upon hour with these guys this year and certainly more time than I've spent with her.

'I'm sorry,' I say. 'We'll see lots more of each other this summer.' Depressingly, I know this to be another hollow promise, like so many that oarsmen give to their girlfriends. My first-year exams are coming up and I plan to race at Henley Royal Regatta – priorities, although not necessarily in this order.

The locked doors of the other student rooms in the corridor suggest that they're not in. I've barely seen my neighbour Alex all year. In fact about the only time that our lives have overlapped has been when I've returned mid-morning, having already done one rowing session and attended my morning's lectures. I'd run into him in the corridor in his dressing gown on the way to his 'morning' shower at around noon. Lucky bugger, I usually thought, as I dragged my drenched, tired body past him.

We descend the staircase, head out into the mini quadrangle and illegally cross the grass. Strolling past the college library, I think of James, slaving away for his finals in some dull, dark Cambridge library. The parents mentioned he's applying to come back for one final year, to have one final Boat Race. He must really want it. I'd happily assumed the parents would just be supporting Oxford – me – next year. He's had his turn, surely it's my chance now? Still, if I get the opportunity I'll be ready to race him.

Maria's car is parked, if you could call it that, just up the road, and we reach it quickly. She turns to face me, glancing up at me with her hazel brown eyes. She looks stunning. On tiptoes, she reaches up to kiss me for a few moments. I embrace her. What on earth am I doing? She's such a great girl, I should be spending tonight with her. Although we've only been on a few dates since we met at Reevo's twenty-first a couple of months ago – Reevo's father pushed us, in full black tie, into his swimming pool together: a perfect ice breaker – I think this could be the start of something serious. We seem to fit together; she's smart, chatty, and importantly, given my shameful shallowness, beautiful. It's true, she can't park, has really awful navigational skills, and once asked me what the capital of Amsterdam was, but that just endears her to me. We've decided to try to keep things going when she goes to Bristol University later this year.

'Bye, see you soon,' she says. She opens the door and gets into the driver's seat. I'll see her at Henley Royal Regatta in a few weeks' time, once she's back from holidays.

I linger for a few more seconds to watch her go. The distinctive yellow Polo reaches the end of the street and she beeps twice before turning right and going out of sight.

I look at my watch again. I am an hour and 59 minutes late. Bloody hell, technically that's seven penalty drinks. Hopefully they won't enforce it. I rush back to the college underground bike park and get out my hunk-of-junk bike. It creaks and clicks as I wheel it up the slope. I whizz down Merton Street, handlebars and arms juddering over the cobbled stones. I cycle past University College and at the end turn the corner that takes me past the gothically ominous Examination Schools where everyone sits their University exams. Turning out on to the High Street I then shoot down towards South Oxford. Crossing Magdalen Bridge, pulling into the right-hand lane and around the roundabout, I step hard on the pedals. I continue up Iffley Road and then I take my final left.

My brakes squeal as I slam them on hard outside the Oxford Blue pub, alerting the guys sitting outside to my presence. I feverishly lock up. There they are, all proudly sporting their bowling shirts. Nick Tuppen, the first to see me, begins a roaring 'Ooohhhh . . .' which the others build into.

'What time do you call this, Livingbone?' slurs Angus Warner as I approach.

Reevo, always keen to make sure people have been properly fined, stands up from his seat. 'That's NINE penalty pints!' he declares proudly.

The group laugh at the severity of the fine, *Schadenfreude* painted all over their faces. Instead of engaging them in a plea of mitigation I raise my hands to acknowledge the fine and yank open the doors of the pub, hoping to get away with a few quickly drained beers by way of penalty. As the doors swing shut behind me I hear the familiar drinking song starting up outside:

'Here's to Reevo, he's true blue,
He's a piss pot through and through,
He's a bastard so they say,
He tried to go to Heaven but he went the other way.
Drink it down . . . down . . .'

Inside, it is a lot more serene; 'Brown Sugar' by the Rolling Stones rumbles out of the speakers on the other side of the bar, and there are various other people, non-OUBC rowers, or 'civilians' as they are sometimes known to us, playing pool or having quiet drinks, no doubt trying to avoid the roaring lunatics outside.

'Hi, Dave, I'll help you with this one,' offers Nick O'Grady, who's followed me into the bar. 'I'm going to let you commute it.' Nick leans over the bar, ready to give the order to Rodney the landlord. Commuting means I get spirits rather than beer – helping me get to my destination quicker.

'Nine vodka shots in a pint glass please, Rodney.' Rodney the barman raises his eyebrows but then picks up a pint glass and starts to pour the vodka shots. As each one hits the bottom of the glass I feel ever more daunted.

'Come on, Nick, there's no way,' I protest. 'I've got Henley and prelims.'

'Come on, Dave, them's the rules,' says Nick rather unforgivingly, his swagger already a sign of his inebriation.

I take a few seconds to myself. Live by the sword, die by the sword, I guess. 'Bugger it. I'll do it!' I exclaim, slapping my hand down on the bar, convincing myself as much as Nick. If I can't drink in the off-season then when can I?

Rodney slips the half pint of clear liquid over the wooden bar top. 'That's £27, please,' he says. I look round for Nick but he's disappeared. I spot him further along the bar, suddenly deep in conversation. Rodney looks at me expectantly. Reluctantly, I hand over my battered debit card. Paying for my own demise; how masochistic.

Outside the guys are joshing furiously with each other.

'Ok, boys,' I announce. 'My penalty, using vodka', and I raise the alcoholic time bomb in my hand. They laugh, initially in disbelief. Then the chanting starts.

James:

Friday 21 June 19:45, Strawberry Hill, Twickenham

A distant jangling of keys and scraping of feet on the mat outside announces Dad's arrival. The evening feels warmly complete. We're all here now. I hear the front door firmly shut and Dad shouts his cheery greetings as Mum comes down the stairs, having changed after work. Both enter the pine kitchen where David and I are trying our hand at cooking for our parents, returning the favour of twenty years or so. I'm looking after bubbling pans while David lays the table. We restrain Mum from trying to help and Dad pours large glasses of wine for them both before they sit down and we all talk about our day. It's great being back together as a family.

We're interrupted by a meowing from the garden. Dave opens the back door to let in the cat, who immediately leaps on to the dining table and trails his tail through Dave's soup. Mum deals with the errant feline.

'So any news from the holiday two?' Dad asks. 'Tough day, was it? Up around twelve and getting into some serious lounging round after lunch?'

'John!' says Mum protectively, 'You know the boys are training hard for Henley.'

In fact, we'd spent most of the day moving out of our respective university rooms and getting ready to move up to Henley.

'Well, actually I did get some news,' I reply, tending to the carrots, 'I got on to the management course. I can avoid the real world for another year!'

'Oh congratulations! This calls for more wine!' Dad smiles.

'Well done, James,' says Mum.

'Another Boat Race then? Fantastic,' Dad continues. 'And of course you'll be up at Oxford, Dave. Could you both make the Blue Boat?'

'Maybe, depends on who turns up this year,' Dave says a little quietly.

'Have there been brothers race each other before?' Dad asks. Dave and I look at each other and shrug.

'I don't know, not that I know of,' I reply.

'Imagine the press! How exciting.'

Mum looks a little less excited; if anything, quite apprehensive.

Blood Over Water

David:

I jog off through the boat tents towards the changing rooms, desperate for my final pee. I've been sipping water all day to make sure I'm hydrated enough for the race this afternoon. The marquees are now almost completely empty of crews, coaches and boats. It's semi-final day at Henley Royal Regatta, with only four crews left in each event. Most have been knocked out and have either gone home or are propping up the Fawley bar, pints of Pimm's in hand, no doubt spinning gallant tales of their push at the quarter-mile marker.

Inside the changing area a few nervous crews wait for their races, most notably the South African Olympic pair of Di Clemente and Cech. In contrast two purple blazer-clad bodies sit slumped in the corner, trying to sleep off last night's revelry. I'm feeling pretty nervous myself, being very conscious that the legendary Boat Race coach Sean Bowden will have his eye on my rowing in the six-seat from the umpire's launch behind. Not only will a good performance put us in the final and give us a shot at winning, but it will be the start of my campaign for one of next year's Blue Boat seats.

Back in the boat bay I squat to the floor, ripping a handful of the plush grass from the ground and rubbing it between my hands. It's been my ritual at this regatta and thus far it's worked. I notice the coffee cup of our resident Dutchman, Big G, under the boat. He'd drink it half an hour before racing so that the caffeine would be in his system by race time. Others have their own rituals which give them that little bit more confidence or comfort, even though deep down we know these have nothing to do with the end result.

Our final preparations completed, we carry our slender, yellow shell out of the huge marquee and on to the landing stages. Taking to the boat, we push off from land and row out into the busy Henley stretch. There's a scary amount of river traffic today, including various slipper launches, punts and skiffs, most with pissed drivers who crawl crabwise along the river. A big cruiser with some Elvis impersonators on deck drives past, halting our warm-up. They belt out a poor version of his classic 'All Shook Up'. It would be funny but we're in race mode and these distractions serve only as annoyances.

Our warm-up begins as we row up the course, boxed in on either side by the wooden booms. Coming alongside the stewards' enclosure, I keep my eyes forward as cheers come from the colourful blazer-wearing crowd. 'Jolly good, Oxford!' shouts one old buffty. We drill through the routine and arrive at the start warmed up and ready to go. Our cox Pete runs through the race plan one more time before falling silent and allowing us our own thoughts. Even though I'm surrounded by others, I find the moment deeply personal.

The umpire's launch comes round the back of Temple Island. I can see Dad's lens focussing in on the crew. Henry touches me on the back. 'Green light, Dave. Let's go for it.'

James:

Saturday 14 September 12:15, somewhere over the Atlantic

Ten of us from the CUBC squad are squeezed sardine-like into the economy flight to Los Angeles. Our pre-season training is to begin on the other side of the world, almost as far from the ancient grandeur of Cambridge and the urban grey of Putney as it is possible to go. Waikato University of Hamilton, New Zealand, have challenged us to race.

This sort of trip isn't unusual in the summer break. Thanks to the iconic status of the Boat Race, and Oxford and Cambridge Universities, there are regular invites to compete in foreign climes. Within recent years we've raced the huge Turks of Boğaziçi University in Istanbul, the smaller Chileans of University Austral on the Calle Calle, Brazilians on the Amazon, South Africans in Cape Town and others closer to home in France, Germany, Poland and Italy.

Our crew is a mix of experienced Cambridge oarsmen, such as newly appointed president Tim Wooge and Goldie oarsmen of last year like Groves and Jon Alexander, as well as a few totally new to the CUBC. We have all been looking forward to the trip immensely, and there is a hyperactivity to our babble in the plane that even the lack of leg-room can't cramp. The summer break has been quiet for many and training alone is a hundred times harder and less enjoyable than training in a squad. It has also not escaped anyone's notice that this is a great opportunity to put in a good early season performance in front of chief coach Robin Williams. In practice, though, this may be hard to achieve given that the organisers have put together a packed itinerary full of extreme sports (zorbing, anyone?) in the run-up to the race. The planned visit to New Zealand's Cambridge Stud also caused much pre-tour jesting about which one of us exactly they are referring to.

After an interminable amount of time we land in the urban sprawl of Los Angeles for a stopover of a couple of hours. 'Let's hit Venice Beach!' I suggest, having been in LA only a few days earlier at the end of a road trip with Sam and some friends. We investigate with the tourist office. The dazzlingly blonde advisor tells us to get cabs and under no circumstances walk, as it would result in a very expensive few minutes and a good insight into the local gang culture.

Half an hour later we are bodyboarding in our boxer shorts under the blazing Californian sun. It's midnight back home but the cool of the water and the adrenalin of being thrown crashing into the sand by the Pacific rollers more than keeps us awake. Everyone is smiling and laughing. It's great to be alive. Hilarious too when we line up for a photo and Groves pulls Ben Clare's boxers down ('debags', to use the technical term) in front of the packed beach. The unfortunate Ben shouts in surprise, turning more heads towards him and his lily-white lower quarters. Groves takes off down the beach, laughing his head off. Ben scrabbles to pull up his boxers and takes off after him, finally catching him and wrestling him into the surf.

Memories of fun on the beach are rapidly eclipsed by the nine-hour flight to Auckland in horrifically damp and sandy underwear. We disembark into the New Zealand dawn with our spirits deflated. The malaise, though, is quickly dispelled when we see sleek black 4 × 4s waiting for us, with 'The Great Race' emblazoned on the back and a long list of sponsors down the side. We are over here for a reason.

Traditionally on these foreign fixtures the 'university' team which Cambridge or Oxford face is made up of the host country's national team, who have all handily signed up for a postal course in water studies or the like at the university. The opposition is often therefore very good. Fair enough, we're a pretty high standard too. The host's trump card, however, is that they are in charge of planning the itinerary. If, after a non-stop round of tourist attractions, numerous drinks functions with local mayors and various other non-rowing and often dangerous activities designed to show the visitors the country, we are, by happy chance, introduced to our boat prior to race day, it is guaranteed to be a twenty-year-old hollowed-out log. Meanwhile the local host team is warming to their newly imported German Empacher, the Ferrari of rowing boats – expensive, fast and flash. By the time race day arrives our crew is nicely tanned, well acquainted with all local eating and drinking customs and expert at white water rafting, but we're each a few pounds heavier, suffering a week-long hangover and are in no condition to row, let alone race. When, finally, the perfectly drilled local crew heave into view on the start line it is tempting to all but admit defeat, quietly give thanks that at least no one you know is out here to see you lose and mentally prepare for the celebration dinner that evening. The Great Race? Perhaps. Perhaps not.

'10, 44, 17. Hut!'

I snap the ball to Wooge, who shuffles backwards, arm poised, while the front rows grapple. Sammy sprints clear into the 'end zone' and the American football arcs through the air, spinning perfectly on its axis to his waiting arms. Wooge's time at college in the USA obviously wasn't only spent rowing.

As soon as we'd dropped our bags on our bunks, Robin had sent us running along the shore of the vast, flat Lake Karapiro. We ran over the soft, rolling hills of North Island, New Zealand, past green fields, cattle and small farms; heaven to stretch our legs in the sun after the flight. We ran carefree, together, chatting over snatched breaths or chanting along after Groves's lead.

On the return leg the pace increased, and our group broke into twos and threes before we each arrived sweating and panting back at the lodge by the lake. We'd rigged the boat lent to us, and while Robin went over the boat inch by inch, tweaking it a fraction here and there, the game of touch American football had started up spontaneously.

The scores are tied. Sammy passes the ball to Wooge. Groves and I pelt across the field and the ball arcs up high once more. My eyes are zeroed in on it as I scrabble to avoid Andy and run to catch the ball, leaping up as it spins down to earth. Too late, I see my 100-kilo teammate Groves in mid-air as well, flying towards me with a grin that freezes as he realises our impending collision.

Crunch. 'Ooommphhh.' The wind is crushed from both of us.

Instantly, I'm horizontal, with my right arm trapped beneath me. Lying with my head on the ground it strikes me that the grass here grows higher here than back home. The shock fades slightly and is replaced by dizziness and pain.

'Shit, sorry, Bungle.' Groves offers me an arm up. 'You all right?'

I sit up. 'Think so, mate. You guys keep going. I'll sit out for a sec,' I say, nodding his offered arm away.

Sitting to the side of the game I watch the boys play while I gulp down air. My shoulder hurts like hell and I feel a little sick too, which is odd. A few minutes later and we're down two touchdowns, the one-man overlap making the difference.

Sammy fires it to Wooge, whose head twitches left and right, desperately looking for a receiver, while Ben 'The Rock' Clare, runs him down.

'Tim!' I scream, and I'm up and running, totally unmarked. The ball goes up high.

Laughing at the cheekiness of the manoeuvre, I lift my arms to receive my prize.

As I raise my right arm there's a nasty 'Crchh.' I stumble to a halt in pain, the ball dropping to the ground. Jesus, that hurts. Must be some tendon. Or a trapped ligament. Damn.

I'm about to announce my retirement from the game when Robin shouts, 'We're not here for rugby, boys. Let's go and earn that flight,' beckoning to the readied boat.

I jog over to him. 'Robin, my shoulder doesn't feel so good.' He's obviously unimpressed; the last thing he wants is an injury when we haven't got a spare man to fill in. An injury before even touching an oar. We only landed five hours ago, for Christ's sake.

Now some New Zealand press are arriving to watch our first session. They start interviewing some of the boys, much impressed by their height. Robin takes my right arm and tugs on it steadily, simulating the pull of the oar when rowing. Pain shoots across my chest.

'How's that?'

'Not great,' I say through gritted teeth, 'but do-able, I think.' It can't be broken. I'll be fine. I can't be hurt.

Robin looks relieved. 'OK, just tap it along at bow this outing, don't put much pressure on it. Let's go, boys!'

'Heads, up!' calls our cox, and we swing the boat above our heads in a businesslike manner. I can't raise my right arm and just support the boat with my left as we walk it to the dock. 'Out and in!' We lower the boat carefully on to the lake, causing me to wince again. I pick up my oar with my left arm and walk back to my position in the bows. This is a bad idea.

As I bend down further to slot my oar into its gate, the agony is extreme. As I stretch for the gate something in my shoulder goes 'chink!' and I cry out with the intense stabbing pain. Tears come to my eyes. I can't be injured. It's just a tendon or something. Don't let it be serious.

'Robin, I'm sorry, I can't do it.'

'OK, go and rest up in the lodge. I'll sub in for this outing and we'll go and get it checked out when we get back.' Robin takes my seat and they row off into the blueness of the lake. I turn and walk solemnly to the lodge, past several confused-looking journalists.

Sitting quietly at our large dining table I explore my collar bone with my fingers. There's a jagged lump which burns red hot when I touch it. Tugging down my T-shirt with my left hand, I see why. A shard of bone is pushing a tent of skin upwards. The skin is stretched white and taut over a sharp point. Oh hell.

By the time the boys return from their twenty-kilometre row darkness has slid across the lake and hills. Robin drives me to hospital, over a road specialising in both speed bumps and potholes. The X-ray is conclusive. A broken collar bone.

As Robin drives us back I reflect on what the doctor has said. Eight to twelve weeks to mend. Wow, I'll be so unfit by then. I might never make the Blue Boat again and never get that second chance.

James:
Saturday 21 September 17:09, New Zealand

A couple of days later I'm reading the *Waikato Times* sports page in the back of the coach. 'Touch of Bad Luck', reads the headline. The New Zealand press are understandably finding the story quite amusing. The Pom who touches down in New Zealand for a rowing race and injures himself within minutes, bumping into a teammate playing touch American football.

On the upside, I have become the media spokesman for the team. While the others got stuck into some training on the vast lake, now with the chief coach installed in the bow seat, I was giving radio and TV interviews, which was good fun.

When I strolled into some of Hamilton's nightspots in my now trademark sling, with selfless members of the team gallantly accompanying an injured friend, everyone seemed to know about the entertaining misfortune. The free drinks generally didn't mix overly well with the painkillers but had a similar effect. Last night we were chatting to a couple of women who found our accents most amusing.

'I'd better get used to it, I'm moving to England soon,' said one.

'Oh, really, why's that?' I replied.

'My husband's work.'

Husband? This was concerning. Whilst neither Sammy nor I had any intention of doing anything more than talking with these girls, both being very much in love with our girlfriends back home, from a jealous husband's perspective, earnest discussion in a nightclub at 2 a.m. might have looked suspicious.

She continued. 'Yes, he's going to play rugby for Leeds.'

Rugby? Professionally?

'Troy, come over here and meet these nice guys from England.'

The immense All Black, Troy Flavell, emerged from the crowd and scowled at us unhappily. It was lucky I was wearing the sling.

Plenty of other dangerous activities also kept us amused. The rest zorbed, jet-boated, bungee-jumped, swooped, tobogganed and caved while I sat by and read about the Tour de France and legendary British cyclist Tommy Simpson. On the notoriously tough Mont Ventoux mountain stage Tommy's delirious last words to nearby spectators before his death were 'Put me back on my bike', having fallen for the penultimate time. I wanted to get back in the boat. But I couldn't: my right arm now sat a good few inches lower than my left and, according to the doctor, the bones would take weeks to even get 'sticky'. So I stepped on the stepper machine, listening to my aged Discman, staring at the wall, climbing God knows how many staircases while the others enjoyed the lake.

The guys each take time out of their other activities to sit with me. The quiet giant Ben sits with me more than most. We talk companionably about old times or just sit and read, enjoying each other's company. He's grown a rather good beard.

The coach pulls up at one of North Island's many beaches. Climbing down from the bus, we stroll along the sand and watch the surfers waiting for the perfect break.

'Let's take a dip boys,' says Sammy, grinning.

There isn't a chorus of agreement. The Tasmanian Sea is lapping icily at our feet, with huge waves crashing further out. Also none of us have any trunks, yet again.

After a moment's more silence Tim says gruffly, 'Are we going to do this thing or what?' With that he throws off his rugby shirt and shorts and runs headlong for the icy sea. There's a cheer from the rest and suddenly they are naked and sprinting for the sea as well.

Knee-deep in the cold water, Robin and I watch and laugh as the others plunge into the waves after Tim. The sight of the six-foot-eight naked German diving into the surf is not one I will soon forget. Tim is clearly going to lead from the front this year in all manner of things.

James:

Tuesday 24 September 21:53, New Zealand

'And now will Cambridge please come to the stage.' One of the organisers of the race, a New Zealand Olympian looking smart in black tie, beckons. I slip on my sling and follow the rest of the crew up to the stage to vigorous applause. The post-race dinner is buzzing, helped by the home side victory this afternoon. We hadn't known the river well enough and our poor understanding of the current and the corners had cost us the race.

Sammy steps up to the microphone. 'We'll go back home with nothing but good words to say. I'm sure Oxford will be very much looking forward to coming here next year.' The organisers have already begun planning a race with our arch rivals.

Sammy continues, 'Just make sure you beat them by more than you beat us.' There is general applause.

'And make sure they play touch rugby,' Sammy finishes as I raise my sling. 'Every single day.'

We leave the stage to raucous laughter. We move on to the 'after party' where the guest of honour, an old Cambridge Blue, now eighty or so and living in New Zealand, officiates at the drinking games. Some of us even have a brief phone conversation with rugby legend Jonah Lomu after one of the PR girls gets talking about her contacts. Sadly, about the only thing I can think of saying is, 'How much do you benchpress?' The answer is an awful lot more than I do, especially right at the moment. Official Cambridge training starts in earnest in ten days. I pray my collar bone will mend fast. Every day will count.

Chapter 3
New Beginnings

David:
Wednesday 25 September 16:03, Iffley Road, Oxford

We stumble through the gym door out into the cool autumn air and on to the Iffley Road running track, where Roger Bannister famously ran the first ever sub-four-minute mile on 6 May 1954. I remember reading a quote of his. 'Doctors and scientists said that breaking the four-minute mile was impossible, that one would die in the attempt. Thus, when I got up from the track after collapsing at the finish line, I figured I was dead.'

As I watch the forty or so ungainly new triallists for this year's Oxford University Boat Race team dragging their hulking bodies around the track, it's clear there is no danger of any record-breaking today. This bunch has turned up hopeful to make the top eight and race Cambridge next April. As the days tick down to the race, most of them will be discarded by the club. There will be ten fewer by the end of next week. With the race more than six months away, the goal is still only a distant dream, with hours of torturous training, racing and testing needed first, on top of the academic work required to keep ourselves part of the university. The competition will only get more intense from here on.

At least I know what to expect this year. It could hardly be as physically tough as the start of last season, when I'd turned up three weeks late to squad training, a wet-behind-the-ears eighteen-year-old 'fresher'. Somewhat foolishly, I'd thought my bronze medal at the Junior World Championships in Germany that summer guaranteed that I would still be in good shape for Oxford, even after a couple of months travelling around Australia on a diet of cheap pies and chips. I was soon proved wrong.

That medal represented the culmination of my schoolboy rowing career and was my proudest achievement. Although out of medal contention for much of the Duisburg course, our eight had surged past the Germans in the last ten strokes and crossed the line inches ahead, punching the water and screaming with joy. The home crowd had sat in silent shock while my brother and parents burst into ecstatic cheers and flag-waving. I had become a relatively big fish in the baby tank – only to be thrown into the deep end the minute I arrived at Oxford.

I was introduced to the notorious weights circuits before I had even unpacked. When I saw the Herculean weights laid out, as if for torture, I was filled with dread.

'Three times round the circuit, with forty reps at each station,' Sean Bowden had declared. My first impression of the coach was of a small, intense-looking figure in his late thirties standing in the doorway of the gym, appraising us with a cool stare. So this was the man whose tough, determined coaching had masterminded a turnaround in the fortunes of Oxford rowing from the dark times in the 1990s, when Robin Williams's light blues seemed invincible. I could see why he was feared as well as hugely respected.

I started at the first weights station. I could barely complete twenty squat repetitions in one go. Others raced past me as I struggled on. By the end of my first circuit I felt horrendous. I staggered outside into the sunshine to escape and found myself bent over and vomiting my breakfast on the grass. Feeling terrible, I pulled my T-shirt up and wiped the worst of it off my mouth. After a few more much needed breaths, I grimly went back into the darkness to continue. By the time I'd finished, the gym was empty. Most had already showered, changed and left when I dragged my destroyed body into the changing room.

Those initial weeks were some of the hardest of my life. Training was brutal: two sessions a day, one in the gym, one on the river. The standard was unbelievable, and I stood in awe of the man-mountains in the club, some of them Olympic athletes almost ten years my senior.

Outside the gym, I struggled with my first taste of independence, away from my doting mother. The stone passages of my vast and ancient sixteenth-century college, Christ Church, echoed with only my footsteps, the academic term proper being still a few days from starting. The quads, towers and cathedral seemed overwhelming, the crenellated college walls claustrophobic.

The only others in the college were the stern porters, who tipped their bowler hats as I passed, a number of priests who seemed to be staying for a convention and the last remaining tourists of summer. At breakfast, lunch and dinner I gorged myself like a starving man in the vast emptiness of the dining hall, alone but for portraits of famous Christ Church graduates, viceroys of India and former prime ministers; ten of the former and thirteen of the latter (more than any other Oxford or Cambridge college) stared down at me from the panelled walls, not helping my feeling of intimidation and insignificance.

I found myself sleeping fourteen hours a night and was aghast at the thought of how I'd cope when the academic term started. My dread was doubled when, to signal the start of the term proper, Sean scheduled a two-kilometre rowing machine or ergo test, the standard by which oarsmen are physically measured on land. At around six minutes of intense pain, this trial was feared and revered, not only as a challenge of strength and endurance but also as a massive mental battle. The immense pain involved seemed to burn deep enough to test the very soul. Underperformance meant being dropped from the team. Christ, my brother had already survived two years of this at Cambridge. If I couldn't deal with two weeks, what was I but a failure?

The day arrived.

'Pick up your handles,' Sean commanded. I gripped my machine handle tightly, took a few last deep breaths and squeezed my eyelids shut, praying for salvation. 'Attention, GO!'

Salvation didn't come. Within a minute, maintaining my pace became difficult and my score began to slip. No matter how hard I drove my burning legs the machine readout stared back impassively, mocking me with a steadily worsening score. The metres ticked down slowly and each second stretched like ten.

Teeth clenched, eyes half shut, I prayed for it to end. Finally I collapsed off the machine, lungs gasping for more air, legs screaming with lactic acid. Coxes quickly scurried up, stepping over my heaving body, and busily scribbled down the cold statistics of my performance.

It took me several minutes to regain some form of consciousness and not many more to realise that my score was poor by my standards and not even close to those Olympians I idolised. By that evening, having spoken to some of the others, I knew I was the worst in the group. By the end of the following day I was sure I'd be cut from the team.

The day after came and went. I waited for the axe to fall. The day after that Sean granted me a stay of execution until the weekend when they could test me on the water. Racing for my place in the team, I battled with all the pride and power I could muster. I destroyed the other lagging hopefuls I was set against, grabbing this tiny life raft while the others sank from trace. I had earned myself some precious time.

Now I'm back for another year. Within the sterile white-washed walls of the gym, adorned only with signs saying 'absolutely no spitting', the row upon row of rowing machines and weights give the uninitiated a clue of what lies ahead.

The thirty or so men against whom I'll be fighting for a place this year sit on the mats and gym apparatus or lean against the walls. Many faces I recognise; survivors from last year's Blue Boat, Robin Bourne-Taylor, or BT as he's known, and Bas Dixon, the stockily built, emotional character, chat in one corner. A number of my old Isis crewmates are also spread around the room. I catch Henry's eye and give him a nod. I haven't seen him since we raced at Henley in the summer. As freshers at Oxford last year we ended up racing in Isis. Now we both desperately want to graduate to the main boat. Henry doesn't look particularly intimidating to those on the lookout for competition, being only a fraction over six foot tall – small for a rower – but he is fantastically skilled at moving a boat and a great racer.

Others are new. Contenders I've already met include Canadian international Scott Frandsen, a preppy Harvard alumnus called Matt Daggett, and Sam McLennan, a softly spoken, barrel-chested Aussie. They are from the three best rowing universities in the States. Surveying the room I am pleased to see that no one else new is wearing national team kit. A classic catch-22 situation: the more international oarsmen that show up, the harder it will be for me to make the Blue Boat, too few and we will be outgunned by Cambridge.

I notice that I don't feel the same out-of-my-depth intimidation this time. I know what we are in for and that I'm in much better shape. By the end of last season the frequent physiological tests and blood sampling proved my system had responded to the training and become vastly improved. Since then I've done more training over the summer break. I've lifted weights with John Adams, another Isis man, and done the odd session with James and of course I've trained for and raced at Henley Royal Regatta.

The room quietens as Sean Bowden and Matt Smith, our newly anointed president and school friend of James's, emerge from the coaches' office. Matt begins to hand out papers. Even without the title he would be a natural leader this year given his experience of three previous Boat Races – two of which he won.

The assembled throng busily digest the training schedule for the next few weeks. I glance up and notice Sean has a wry smile on his face reading people's reactions.

After people have had a chance to read it, Sean turns on the TV, propped on the wooden box in the centre of the gym which we normally use for circuit training. The group shuffles round to see two rowing crews battling it out and Barry Davies's commentary fills the quiet room. It's last year's Boat Race. Instinctively I pick out James, giving it everything he has. I can't help but feel a conflicted stab of pity for him as Oxford take the lead in the last minute of the race. Sean turns down the volume to make a comment.

'This year it's obvious to me that we face quite a challenge from Cambridge. Last year we won but made a lot of mistakes along the way. We let Cambridge get back into the race when we could have finished it early on. We cannot afford mistakes this year. They have a squad brimming with international experience and we must raise our standards once again. We're going to have to be capable of racing at a higher intensity than has ever been seen before in this race. You will all get a fair chance to prove yourselves good enough to make the crew.'

He pauses for emphasis, then continues. 'Oxford University Boat Club has one single ultimate objective: to win the Oxford and Cambridge University Boat Race. Everything else is secondary.'

I nod to myself, making the club's mission my own. To monitor my progress I'll begin to keep a training diary, counting down the days till the race and tracking my progress. I want that shot at the big time. I'm going to put winning this race above all else; above my girlfriend Maria, friends and academia, and even above my brother if it comes to that. I'll do anything, and I mean anything, to win.

James:
Friday 27 September 17:56, Goldie Boathouse, Cambridge

I've walked this path before, each year for the last three years. It has never led me to Boat Race victory. By walking through the door of the Goldie Boathouse, home of Cambridge University Boat Club for the first meeting of the new campaign, I am bound by honour to see the year through with the club. No matter if I miss selection for the first boat, as has happened twice before, or if, through the course of the year, it becomes obvious that Cambridge haven't a hope of victory, I cannot give up. Cannot quit and put energies back into my neglected studies or my student life. Am I throwing one last good year after three bad?

After only a moment my hesitation is overrun by a vision of Cambridge crossing the finish line victorious, my friends raising their arms in triumph and hugging one other, while I stand alone on the bank, a spectator and outsider.

I have already made my decision.

Passing the trophy cabinet on the left, I enter the wood-panelled and overwhelmingly duck-egg blue Captains' Room. The room is smaller than I remember but then this is the busiest it gets all year. Nearly 40 tall, heavily built men fill it with their awkward bulk and low chatter. Dotted between them sit a dozen much smaller individuals of both sexes who will vie for the coxing seats, the disparity making them look like a gaggle of hobbits at a meeting of men. Most are new to me.

I take a breath. I'm home. Heading for one of the few remaining empty seats I salute old friends like Alex McGarel-Groves, Andy Smith, Ben Clare and Jon Alexander, known to everyone simply as JA, and we slip into the easy banter of old comrades. While catching up on summer goings-on I survey the room again and, with a twinge of sadness, confirm that I'm the only returning rower from last year's Blue Boat. Everyone else has finished their degrees or else been banned from rowing by their PhD supervisors. The only other remaining survivor from the crew is Ellie, our blonde cox.

Coming back has been a tough decision for her. Since our race there have been rumblings from the coaching staff that she was at least partly responsible for our defeat. Ellie had been told she'd made a grievous error by not informing the five oarsmen in front of Seb that he was in trouble. It wouldn't have made a blind bit of difference. We were sunk anyway. But that was last year.

'Just us then.' I grimace at Ellie.

'Yeah. Looks like it. Pity about Josh.'

Josh West, the softly spoken biggest man ever to row a Boat Race, still has another few years of work to conclude his epic PhD on chemical erosion in the Himalayas. He is up in the appropriately gigantic mountains now, taking his samples and no doubt spawning a flurry of abominable snowman sightings. He has already competed four times for Cambridge but thanks to Boris Rankov can't add to his tally. Boris, the designated umpire for this year's race, rowed for Oxford a record eight times across the 1980s. A joint agreement between the clubs that no one could row more than four races as an undergraduate, and four as a postgraduate was subsequently reached to deny any one man decades of domination and to persuade the oarsmen to get out into the 'real world' at some point. There wasn't much else jointly agreed upon – the club committees met grudgingly and head coaches snarled at each other under the pretence of professional courtesy. Some time in the past a maximum number of hours' training each week was decided, with the aim of preventing rowing for university 'conflicting with academic commitments'. Handily, the endless hours spent commuting, changing, rigging and stretching weren't recognised.

A hush suddenly descends as the door opens, revealing a vast silhouette highlighted against the brightness of the hallway. Tim Wooge, our colossal German president, ducks his head under the door frame and enters, followed by a wiry, older man, Robin Williams, head coach and ex-lightweight international, who couldn't be more different from his comedian namesake. Both smartly dressed for this important occasion, they take their seats behind the oak table facing out into the room.

'Good evening,' Wooge begins. 'For those of you that don't know me, I am this year's president, Tim Wooge.' Everyone knows who he is. He's something of a Cambridge legend, having stroked the 1999 and 2001 crew to imperious victory. After seeing us lose in 2002 he has come back in the last year of his PhD to help Cambridge return to winning ways. 'On behalf of myself, the coaching staff and the names surrounding me I would like to thank you for your commitment to trial with us this year.'

Names. Everywhere you look in this room are names; glittering words illuminated in gold against the Cambridge blue paint, recording every oarsman who has ever raced in the Boat Race for Cambridge, from 1829 right up to last year. The large walls are entirely covered with over a thousand names, each crew on its own panel. In fact those lucky enough to be in this year's crew will be commemorated on the ceiling. The room is, literally, covered in history.

Robin picks up Tim's thread. 'Each of these names has a story behind it. And behind each name are at least three more men that pushed him on to greater performance. Only eight rowers will make the boat but all of you here today are crucial to Cambridge's success.'

Lifting my eyes I proudly note my own name on one of highest panels and find myself half-grinning, reminiscing about my old crewmates. The smile vanishes when I read the single word at the top of the panel. It simply says, 'Lost'. Nothing on how we were the most powerful Cambridge crew of recent years. No elaboration on how close we were to victory. I seethe with the injustice of it. The panel to the right is empty; this year's result is yet unwritten. I turn back to Robin, whose inspirational speech continues.

'No one's seat is reserved. Right now everyone is equal, regardless of their past performances. Tomorrow it starts counting.' The new arrivals must think they've walked into a re-run of *Top Gun*.

David:

Saturday 28 September 13:34, Cowley, Oxford

Dropping down a couple of gears, I push on up the steep hill, turn right on to Iffley Road, and then immediately dart left down Oxford's back streets until I reach Cowley Road. I park my bike outside the Save the Children charity shop and climb the fire escape stairs behind it, letting myself into the flat I'm dossing in. This is home for the next few days until the start of term, when I will be allowed to move into my new college room, overlooking the college library in Peckwater quad. Cowley feels a world away from the venerable institutions and tweeded dons in the centre of Oxford, but most of my club mates live here, close to the gym, giving them more precious minutes in bed before the early alarm call. This enclave, south-east of town, has sprung up in the last thirty years as the student and immigrant populations have exploded, giving it a constant bohemian buzz.

As I head to the kitchen and prepare a late, post-training breakfast I reflect that despite the earliness in the season there is a great sense of togetherness among the team helped by existing friendships between those who've returned. Nick Tuppen and Bas, both at Pembroke College, share a flat and give their utmost to the cause. Nick was particularly good at squad organisation; he'd even organised a pub golf night last week. He'd had the best charity shop golf outfit I'd ever witnessed. Another cell is in Oriel College, traditionally one of the most successful rowing colleges, where Reevo and Mark Vickers are both studying. They are frowned upon by their tutors but loved by their college compatriots for their sacrifices to beat Cambridge.

Of the new triallists, Sam McLennan, or Macca as he's become known, Brian Romanzo, a fun Princeton alumnus, and Scott have become close friends. They've bonded over a shared ridicule of Oxford, and England more generally.

Another character we're still getting to know is the amazingly named Montana Butsch. His gruff voice has already found a home on Oxford Radio under the stage name 'The Rock Messiah'. I'd learnt more than I wanted to about his latest conquest when I noticed the scratches all over his back in the shower the day before.

Finishing breakfast I pull out my old mobile phone. The battered screen shows no new messages or missed calls. Parents must be running late; they said they'd be here half an hour ago. No surprise there. My father is shockingly unpunctual. Going to visit relatives, we'd often leave around the time we were actually meant to arrive and spend the trip making embarrassed phone calls about traffic and have to enjoy a cold lunch when we arrived.

Thinking of them heading to visit me in Oxford reminds me of family trips to see Great-aunt Beryl, who lived on the west side of town. After Dad's father died when Dad was in his first term at Cambridge, Aunt Beryl cared for him like a second son – helped by the fact that Beryl's son Edward and Dad attended the same Cambridge college.

Not surprisingly, everyone had seen Cambridge as the natural choice for me when it came to application time. My brother was up there and enjoying it. Half my family, including my uncle, grandfather and great-aunt, were alumni. My parents had met there, for God's sake, so I owe my existence to the institution. My mother, Catharine, was even named after St Catharine's College in Cambridge, where my grandfather had studied in the 1920s. When James's post-interview letter from St Catharine's dropped on to the doormat at home, Mum and Dad had steamed it open while he was still asleep, desperate to know if he'd made it in.

From that family history you might surmise that the Livingstons were blue-blooded and owned half of Kent. In fact, Dad had grown up in modest surroundings, on the south coast, the son of a well-respected prison warder. At thirteen he won a place at the grammar school in Winchester and a few years later sat the Cambridge entrance exam. He was accepted by St John's without ever having seen the town, let alone the college. While studying there he ran a poster business and sold flights to the USA to help with the bills.

Mum grew up in York, the daughter of a strict schoolmaster known to kids and teachers alike as 'Boomer'. He was as keen on sport as education and often corresponded with his friend Harold Abrahams, who was later immortalised in the film *Chariots of Fire*. If James and I inherit our competitive streak from anyone, it's from him; he was pretty intense. For her sixth birthday Mum received a miniature shot-put. At eight she was made to walk an impromptu full marathon one Sunday, with extra laps of the airfield on her return just to make sure she had covered the distance. O levels and A levels were pressed upon her similarly early. She excelled at languages and swimming, if not the shot-put, and spent a year in Spain as a student before taking her place at Cambridge in 1967, where she studiously avoided all sport. The competitive sports gene must have skipped a generation; Mum's proud of our achievements but I can sense she is also scared that we have become obsessive, like her father.

In her final year Mum, having tired of languages and now reading fine art, attended a lecture on Russian building design given by a young man from the architecture faculty, who'd spent the summer driving across the Soviet Union in a clapped-out Rover 90. He wore a snap-brim trilby hat and this dashing look, combined with stories of the east at the peak of the Cold War, made quite some impression. Two days later they met at a party. Two years later they were married.

Although he'd never said it directly, Dad was so enthusiastic about St John's that he was disappointed by James's decision to apply to St

Catharine's. Still, there was one son left to follow in his father's footsteps.

Yeah, I was feeling the pressure all right in the last couple of years at school. James had won his place at Cambridge with stellar A level results and all I had achieved were distinctly average GCSEs. I buckled down and began to post good results in A level modules, despite a hair-raising time with chemistry, where I got Ds in every mock only to scrape an A when it came round to the actual exam.

Cambridge was the obvious choice, the trodden path. Like a good little brother I went up to visit Cambridge to look round the various colleges, including St John's. I didn't manage to see James; he was on the river that afternoon. On the train back to London I sifted through the various university brochures. I couldn't escape the feeling of being trapped. I didn't just want to follow James; be him but younger. I wanted to forge my own life, my own relationships, to be my own man. Cambridge would not allow me to do that. I would be James's brother, both in the rowing squad and in the faculty. I couldn't be just another student.

Would I be letting my parents down if I didn't apply to their alma mater? I turned the question over and over. What I knew was that being in the shadow of James was no easy task and I didn't want to have to live up to expectations set by him any longer. As the train rolled into King's Cross my mind was made up: I was shooting for Oxford.

James:

Monday 30 September 11:21, Goldie Boathouse, Cambridge

Back in the Captains' Room Robin's light-hearted demeanour and general good humour give away his happiness at the ergo test results that he is reporting. The three new Harvard oarsmen – Wayne Pommen, Hugo Mallinson and Steffen Buschbacher – feature highly, as does our new Yale man Nate Kirk, despite their suffering heavy jet lag. President Wooge and another German, Matthias Kleinz – or Matze as he'd quickly become known – also did well. Wow, didn't see him coming. Slight of build and obviously mild of nature, he doesn't have the size or the vocal volume of the new North American contingent. Turns out that he has represented Germany at all levels and just missed out on the Sydney Olympics in their lightweight four. Thankfully he rows on strokeside and won't be competing against me for a place on bowside. Robin couldn't believe his luck: normally such oarsmen contact the club in advance to talk to the coaches and find out about the programme. But no one knew Matze until he walked quietly through the door and pulled a fantastic erg score.

Two big British undergraduates set the pace though. Survivors of last year's Goldie, the Cambridge reserve crew, Alex McGarel-Groves and Ben Clare have been training hard all summer to ensure they make the first crew this time. It's Groves I have to thank for my snapped collar bone, which now, three weeks later, is on the way to knitting but has still prevented me from taking part in this first ergo test.

Robin takes noticeable pleasure in reminding us that there is still a promising Aussie called Kris Coventry yet to arrive who's done the test at his club, Mercantile in Melbourne. He'd pulled 6 minutes 10 seconds, a damn good score early in the season, which puts him fourth. A thoughtful silence fills the room. One of our freshers, Tom James, puts his hand up, still in schoolboy mode.

'Yes, Tom?' says Robin.

'Er, what side does this guy row on?' The room bursts into laughter. Everyone is desperate to know but nobody had been willing to show their concern that this mystery Antipodean might be a threat to their seat. It has taken a schoolboy to ask the obvious question.

Robin smiles. 'He can row on either side.' There is a general groan.

Ellie and I leave the boathouse in the direction of St Chad's, a modern low-rise block of red-brick flats where the St Catz second years and my few fellow fourth years are billeted. It's a mile or so west of the old town, near the vast university library. Ellie cycles slowly alongside me on her little purple bike. She lives across the road from me, at her college, Robinson.

Once we're a little way from the boathouse we start dissecting the new squad, 'Not so many of the big medalists this year then, or the big personalities,' I offer. Many of the international medalists that arrive to trial have so much belief in both themselves and their chosen 'best way to row' that getting them to buy into the Cambridge way of doing things can be a fraught experience. And the fact that most of the squad idolise them certainly doesn't help.

'Yeah, but Bas says they haven't got a big crop this year either.' 'They' refers to Oxford. Ellie and Oxford rower Bas Dixon have been clandestinely going out since meeting at a regatta in Princeton over the summer to which both Oxford and Cambridge were invited. Ellie has kept it very quiet, particularly to the coaches, and according to Dave, Bas has too. It is very Romeo and Juliet.

'In fact,' she continues, 'sounds like we're going to be quite a bit bigger. Bas didn't tell me the results of their erg tests but I could tell from his chirpiness he was quite high up the rankings, which means most of them must be slower than 6.15. You haven't caught up with Dave recently, then?'

'No, not really, we're both busy settling in. That's good news about their ergs. Any big internationals?'

'A Canadian and a couple of Americans but no senior medals, I think.'

'Sounds good.'

We have a laugh about a couple of the weakest triallists and bet on how many days they'll last, then at the Magdalene Bridge crossroads El cycles off.

'See you mañana por la mañana, Bango.'

'See you then, El.' I'd picked up the nickname Bungle at school, my size and precocious chest hair contributing to an extremely vague similarity to the bear from *Rainbow*. It had followed me to university. When racing at Henley this summer with Seb, Ellie and Sammy, Seb had misheard my nickname and so I'd become Bango to him and pretty soon to Ellie and Sammy too.

El disappears among the other cyclists, heading off to her college. I can't get back on my bike yet as my arm and shoulder are still painful to put weight on. I'm also worried about what would happen if I fell off my bike, jarring the shards of bone apart again. Terrified by the pain it would cause and by the further delay in recovery.

I was the only one not taking the erg test and it is galling to see the other guys, not to mention Oxford and my brother, moving further and further ahead of me while I'm still confined to the stationary bike. My name isn't even down on the list at the moment. Am I to be left behind?

I'm glad when I get back to Chad's as it's a grey and dispiriting day outside. I've lucked out this year. Big room. Lots of shelves against one wall which are probably meant for heavy books are already covered in neat piles of rowing kit. Expansive bay window, looking over the garden two floors below. But it's strange to be in Cambridge without my old college mates – they're out in the real world, starting careers or else lurking at home in some sort of holding pattern. Many of the CUBC guys that I'm close to have also gone, down to London or to the USA, quite a few of them trying out for their national teams.

I pick up the almost embarrassingly large plastic phone and dial Sam. She answers quickly.

'Hey, you, it's me.'

'Hey I was just thinking about you.' She sounds slightly fragile.

'Ah, how are things going up there? How's the house?' Sam moved in last week with eight other girls, all school or uni friends, all in Nottingham to do the legal practice course. It had been difficult to find a nine-bedroom house in the months beforehand and when the estate agent did, they'd signed up quickly.

'Er, not great, actually. We've just had a visit by the police to tell us that the area is unsafe and under no circumstances should we walk home alone.'

'You've what?' I stammered in surprise.

'The street's pretty horrible. This morning there were a few women hovering around, after the school run to the school across the street. Only it turns out they're not mums. They're prostitutes.'

'No way.'

'It's true. The police told us there's a real problem with it. Some tramworks further into town has apparently pushed the red light district up our street. And it means the girls can pick up the dads who are dropping their kids off for school.'

'Oh gross.' I wince.

'It gets worse.'

'Worse?' I say, quite concerned.

'You remember the graveyard I told you about at the end of the road?'

'Ye-es.'

'That's where they bonk their clients. That's why some of the gravestones have been knocked over!'

'Oh Sam, I'm sorry. It sounds terrible. The house itself, though, that's nice, isn't it?' I say, trying to find a way to cheer her up.

'Well, we've got slugs in the kitchen. They leave streaks on the walls.'

'Oh grim,' I reply, half-laughing now.

'I know!' She giggles. I'm relieved to hear her laughing. She was sounding like she might cry.

'Which room did you get?' I knew the girls had drawn straws. There was a lot of difference between the best and worst bedroom, particularly in terms of space to hang clothes, apparently.

'Oh, I did OK. On the second floor, next to Nikki. Her alarm woke me up this morning. The dividing wall is like paper.' I hear someone knock on her door.

'Coming!' she shouts, holding a hand over the phone. 'That's Nikki, I'm late for registration. Can we talk tonight?'

'Sure, I'll give you a call.' A moment passes. 'I miss you,' I say.

'Oh, I miss you too.' She sounds sad. Then I hear someone shout her name. 'Got to go, don't want to walk round here on my own. Love you. Bye.'

'Bye. I love you.' But she's already hung up, rushing off to the safety of numbers.

Outside I see a second year wheeling a trolley of boxes to her new room. I saw that girl at the college bar last night with some of the freshers. They looked very young. I felt a lot more than just three years older.

David:

Tuesday 1 October 07:34, Iffley Road gym, Oxford

The dull drone of whirring ergos fills my world in the Oxford University gym. I sit on one of the machines, going forwards and backwards, the bland gym wall a few feet in front of me. Usually there's music to listen to, which allows you to zone out and alleviates the boredom, but today we train in silence with only the machine fans and internal thoughts for solace.

The squad has a variety of pet names for the rowing machine. 'Iron Horse' and 'Misery Machine' are two of the current favourites. I have always had a volatile relationship with the rowing machine, sometimes loving it, mostly hating it. Today is one of the hate days. I swear that the spiteful machine is giving me poorer scores than normal. At least this is my last piece of work for the testing session. By the sounds of Bas's huffs and puffs next to me he's also having a bad day.

Theoretically I have covered hundreds of kilometres on these machines. If the ergo moved I would, by the time this season is over, have covered 1,600 kilometres, roughly from Oxford to Lisbon. I feel a long way from soaking up the sun or being served sangria by some attractive Portuguese girls. A Dostoyevsky quote pops into my brain. 'Suffering is the sole origin of consciousness.' At least I feel alive, I guess.

The seconds tick slowly by at the top of the screen; 1 minute 37 remains on the clock for this piece. Each six-minute section is followed by a blood sample, taken by the coaches, who will later recede into the mythical, out of bounds, back office to analyse the samples for the amount of lactic acid present. The results tell you how physiologically fit you are; it is a measure of fitness, strength and endurance all rolled into one and this helps the coaches set training intensity for the next phase as well as begin to identify the athletes they want to select to face Cambridge.

With a minute to go, the bespectacled cox Acer appears at my left-hand side. '156, Dave?' He peers down at my heart rate monitor watch.

'Yep,' I grunt between breaths on the way up the slide to the next stroke. Acer scribbles the result down on his pad with the same diligence that earned him a funded place on his PhD. Acer's mixture of indisputable intelligence – a top first in physics and philosophy – his sharp wit and eclectic music taste make him a likeable guy, despite his subjecting the minibus to songs by his schoolboy band Yesterday's Juice. Luckily for the captive audience that tape was slung out of the minibus window somewhere on the way to training. His brains and steering ability make him invaluable in the cox's seat. 'Thirty seconds left over here,' he shouts behind me. This alerts the coaching staff to take the sample.

Physiological testing is an integral part of the life of a serious athlete. Our race may not be for money since we are unpaid, but we aim to be professional in every other sense. Defining improvements over the past month and setting new goals is a constant, relentless process, and progress has to be made at each new test if I want to keep myself in with a chance of making the boat. I cannot stand still.

I have become used to this sort of testing. The medical team for Great Britain Juniors made me provide urine samples every morning during competitions to ensure I was keeping myself properly hydrated. The amusing joke was to fill the cup up to the very brim outside the drop-off point so that the medical team could not lift the cup without spilling it. I'm not sure they always found it as funny as we did.

I'd also had to give a urine sample for a drugs test while on the GB

Junior team. Without any warning the UK drug testing authority showed up at our training camp in Chester. My name was on their list of those randomly selected for testing and I had to accompany several others to the testing station. The UK Sport Anti-Doping Officer introduced himself as Phillip and invited me to produce a urine sample.

I attempted to go but things weren't working for me. 'I can't go,' I said to Phillip, who stood at my side looking at my penis to make sure the test was not rigged. 'I just can't go,' I repeated. It was not the stage fright of having a bearded man standing next to me, watching me trying to piss, but the fact that I'd been to the toilet shortly before they'd unexpectedly arrived.

'OK, don't worry, just go outside and take your time and let me know when you're ready,' he said.

I waited for half an hour and I still didn't need to go. The others in the waiting area quickly fell away. Two bottles of water later, and another half hour, and still nothing stirred in my loins. Phillip, seemingly used to this, suggested a walk. We walked along the canal together in awkward silence. He could not leave my side in case I got someone else to wee into my pot. I tried to think about waterfalls and running water. On the way back Phillip kindly informed me that failure to produce a sample within the allotted three-hour window would mean that I hadn't complied and had failed the drugs test. Fucking brilliant.

Back at the testing station, I stood in the toilet once more, psyching myself up to piss. After an age I squeezed out a few precious drops, then a few more and finally full flow. I had never been so overjoyed to pee. I think even Phillip felt the relief. We both had beaming smiles as I handed him the overflowing, warm jar of urine.

Going in to the final strokes of the ergo test, I mentally count them down. I want to push the pace up but today the scientific testing means I have to keep it steady. Sean appears in my periphery, pulling on surgical plastic gloves. He wears his customary blue jeans, dark blue jumper and OUBC cap. On his feet Sean's skateboarder trainers are a sign of his previous, more alternative life as a surfer. I can't imagine it now. To me he is the complete antithesis of a chilled-out surfer dude. But, then again, not many of us know Sean well as he is an introspective man who doesn't open up a great deal to his athletes. Like most successful coaches he is guarded about his personal life and likes to keep his distance –

perhaps because he'll drop whoever he has to in order to make the crew work.

'Three seconds . . . two seconds . . . one second', the machine readout tells me. Finished, I put down the plastic handle connecting me and the machine. Acer, now in front of me, pulls up the display panel to write down my results. How many watts I've produced, how many strokes per minute I've taken; all the minutiae of details that the coaches will later analyse, alongside the results of the blood sample.

'Here you go, Dave,' he says, handing me some paper towels. I use them to wipe the sweat away from my right ear. Sean grasps the bottom of my right ear lobe with one hand; in the other he brandishes a sharp needle. He pricks the bottom of my ear lobe. After three tests already today it resembles a bloodied pin cushion. I wince as he squeezes hard and extracts blood into a sampling pin. 'Number 32,' he announces. Acer furiously scribbles down the sample number next to my test details. Sean sits down on a wooden box to my right-hand side. Somehow I think Sean gets satisfaction from performing this clinical task, as if checking the fitness of his race horses.

Bas, who's now finished with his ergo on my left, reaches out a sweaty closed fist into the space between us. I nudge it with mine. A simple sign of respect between us.

Sean snaps off the plastic gloves and moves on to his next subject. I'm conscious that my scores on the rowing machine are my big weakness, a problem that James never seemed to have.

James:

Wednesday 2 October 06:45, Goldie Boathouse, Cambridge

The rowing machines purr in the next room while I pump my legs on the stationary bike and watch the giant Ben Clare finish his set of squats. Thuds of metal bars hitting benches and grunts of straining athletes fill the room. The inch-thick metal bar straddled across the back of Ben's shoulders visibly strains and curves with the number of heavy metal discs loaded on to each end. He drops slowly into another squat and then gradually drives the ton and a half back upwards against the pull of gravity. There's a loud expulsion of air through his gritted teeth as he reaches his full height. Arnold Schwarzenegger, Ben's idol, flexes down from a poster on the wall approvingly, alongside several posters advertising various international rowing competitions and one of Pamela Anderson in her *Baywatch* days.

'Good stuff, mate. This one is for the Filth,' I pant as he drops into his eighth and final rep. If OUBC aren't referred to as just Oxford or the Other Side, they are generally known to us as either the Filth or the Scum. Veins bulge in Ben's reddened face as he drives up slowly, inexorably, for the final time before inching forward to lower the straining bar on to the stand.

'Twenties off, please, mate,' JA says and they remove a 20-kilo disc from each side of the bar. It strikes me that when I lifted weights with Dave a few times over the summer in our local gym he never once asked for any weight to be taken off after I'd taken my turn. He'd always let me do the first set, watching as I chose the weight, then he'd doggedly attempt to lift whatever I'd done. His longer, thinner frame and fewer years spent weight training meant he had to strain and strain to lift the weights. Often he failed and I had to help him with the last couple of lifts. His stubbornness aggravated something in me and I piled on the weights till it took eye-bulging effort to finish. Dave resolutely took his turn, stony-faced, desperately heaving to lift the weights, body shaking with pain. He failed, of course.

'Last set,' says Ben to JA. Squats are the toughest and most painful of the weight training this morning. Get them out of the way and it's downhill all the way to breakfast. I watch with a strange envy and stand up off the seat of the bike machine to push on for the last few minutes, replaying the ecstatic yells of last year's Oxford victors in my head.

Rowing races tend to follow the form book – the 'better' crew will very often win the race, unlike in games such as football, where minnows can giant-kill their way along the FA cup draw. Our sport depends less on chance or luck or inspiration on the day and more on preparation: strength, strategy and training. We very much earn our right to win. There is a purity, something almost religious, to our striving for incremental improvements in training. A few extra kilograms of weights lifted each session, fractional improvements to the split times on the ergometer, all stored in our personal training diaries.

Across from us on the torso rotate machine, one of the less experienced triallists, Chris, finishes his set and looks slightly startled to see coach Robin standing in front of him.

'Hi, Chris. Can you come my office after the session for a few minutes?' Robin asks quietly, in a professional but slightly apologetic tone.

Chris can only nod. Those of us near enough to hear Robin's request pretend not to have heard and continue our lifting. This is the end for Chris. Robin will now 'bin' him as he has binned the other twelve or so hopefuls over the last couple of weeks. Chris turns back to the machine, puts the weight up a couple of notches and starts another set. In the showers afterwards he stands alone and silent, a marked man, while the rest of us plan our evening out.

'Burgers at the Hawks at eight, then on to Life?' Hugo confirms, while toweling himself down. There's a chorus of agreement from Wayne, Matze, Wooge, Groves, Buschbacher, myself and a few others. The Hawks Club bar, in the basement of the Hawks Club, the club for university sportsmen, is the de facto location to start our nights out, the Hawks Burger the de facto meal to fuel them.

As I head for the door and lectures I notice Chris slowly ascending the wooden stairs to the office. He lingers for a moment beneath the Goldie honours board on the landing, before turning to ascend the final flight of stairs to the coach's office.

'See you, Chris,' I say to myself while unlocking my bike outside. We won't see him again. His name will disappear from the crew list for the afternoon's rowing and will never reappear. The slimming down of the squad is a very necessary evil. Coaching effort needs to be concentrated on those who will finally face Oxford, and the training needs to be as high quality as possible. The weak must be cut to keep the quality undiluted. Robin says it is the hardest part of his job, and I don't envy him, ending people's dreams before they have even really begun. Some come back the next year to try again. One guy trialled for four years consecutively and lasted a grand total of three and a half days. He is known only as 'the Legend' as he wasn't around long enough for anyone to learn his name.

David:

Saturday 5 October 07:34, OUBC Boathouse, Wallingford

The flotilla of rowing boats launches from Oxford's Wallingford base. Save for the movements of the local bird life, nothing else stirs on the river this early on a drizzly Saturday morning. Without any effort the boats float quickly downriver with the strong prevailing stream.

'Right, are you ready?' calls John, my partner in the boat. I square my blade to indicate my readiness. 'Row.' With strokes powered by ambition the boat accelerates away.

The top end of the squad have been training in pairs to develop our basic boat-moving skills and to allow Sean the opportunity to race us and determine an early season rank order. I'm pleased to be rowing with the tall and incredibly confident Old Etonian John Adams. We knew each other before Oxford, having attended the same Junior World Championships where his father could be seen rollerblading alongside his races, screaming encouragement. John had come up to Oxford with me last year and we had rowed together in the winning Isis crew. He has become a close friend and is a tough competitor. Despite his Christian faith and selflessness, he wants to win this as much as any of us do. His belief in God gives him confidence in some sort of master plan and world order which in some ways I envy. We've spent some of the summer lifting weights together, putting more muscle on our tall young frames.

The meandering tree-lined banks speed past with our strong strokes. The red-brick outline of the Wallingford rail bridge recedes into the distance and we approach our turning point at the lock.

After a quick break for some water and removal of extra kit we begin our row back. We pass Scott and BT going in the opposite direction, looking like a fast combination. They are tailed by Sean in his coaching launch. He drops them, spins his launch and catches up with John and I. He peers at our rowing with his head tilted slightly to one side.

Sean carefully raises his megaphone. 'Take a stop there.' John calls us to a halt.

As Sean pulls alongside and turns off his engine, ready to critique our technique, I'm reminded of my insecurity and general wariness towards him. Last season, after a poor start, I had risen through the team to win a seat in the provisional Blue Boat. I believed I'd made it. However, when we got back from training camp in January I'd underperformed on the five-kilometre ergo test. The next day at the boathouse Sean was giving his pre-outing briefing and he announced a change to the crews. Bas would row in the A crew that day and I would row in Isis. Minutes later we were out on the water. I seethed with resentment. I understood it was not his place to soothe my ego but I thought he had dropped me from the Blue Boat in the coldest manner possible. I was crushed.

In the end Sean had made the right choice, Bas did a great job in the winning crew, but the way he dropped me still haunts me. This season I feel his sword of Damocles hanging over me constantly. Even if I'm selected I'll never feel safe.

James:
Sunday 6 October 08:54, St Chad's, Cambridge

This afternoon we finish our two-week, pre-term training camp. A great feeling of optimism has bubbled within the squad, and people are making new friends, sharing a common goal. Robin's binned some more rowers and a couple of coxes but this has only served to bring the rest of us closer. The loss of one of the coxes was a particularly easy decision after she nodded off during an outing, only to be rudely awakened by crashing headlong into a bridge.

An exasperated and angry Robin surveyed the damage to the boat and asked the crew, 'How did you not notice she was asleep!? She must have been silent for some time?'

'To be honest, Robin,' one of the nervous oarsmen sheepishly admitted, 'that came as a blessed relief.' Needless to say, she wasn't seen again.

Sitting in my college room, I stare at our training programme. The words 'Club Triathlon' stare back at me. At the end of last season Robin mentioned that this would form the climax of the first fort-night's training, and its inclusion was meant to encourage cross-training over the summer and help identify guys who were physically in good shape but whose rowing technique might be restricting their speed in a boat at present. Robin liked to believe that anyone could learn to row but if you didn't at least have the beginnings of the big heart and lungs required to tear along the four-and-a-bit-mile course then there was no hope. You could row as prettily as you like, but as Olympic coach Jürgen Grobler once said to Matthew Pinsent, rowing 'isn't dressage'.

My collar bone is pretty much healed so I've persuaded Robin to let me take part, desperate to make my mark. We've been out on a few training bike rides around Cambridge, our natural competitiveness causing constant juggling for position, with bold breakaways and insane overtaking manoeuvres on blind corners, just to get one over on the guy in front. The regular sudden surges in pace meant there were a number of casualties who slipped off the back of the pack and then never had the momentum to catch up. It was a cruel wake-up call for those guys trialling for the first time.

I can hear my flatmate Andy next door, strumming the chorus to 'A Long December' by Counting Crows, and humming. A cheerful engineering grad, he is one of my few old friends still to be around in Cambridge as his degree is four years long.

I turn into his room. 'Hi, mate, how's the unpacking going?' I ask him. He's sitting at his small desk, still in his trademark navy dressing gown, acoustic guitar on his lap. His scruffy short hair hasn't yet seen the shower.

'Hey,' he smiles. There are boxes everywhere as he arrived only last night. All still full of stuff, I notice. His computer is one of the few things unpacked and his screen glows behind him.

'Just working on the site. Almost there now.' After finishing this year, Andy is planning to drive from London to Sydney in a convoy of two VW camper vans, with a couple of school friends and, potentially, me. I could almost recite the route myself. Eurotunnel to France. Autobahn through Germany, then Austria, Hungary, Romania, Turkey, Iran, India, China, Thailand, Malaysia. A few ferries along Indonesia. Another to the Australian north coast. A long drive south through the outback, dissecting Australia, then a dog-leg east. Get to Sydney in about nine months. What freedom. No training programme, no lectures. No club triathlon.

David:
Saturday 12 October 08:45, Windsor

G-force pushes me against the capacious shoulders of fresher Sam Parker, as the minibus careers round the tight corner. He stares bemused at his first-year organic chemistry notes. Matt Daggett, who frantically highlights case studies for his MBA course, sandwiches me in on my other side. President Matt swings the steering wheel again and keeps us on the racing line. In the juddering mirror I see we haven't lost the other minibus which follows in our wake. Water flashes by on our right.

The low wooden curves of the Eton school boathouse appear on the horizon. I look out of the window across the open grassland, to the man-made rowing lake. The water is relatively flat with a slight crosswind. Good conditions for rowing and racing.

Normally we would use our training base on the Thames in Wallingford, a quiet Oxfordshire market town, thirty minutes away from the grandeur of the city centre, but today we're being measured on the straight man-made course.

I hear my phone ring from inside the depths of my bag.

'Hey, Maria! How are you doing?'

'Hey, baby, really good.'

'Term going well? Was the end of freshers' week awesome? I'm so jealous.'

'It's been amazing! So many parties. The freshers' ball on Friday was epic. I got home at five! How are things with you?'

'All going well so far. In the minibus on my way to rowing right now.' Radio Oxford starts blaring out of the speakers next to my head. I hold the phone closer to hear her over the ear-meltingly loud music.

'So when are you coming up to visit me?' she asks expectantly. 'You've got to see my dingy halls and I can show you Bristol. How's next weekend?' I remain silent for a moment.

'Er, I can't, Maria. I'm really sorry. Like I said before, I'll get to see you lots at Christmas time but I've got rowing every weekend this term. I would love to come and see you but it's just not possible.'

'No weekends till Christmas! Are you serious?'

'I'm sorry. We'll spend loads of time together then, I promise.' She is quiet.

'Fine, well, I'll see you then, I guess.' She sounds irate. 'I've got a lecture to go to now. Speak later.'

'I'm sorry. I can't wait to see you. I'll give you a call later,' I say, fumbling for words to smooth over her disappointment.

'Bye,' she says. Before I get a chance to reply she's already hung up.

Henry turns to me from the seat in front, having heard my conversation. 'Things all right?'

'Not really, mate. Not really.'

Rain begins to fall and droplets form on the windows. 'Liquid sunshine,' I whisper to myself doggedly, 'liquid sunshine.'

James:

Wednesday 16 October 18:57, The Judge Business School, Cambridge

'And, now, who can give me an example of oligopoly in the British market?' the bespectacled and rotund Austrian PhD student continues. He looks half owl, half toad and about twelve.

Silence. My eyes are drawn magnetically to the clock over the left shoulder of the owl-toad. It seems to have frozen. Toady glares at me.

'James?'

'Er . . .'

My conscientious Spanish classmate interjects. 'Petrol stations. Only five or so firms in the UK, I believe,' going on to elaborate on price fixing. The owl-toad nods grumpily at the Spaniard's comments, unhappy that I've been let off the hook.

Relaxing back into my chair, I lament my lack of preparation for the first supervision of term. For every lecture course, of which there will be three or four, every student receives a weekly hour-long tutorial alongside one or two classmates, with an academic expert in the field, perhaps a professor or a PhD student. Each hour begins with a critique of the essays the students will, ideally, have submitted before the super-vision and once that's done, a more general grilling on the course content begins. Pretty gruelling, particularly for those with dubious lecture attendance records. Four years in, though, I've learned a few tricks. First impressions count – work slavishly on the first essay of term (ideally citing several of your supervisor's more renowned research papers) and be exceedingly keen, polite, inquisitive and knowledgeable during the first supervision. That way, for the rest of term lengthy silences of stumped confusion will appear to be moments of quiet contemplation or nodding appreciation, and essays subsequent to your epic, completed in about a quarter of the time, are labelled as 'not quite up to your usual high standard', rather than 'your usual poor standard'. And never mention that you're trialling with the CUBC – or at least not to start with. Any work that is a few minutes late, or below Nobel Prize-winning standard, will be waved at you by the disapproving tutor, admonishing you that 'This is what comes of spending all your time on the river!'

I'm certainly never going to mention the dark secret to Toad of Toad Hall in front of me. He'd probably spontaneously combust. Towards the end of term, if your tutor is one of the younger and sportier supervisors (an extremely relative description), you might drop into conversation after a particularly good supervision that you're training for the Blue Boat, resulting in a day or two's grace with essay deadlines or a softer attack on your understanding of theories of comparative economics. Towards the end of term, when the supervisor is only going to have to put up with you for another hour or two, you can at last come clean so that he or she can brag to their colleagues on Boat Race day.

The last minutes of our allotted hour slowly pass. I can tell that the first impression I've made on the toad has been poor. My bluffing and dodging has not gone unnoticed.

Strolling out of the art deco business school, I reflect that it's not just training that's been keeping me from my studies. I've spent most of my time this week working with president Tim, having previously been rather lax on my vice-presidential duties. In fact last week, as Ellie and I cycled back from morning training together, she passed on that Wooge was 'unhappy with me for doing nothing'. I was fuming when I got back to my flat and stomped around the kitchen grumpily, waking my flatmate Andy. It wasn't as if Tim had actually asked me to do anything. Later, in one of the duller moments of a lecture on organisational design, I saw his point: I'd been too caught up focussing on my own recovery. Since then I've been more involved, and Tim and I conduct one-to-one meetings with all triallists, welcome them to the squad, discuss their goals for the year, advise them and enlist their help with certain matters. In several cases, no sooner have we talked through an athlete's lofty aims for the season than Robin gives them their marching orders.

David:
Thursday 17 October, Iffley Road gym, Oxford

I lie down on the thin mat on the freezing gym floor and try to calm my breathing after my short cycle to the gym. The mat feels cold against my neck and each breath sends out a cloud of fog.

Soon my body begins to relax and my breathing deepens. Closing my eyes, I'm almost asleep again. The gentle hum of ergo machines comes from the next-door room. Some must have started their morning session after their Omega Wave tests. The Omega Wave test is used to give an assessment of the overall physiological state of an athlete through the attachment of electrodes to the chest, wrists and ankles. Unlike other testing methods it's not physically invasive or time-consuming but it's not widely accepted in the sporting community, partly because it's so new and partly because the machine costs close to £10,000. Mainly, though, it's because the science isn't well understood. The Omega Wave does feel a touch magical; it's rumoured to have been developed by the Russian space agency.

Sean and his assistant coach Derek are countering Cambridge's winning streak by redesigning the programme, using the Omega Wave to walk the fine line between too much and too little training, while also personalising the programme for individuals. It's working; Oxford have won two out of the last three Boat Races, with the other contentiously restarted. I believe in their innovative methods; they're pushing boundaries and trying different things.

Scott mutters obscenities under his breath, walking out of the back office after his test. I can tell it's him even with my eyes closed. I've heard a few complaints from him this season. Scott got a bad result in the first couple of Omega Wave tests, his results coming back as 'overly stressed' more often than they should. For a relatively small guy (compared with rowers in general) at six foot two, he pulls amazing scores on the rowing machine, refusing to allow himself to be tired.

Some people never get positive test results on the Omega Wave. Bill Fedyna, an energetic new triallist this year, who won the World Championships for the USA as a lightweight in 2000 before hitting Wall Street for a couple of years, consistently scores 1,700 in the tension index, his stress levels effectively off the scale while most people are in the teens. Poor scores are the sign of desperate tiredness or sickness and sometimes, depending on the coaches assessment, result in an easy recovery session on the rowing machines.

The door of the back office creaks open. I open my eyes and roll my head back. 'OK, Dave,' says Sean, from the doorway. I remove my jumper and T-shirt and follow him in. I lie face up on the physio bench, closing my eyes once more to relax my breathing. Cold, greasy electrodes are attached to my wrists, ankles and chest. The wires off these run to a computer measuring the rhythm of my heart rate and breathing.

'Here we go.' Sean clicks on the mouse and I'm being measured.

Blood Over Water

James:

Thursday 17 October 13:45, Ely

A vista of flat, flat fenland greets us through the misted windows of the minibus. Green fields cross-hatched with drainage ditches as far as the eye can see, with the occasional yellow burst of oil seed rape brightening the scene. In a few months these fields will be a uniform muddy brown.

In the seat in front of me Hugo is talking to Jim O'Martian, 'Have you seen a mixer tap since you got here? At my college every basin has two taps – one for ice cold, the other scalding. And the washer dryer machines – is it just me or are they much smaller than their US brethren?' Hugo, who is half-British, half-American, has inherited a very British dry and ironic sense of humour. He loves shows like *Blackadder* and *Red Dwarf* and so relishes quoting them to other fans, like me, that I get the impression this love of Brit comedy was kept a bit of a dark secret at Harvard. Jim coxed Hugo and Wayne at Harvard. Jim's small frame is bursting with competitiveness and he gets a thrill out of the control and power innate in coxing. I wasn't surprised when I heard he got his pilot's licence at the age of sixteen. He is exceedingly loyal to his friends, proud of Harvard and without doubt will be Ellie's competition for the Blue Boat cox's seat.

Behind me, Ben and Tom are debriefing the back of the bus in hushed tones about Tom's initiation into the Trinity Hall Half Moons drinking society last night. Groves and Buschbacher try to guffaw quietly, so as not to arouse the interest of the coaches sitting up front. Tom is a fresh-faced first year, in the first couple of weeks of his Cambridge life. Ben is a boisterous second year I've known since he was eleven, the easy-going younger brother of the current Oxford president and my old schoolmate Matt Smith. Ben has all the talent of his sibling but, in equal measure to Matt's legendary drive and determination, Ben has a happy-go-lucky, relaxed, Zen attitude to life. He didn't trial last year, wanting to warm gently into first year. Things just seem to go right for him without apparent effort.

Overhearing some more of their antics, I turn and join the conversation, grinning. 'Hang on, Ben, where did they stick the toilet paper?'

'Yep. There,' smiles Ben cheekily. 'Then we gave TJ and the others their dirty pints.'

'And they lit the toilet paper,' adds Tom. The audience collectively wince.

'Lucky they were pretty quick on the draw. They downed the pints and we put the flames out before the paper burned all the way up. TJ was a little close for comfort, though.' Ben grins.

Tom James, our promising fresher, already known to everyone as TJ, looks a little sheepish. 'Think I might have singed a few hairs.' TJ rowed with my brother at the Junior World Championships a couple of years back and was the top GB under-18 oarsman last summer, just missing out on the gold. Without Dave around these young guys are starting to feel like my little brothers.

After some more laughing the banter dies down. The familiar Gothic protuberance of Ely Cathedral is rearing up out of the fields ahead of us, its enormity making the surrounding fens seem all the flatter. Ely, a small town half an hour north of Cambridge, is where we do most of our rowing, on the Ouse. The slow-flowing, narrow river is our own, apart from the occasional family of swans. Canal boats do pass on occasion; holiday craft are rare. The banks of the river are raised so the views on either side are limited to reeds, grass and cattle.

The Cam, the river running through Cambridge, offers better views but is too busy with college rowers or pleasure boats and curves like a sidewinder rattlesnake, an issue when you're in a coxless boat, facing backwards and steering the boat with your foot. No such steering issues for us here – most of our stretch is man-made and arrow straight, running for miles without interruption. If you have to stop to turn around during a rowing session, because of a lock or other obstruction, this causes heart rates to drop and isn't as beneficial for training. Out here we can go on and on, much to the delight of the coaches.

Despite my sleepiness I'm excited at hitting the water, my first time in a boat since breaking my collar bone. I'm looking forward to feeling the surge and flow of a boat once more. The serenity and peace that an outing can bring will be a welcome contrast to the chaos of the start of term and academic demands mounting up already. The river can bring freedom – if the coaching launch isn't too close by.

A few minutes later our packed minibus is roaring through the quiet market town and into the marina where our boathouse nestles. The dark and empty changing rooms are soon filled with chatter and the benches covered in kit bags. The less experienced guys tend to change on the periphery of the core group, always ready to laugh at a joke from one of the older or more experienced hands towards the centre.

The new guys don their college boat club lycras. Some only own a couple of training outfits, which means a lot of washing. By comparison the internationals and old boys like me have cupboards of kit; national team T-shirts and dozens of Cambridge lycras. The Harvard boys (Wayne, Hugo and Buschbacher) have piles of Harvard crimson and hundreds of T-shirts from other US colleges, thanks to the American custom of giving your shirt to your vanquisher – literally the shirt off your back. Poor Nate, who'd been one of the top guys from a less successful Yale team, had given away a lot of shirts, some to our Harvard boys after Yale's losses in the Harvard–Yale Boat Race, America's oldest collegiate athletic competition. Nate had been captain last year at Yale and despite his crew's huge 40-second loss to Harvard, captained by Wayne, Nate was still intensely proud of his roots, even having a 'Row Blue' number plate on his Oldsmobile back home. Tactfully, the Harvard boys don't wear their won Yale shirts around him out of respect.

In the main room, a huge map of the Boat Race course is propped against the right wall, lest we forget why we're here. The room is filled with contorted oarsmen stretching hamstrings or backs, except for Tim and Groves, who lounge on the battered pale yellow sofa.

Tim doesn't believe in stretching, having been told once by a physio from the German team that he was too flexible, which he attributes to his childhood days as a gymnast in Germany. Everyone, Hugo in particular, finds this hilarious as none of us can imagine the huge and often grumpy Wooge gaily somersaulting or jumping around, waving a streamer. Just dropping in 'former gymnast T. Wooge' to any conversation concerning Tim reduces Hugo to stitches and elicits a grin from Wooge. After one such conversation a couple of days ago Hugo searched for evidence of the previously waif-like Tim on the Internet and found a mugshot of a skinny fresher from Northeastern, unmistakably our president, only 40 kilos lighter. The header on the email read – 'Tim, what happened to this kid? Did you eat him?'

Donald, our larger than life assistant coach, strolls in, red-faced as usual with his customary 'jolly good' and puts the kettle on, scattering shy new coxes before him. Don proudly raced in '64 as 'heaviest bowman ever' and has been coaching Cambridge more or less ever since. A well-loved institution, having coached decades of light blues, last outing he'd come out with, 'Groves, you're rowing just like your father!' His coaching vocabulary is colourful, particularly in contrast with Robin's sensible, measured tones. Once, when exasperated with Groves, Donald labelled him 'fourteen and a half stone of shambling shit!' Everyone laughed, particularly Groves.

Donald coached the GB eight for a few sessions in 2001 and they were a little shocked by the treatment. One minute it was 'Bow four! What's going on? It's a complete bloody shambles!', the next shouting at an Olympic gold medallist, 'Lewis, if you can't be bothered at least help the new guys out, they haven't got a clue!' He didn't care if you had three Olympic medals or three weeks' experience, he'd harangue you just the same.

Everyone knows the annual result of the Boat Race means more to him than to anyone else in the world. The long run of Oxford victories in the 80s had been dark times for him. The Boat Race series tends to go in runs, the same university winning race after race. One team might have a particularly inspirational coach or group of athletes while the losers have to change their approach year after losing year, hoping that their new recipe will finally bring them victory. Most of it is about confidence. My first year, 2000, had seen the tide turn disastrously in Oxford's favour with them winning both the Boat Race and Isis/Goldie race, after seven years of Cambridge supremacy. We'd all been so proud to be part of the Cambridge system in the run-up to the race, but at the Blues Dinner that night, we all felt horribly ashamed. We'd let ourselves down but, more than that, the triumphs of our predecessors had melted away to nothing. The dark blues had returned.

Our happiness at avenging ourselves in 2001 was short-lived, with last year's results. We all knew that this year could set the tone for the next half decade.

Finally Robin enters and excitedly reads out the crews for the session. I'm in the stern pair of an eight with Wooge. President and vice-president together, with less experienced rowers in the bows. A typical early season crew, using more senior rowers to set the rhythm and rowing pattern, which the others can follow and learn from.

Robin continues. 'Also, I'm sure you've noticed we've lost a few more. We're down to twenty-eight triallists now. If you see the guys around town do stop to talk to them and wish them the best.'

'How far today, Robin?' one of the new coxes asks.

'Out to the pylons this afternoon, boys.' There is a general groan. Electricity pylons straddle the river eleven kilometres upstream from our boathouse. Out and back means twenty-two kilometres, a long outing this early in the season. Robin smiles at the response. Bring it on, I think to myself, mindful that I need all the water mileage possible to get back on my game.

The pylons fade into the distance as we drive the boat back, stroke by stroke, to our boathouse and home. We pass the ever-empty White Horse pub garden with nine kilometres to go, and an engine growls beside us as Don's coaching launch swings round to pick us up. Silently, he considers us for a few minutes and then the megaphone is raised.

'Boogie Woogie, drop the shoulders. Looking a bit uncomfortable.' In front of me Tim visibly tries to relax. Happy with the change, Donald moves on.

'Livingston. Hampton Hammer House of Horrors. Yep. Loosen up that inside arm. Yep.' A few more strokes and I feel his gaze move behind me to Kartik, who throws discus for the university and who, like Ben Clare, is a maths genius. He's trialled for the previous three years but never made it past the first six weeks. All summer he's trained, hoping that this year will be his year. A brilliant character who brightens the squad. In the run-up to last year's race he'd bumped into the president, wished him luck and confided, 'Watch out, I bet Oxford have put their best eight rowers in the Blue Boat!' He was right, of course.

Donald's megaphone comes to life again, 'Kartik. Hmmm. Not bad. Not bad. Might make something of you this year!' Kartik swells with pride and sits two inches taller. The puddles left by his oar double in size.

Silence for a few strokes then another crackle. 'Hmm. Maybe not,' and the spell is broken.

David:

Friday 18 October 09:14, Oxford University Department of Zoology

I close the lecture theatre doors gently behind me, trying not to make a sound. As I sneak along the back of the lecture theatre as inconspicuously as my height will allow, my size thirteen trainers squelch with every careful step, soaked by my cycle in the pouring rain from the gym to the monstrous concrete faculty on the other side of town.

'Cellular mitosis is the process of cell division for a eukaryotic cell,' drones the grey-haired lecturer to the fifty or so students present. Walking down a few rows, I spot Sally, who sits next to Hammers, my rotund flatmate and fellow biology student. I slip in next to Sal. I must look a mess after the painful circuits this morning and cycling here in the rain.

'Hey, Dave, glad you could make it!' Sally whispers, pushing a set of lecture notes along the wooden desk to me, before returning her attention to the lecturer's gesticulations. I unzip my huge OUBC waterproof jacket as quietly as I can and then wrestle through my enormous kit bag, finding first a banana fruit loaf and secondly a biro. Mercifully, the loaf packaging opens pretty much silently and I rip off a chunk and start chewing. With our training load we need 6,000 calories a day, three times what a normal person consumes. It has become a chore to eat so much: endless troughs of pasta, bread and rice, the carbohydrates needed to keep the body fuelled. Despite the constant eating, some of the guys like John Adams are still barely two per cent body fat, even with his attempts at weight gain with supplements such as 'Invincible[2]'. Even I, with my tendency to develop sizeable birthing hips and 'man boobs' seem to be losing weight.

Timing your food intake is as important as quantity. That's why I'm always stuffing my face in morning lectures, hitting the 'glycogen window' in the 30 to 45 minutes after training when muscles store energy more effectively. I get a few odd looks from the other students as I chomp my way through the malt loaf.

'The sister chromatids are drawn apart,' continues the lecturer. I begin to take some notes but cannot hide the fact that the cells and genes do not capture my imagination a great deal. My real passion is for zoology, environmental biology and behavioural ecology, the seed of which I think was planted by David Attenborough's various programmes and a visit to India as a child. We were lucky enough to see a tiger stalk out of the jungle and kill a wild boar in Ranthambore National Park in northern India. At school James's and my passion for biology was also helped by our rather attractive biology teacher at Hampton. She also coached us in our early days of rowing, and the fact that our teenage bunch would go to any lengths to impress her certainly contributed to our winning quite a few races.

Looking around the hall, I see it contains the usual eclectic mix of an Oxford year group: aspiring academics, pleasant headboy and headgirl types, clean-cut sportsmen and women and the outright weird. The little chap in front of me has quite a phenomenal moustache, rare among nineteen-year-olds, but 'Weasel Tash', as he is known to Sally and I has a style all his own. Some of the girls are equally diverse; one is best known for trying to pull twenty boys on her twentieth birthday. Classy! Despite the mixture of characters our class works well, accepting each other's foibles, and I have developed some close friendships.

'Endoreduplication is common among the Appendicularia.' Sally leans over and draws an unhappy face on my notes. I had first met the tall, curvy brunette at a drunken freshers' beach-themed party or 'bop', where I vaguely remember challenging her to strip down to her bikini. Being a gentleman, I offered a commensurate level of embarrassment by stripping down to a pair of Speedos. If there was any attraction between us – and everyone from the OUBC squad to her granny thought there was – now we are just close friends and allies, although she thinks I am mad to spend so much time rowing. Her organised and dedicated approach to her biology studies has been my saviour. I'd often come back to my room to find my missed lecture notes under my door with my name in her sickeningly legible handwriting and a smiley face at the top. But even she can't help me now as my eyelids begin to drop and my head nods against my chest.

James:
Wednesday 23 October 20:32, St Chad's, Cambridge

While the pasta bubbles away I dial home, the familiar pattern of numbers injecting me with calm. It rings several times before being picked up.

'Hello?' says Mum's soft voice.

'Hi, Mum.' It's always nice calling home; zero stress, a safe world.

'Oh hi, James.' She brightens. Again I sense that that since Dave and I left for uni the big house has felt a bit empty. 'How's term going?'

'Good, thanks. The new squad are a nice bunch. Pulled some decent ergs.'

'Oh good. How's your collar bone? You mustn't rush back too early, you know,' she frets.

'I know. It's much better, actually. No sling or pills needed for a while now.' I decide not to tell her I've been back in the boat a few days – rather earlier than the doctor advised. I couldn't wait any longer.

'How are things at home?'

'Fine. Singing tonight. We're doing *Carmina Burana*. It's wonderful.' Mum loves singing with the local town choir.

'Great. Oh, by the way, the Fours Head is in a few weeks.'

The Fours Head of the River is one of the big races of the British rowing calendar. Hundreds of crews come from far and wide to see how they compare over the timed course on part of the tidal Thames (the Tideway) from Mortlake to Putney; the Boat Race course in reverse.

'Oh yes, we've got it noted on the calendar in the kitchen. You'll be coming home, won't you?'

'Yes, I'm looking forward to it,' I say truthfully as I stir my boiling pasta. 'Would it be OK if I bring three of my teammates? We've got a very international top end this year so I think they'll need a place to stay.'

'Oh, I'm sure we can make room. Yes, that'll be lovely.'

I know I'm asking early – the fours haven't been selected yet. But this race matters. It's a crucial indication of how our season is progressing and kicks off selection for the Boat Race crews. Although we will not be directly alongside Oxford, as we are racing the stopwatch like everyone else, it might as well be just us and them. Robin will already have placed the entries for the event. I just hope he has had enough faith in my rapid recovery to put me in one of the top two crews.

Besides, I want Mum and Dad to meet my Cambridge boys and see what good guys they are. To help swing their allegiance.

Chapter 4
First Blood

David:

Friday 1 November 20:31, Strawberry Hill, Twickenham

I lean forward over the front row of minibus seats. 'Next left, Ace.' We swing into Waldegrave Park, the pleasant tree-lined suburban road where I grew up. 'OK, anywhere round here's great, mate.' Acer puts the brakes on sharply, a couple of empty Lucozade bottles rattle along the floor past my legs, the remnants of our pit stop on the way to rowing earlier this morning. It seems an age ago. He reverses the minibus into a parking space just opposite my house, the small cox expertly manoeuvring the big van. The house is gently illuminated by the glow of street lights.

John and I cross the road together; we're followed a few paces behind by Acer, buckling under the weight of a kit bag almost half his size. In his kit will be his weighing scales. For Acer, getting down to 55 kilos, the minimum weight for a coxswain, will be a constant and enduring challenge over the season; very different from what we rowers face but no less difficult. A few paces behind, Scott wraps up his iPod headphones, putting away his copy of the book *Atlas Shrugged*.

Parked just along the street is the instantly recognisable light green minibus of the Cambridge crew. 'The Tabs are already here, by the looks of things,' I grunt. My dislike of Cambridge, or the Tabs as they're known derogatively amongst us, is developing. And I wasn't happy when I found out from Mum earlier this week that James had already asked if his crew could stay tonight. He's been intruding with his team for years, surely it's my turn now? 'It's fine,' Mum had said, accommodating as usual, 'there's room for everyone.' I was sceptical that there would be space for all of us to sleep in comfort.

I ring the doorbell and soon see Mum's silhouette approaching through the misted glass of the door. Mum opens the door with a jolly hello, wiping her hands on her apron. In a blur Sammy, our ginger cat, hurtles out of the door, through my legs and into the garden.

'Good to see you, Mum.' I lean down and kiss her on the cheek. At five feet seven inches, relatively tall for a woman, she's dwarfed by my brother, father and me.

'The others are already here,' she says, referring obliquely to the Cambridge guys.

'Hello again, Mrs Livingston,' John says cheerily. He has stayed with us before.

'Hi, Mrs Livingston,' follows Acer, also a previous visitor. As I introduce Scott, I hear guffaws of laughter from the living room. The Cambridge guys are already installed next door by the sounds of things.

'Dave, if you show these boys to their rooms, they can drop their things. Dinner will be ready in twenty minutes. One can sleep next door in the front room, one in your bedroom and one in the library.' The library is a grand term for Mum's office, which is filled to the gunwales with bookshelves and books of every variety – pop-ups and children's books of our childhood, my grandfather's weightlifting and athletics volumes, moth-eaten classics from a random aunt and my father's architecture tomes are all part of the mix. I'd like to turn to the guys and say we're about to have a clear-out but it's not true. Nothing is ever thrown away.

'Sounds great, thanks, Mum.' The sleeping situation doesn't seem as bad as I'd feared. I'm just glad none of us needs to share rooms with any of the Cambridge lot. That would be unthinkable. Dumping my stuff, I head down the hall to show the guys to their various billets, past kit bags and piles and piles of musical scores from Mum's local choir, which she looks after as 'librarian'.

The phrase 'lived in' best describes our house. Only Mum truly knows where everything is. Piles of papers, magazines and books cover most flat surfaces. Old regatta programmes surface on occasion, thrown up by the tide of life, generally filled with Mum's neatly pencilled notes of times and margins, of victory or loss. And it wasn't just our boat's results she noted. She also charted everyone we'd ever raced, any Hampton boat, of course, and indeed anyone whose name or face she recognised from the towpath or thought was entertaining.

Mum has made beds up and laid out towels for everyone. Further evidence, if any were needed, that she really is a saint. When we were growing up any insects discovered in the house would be humanely released out of a window. My biosphere of sea monkeys (geekily I knew they were actually tiny shrimp) were repositioned several times because 'the noise of the TV might scare them' and she was afraid of 'waking them up too early in the morning'. On trips to India and China she'd eat up horrendous local delicacies, like blocks of fried goat's cheese or jellied eel soup, so as not to hurt the waiters' feelings, which often meant having to eat Dad's portion as well.

Although she worked as a partner at a stressful city law firm, Mum spent every available moment of our childhood with James and me. She helped us through our GCSEs and A levels, testing us and cajoling us into getting down to the books without ever applying the type of pressure that so often seems to cause a complete swing away from a parent's intentions. I swear she could have sat the exams and done better than either of us. As soon as we started to row the parents were our staunchest supporters. Always on the river bank, even at the smallest of regattas, Mum with the obligatory pack of jelly babies to hand to me before the race, Dad with his cameras. Both ready to celebrate or commiserate.

Acer and I drop our gear in my bedroom. Outside, on the upstairs landing, Acer stops by my wall of rowing photos. 'Awesome photo, Dave, nice curtains,' he says, chuckling at my hairstyle in the Hampton School first eight rowing photo.

'They were big at the time,' is my defence.

'So I see. O'Grady and Smithy have got 'em too.' He fails to mention James, who sits in front of me in the photo, who perhaps has the largest curtains of us all.

As Acer moves off downstairs, I linger at the school photo a few seconds longer. James and I rowing next to each other in our top school eight; National Schools Champions and winners of the Schools Head of the River, two of the most prestigious schoolboy events. We'd become close that year; his mentoring had helped me get in to the crew at the age of sixteen, while he was a final year student, his place at Cambridge all but assured.

We hadn't always been so close. James and I had a rollercoaster ride of a relationship from childhood to our teens. In the early years, like good little boys, we got on well. Then I followed James to Newland House School when I was seven and we began to fight increasingly often, beating the hell out of each other. Sometimes I would intentionally bait James just to get attention or to amuse myself, which often led to fights. On other occasions, albeit rarely, he would initiate a fight and then, when Mum and Dad pulled us apart, blame me for starting it. Infuriatingly, they believed him most of the time.

Our parents got fed up with our near constant fighting and bickering, but mostly managed to mediate in a diplomatic way. Occasionally they did lose their cool. We were on holiday in Kos, a Greek island in the Dodecanese, when I was about eight. One day we took a boat trip out into the waters of the Aegean Sea to attempt to escape the oppressive 104-degree-Fahrenheit heat. As the boat left the harbour I spotted my burgundy bound copy of H. Rider Haggard's *King Solomon's Mines* sitting open on James's lap. My book! How had he got hold of it? What's more, he was really getting into it. As the boat passed the fourteenth-century fortress on the edge of the harbour, James remained gripped by the story, silent and transfixed, eagerly turning page after page. To make things worse, one of the other passengers was equally spellbound, reading it over his shoulder. The more James enjoyed the story the more it annoyed me. That was *my* book, I'd started reading it first. We began to squabble. What would the book's hero, Allan Quartermain, do? I pulled the book away from James's loose sweaty grasp, but he ripped it back, delivering a massive punch to my upper arm as he did so.

'Ow!' I whined. 'Daaad!'

My usually mellow father snapped, bearing down upon us, exasperated.

'I've had enough of you two squabbling!' he shouted, grabbing the book from James. There and then he tore the book clean in half. 'Now you have this half,' he passed me the thinner second half of the book, 'and you have this half.'

It took until James's final year at Hampton before we became close as brothers once again. As we raced and succeeded together it seemed easier to put my lifelong feelings of jealousy and inadequacy to one side. Little did I know that going to Oxford would change all that for ever.

James:

Friday 1 November 20:37, Strawberry Hill, Twickenham

I heard them traipse in a few minutes ago. When Mum told me last week that Dave was also bringing teammates I was surprised, given I'd already made our booking. Dave's as stubborn as me. Well, we've claimed the most comfortable beds and now we have the living room at full capacity with the good TV. Matze, Wayne and I are sandwiched on the sofa, with Hugo on the armchair.

Ferris Bueller's Day Off plays on. A teacher addresses a bored class. 'In 1930, the Republican-controlled House of Representatives, in an effort to alleviate the effects of the . . .' The teacher looks out across his pupils hopefully. 'Anyone? Anyone?' No response. 'The Great Depression, passed the . . . anyone?' No response again. The awkwardness of the scene compels me to face my own slight discomfort so I get up and head out into the hall. Acer is coming down the stairs, with Dave behind him, both of them wearing dark blue Oxford fleeces.

'Hello, little brother.' He looks different. A bit older. A slight change of haircut. There was a time when he'd just copy my hairstyle, however inadvisably.

'Hi, James.' When he gets to the bottom of the stairs we go to embrace but end up just patting each other on the shoulder a bit stiffly. We've spoken once since the beginning of term, two or three weeks ago, but both spent most of the call fishing for information on what crews the other team was putting together for the Fours Head and how initial trialling was going. Already things seem worse between us than at any point last year, even though we were on opposite sides then as well. Maybe Dave resents me coming back this year, when perhaps it should have been his turn in the parental limelight.

Acer and I shake hands professionally. I remembered he'd coxed Dave in Isis last year. Then John Adams appears out of the front room, smiling genuinely. He shakes my hand vigorously and clearly without any agenda.

Hearing the commotion Wayne, Matze and Hugo come out and line up alongside me. There's a flurry of introductions and hellos and polite shaking of hands. My friends' American, Canadian and German accents are very noticeable compared to those of Dave's English teammates. The introductions are interrupted by a curly-haired man of wiry build coming down the stairs.

'James, this is Scott.' Dave introduces us. As we shake hands his fiery blue eyes bore into mine. Scott and Wayne greet each other familiarly, having raced in the Canadian National Team together. After everyone's been introduced and chatted non-committally about how things are going, conversation runs a little dry. John Adams seems to be the only one immune to the tense atmosphere. It's a relief when Mum comes out from the kitchen and calls us in for dinner.

David:

Friday 1 November 20:52, Strawberry Hill, Twickenham

The Oxford contingent, John, Scott, Acer and I, sit on one side of our family kitchen, scoffing bread, waiting for supper. Across the breakfast bar on the other side sit Cambridge. Mum has refused all offers of help in preparing dinner, insisting that we would get in the way.

We've been discussing how today's rowing went. Luckily none of us got heavily 'Bowdenated', our slang for an intense burst of coaching from our Sean, which could shatter the confidence of even the most self-assured oarsman. Countless times I've seen crews rowing past the Wallingford Boathouse in the winter gloom, at the end of a session, practising a strange rowing exercise, up to the top lock, followed by Sean. His passion is unquestionable; in his eyes there is only one right way to row. Anything different is simply wrong.

I hear James laughing with his Cambridge cronies, Hugo, Wayne and Matthias, who are ready to eat as well. It's the first time I've met them and I'm struck not only by them all being internationals, but also by how much older they are than us. Wayne is bald and could be a double for Captain Picard from the Starship *Enterprise*. He'll be racing in the Cambridge coxed four tomorrow, my direct competition. Hugo is as tall and broad as James and sports designer stubble and a grey Harvard sweatshirt. He races with James and Matthias in the top coxless fours event. Matthias, or Matze as they call him, must be in his late twenties and his English has a gentle, yet precise German accent. I bet he's a good rower; his white, Deutschland T-shirt adorned with the German black, red and yellow flag on his left breast indicates he has been part of their famously successful national team. Tomorrow afternoon we're going to find out just how fast all these Cambridge guys are.

I'm racing at stroke in Oxford's top ranked coxed four, alongside Scott, Macca, BT and Acer on the rudder strings. My season has started well; I'd ranked second in the early season pairs racing with John, behind Scott and BT, done fine in the physiological testing and technically I'm starting to row more fluidly. The scrawled handwriting in my training diary on the bumpy bus journeys marks my personal improvements at both. I feel fit and my body fat is down. I don't want to carry any excess weight; Dr Sitchel measured my body fat at 6 per cent. I want it down to 4 per cent.

Our crew is going up against the Cambridge coxed four of Wayne, Tim Wooge, their supersized German president whose Oxford-crushing confidence oozes from his every pore, a strokesider called Buschbacher, and Alex McGarel-Groves, who I beat last year in the Isis–Goldie race. They will start directly in front of us and we will be trying to close the ten-second gap the organisers leave between crews. Acer will closely judge our progress against them. James is racing in the top coxless fours event, with Matthias, Hugo and another American, Nate.

'Dave, can you go and get some more squash out of the cellar, please, we're almost ready to dish up,' Mum asks, waking me from my thoughts, while stirring a massive trough of pasta sauce on the kitchen hob. She seems to really enjoy these rowing crew get-togethers.

'Yep, sure,' I say, rising to my feet. Walking out of the kitchen, I overhear Hugo talking to James about his PhD – something about radio tagging and Hugo Boss handbags. The cellar door creaks open and I reach into the dark for the light switch. It illuminates the dusty, stone steps down to the cellar. The shelving on the right houses a cork collection and hundreds of random keys. Nobody knows what they open. I pace down a couple of the stone steps and reach for a bottle of orange squash, beside one of the markings on the left cellar wall: 'David age eleven, almost five foot six inches'. I'd grown a whopping four inches that year.

Dad used to mark James's and my heights on the wall, around birthdays or Christmas time, the first as a joke on New Year's Eve 1991, alarmed by how fast James and I were growing. From then on it had become enshrined as a family tradition. James was usually the first to be measured. Dad would use a set square pressed against the top of our heads to draw a line in permanent marker, to which was added our age and height. By the time James was twelve he was five foot six and three-eighths inches, and as tall as the average fully grown man. I was always second to be measured. By the time I was twelve I was two inches taller than James at that age. A small but satisfying victory.

Being the elder by almost three years, James was first to do everything. He was the first to go to Hampton School, the first to get GCSE results and get a girlfriend, even if she didn't last long. All his school results were just that bit better than mine, and it seemed he breezed through everything with consummate ease. On my first day in A level economics my teacher, Mr Medcraft, asked me, 'David, are you James Livingston's younger brother?' 'Yes,' I'd replied sheepishly. 'Oh good, you know he is the best economics student I ever taught? He took the A level in AS time and managed to get 100 per cent in an exam I didn't even teach him! Such a brilliant student.' Oh great, I thought, another impossible standard to live up to. He had just left school with five straight As and a place at Cambridge, having already rowed for his country and been a school prefect.

My emotions swing between pride and love, to dark envy and hate. I resent him for being so good at everything. The parents always seem to be more impressed when he achieves something than when I do, as he is their first son to have done it.

I stand up and read the last two measurements on the cellar wall: 'David no shoes, six foot seven inches, 20 years old'; 'James six foot four and a half inches, 21 years old'. At least I really have overtaken him in the height stakes.

Closing the cellar door, I bring the bottle back into the kitchen and mix a jug of squash.

I follow Mum over to the Oxford table. 'Here you go, please help yourselves.' She places a cauldron of pasta sauce in front of us to go with the mountain of fusilli piled on our plates. I plonk the replenished jug of squash down on the table.

'Thank you very much, Mrs Livingston, this looks great,' says John as he dishes it out to our table, before tucking in. Acer's meagre plate, which is mostly sauce, looks comical compared to the heaps around it.

'How long will it take us to get to St Paul's tomorrow?' Acer asks. 'We'll need to be there by eight.'

'About 25 minutes, at that time in the morning, so let's say breakfast at 7ish,' I suggest.

'Sounds good,' he replies. The others nod in agreement, mouths full of pasta.

'Where's that from?' John points above the mantelpiece towards the large framed newspaper cutting of two rowing crews at the start of the Boat Race. The umpire has a pistol in hand and he stands on the prow of a massive paddle steamer. The date reads 5 April 1877. Below the two crews, the caption reads, 'Are you ready?'

'Dad bought it at an auction in Henley. It's an illustrated pull-out from the *London Gazette* from 1877. It was the year of the dead heat. Apparently Oxford won by six feet but the judge on the finishing line was in a drunken stupor so called it a draw.'

'A draw! That'll never happen again,'exclaimed John.

Across from us the Cambridge guys are talking in hushed tones. They seem awfully relaxed; the Oxford table is even quieter, partly as Scott is visibly hyped up, being so close to the competition. Only John seems to be himself; only he does not fear or hate them.

I'm aware of the responsibility I'll be taking on tomorrow – stroking the boat means setting the pace for the long course. It's also my opportunity to prove to Sean that I should be in the Blue Boat this year. BT will sit behind me, giving me the odd word of encouragement. Some of the college rowers know him as 'BT 3000' as his tough, automaton-like attitude is mistaken by some for coldness, yet I know he's a passionate racer. Scott and Macca are also both tremendous competitors, placed first and second respectively on the American University racing circuit. I'm sure we'll be fast but my real worry is beating the Cambridge crews. We will get to race Cambridge once more before the Boat Race, on the rowing machines at the national ergo championships, but this is the only time we will race them on the water.

Bedtime comes around before I know it and we ascend the stairs to our various rooms. On the way up Scott pushes past James, shoulder-barging him. It looks like an accident but neither Scott nor James says anything.

Scott's mattress is laid out on the floor of the 'library', which looks more like a second-hand bookshop with dusty books everywhere. 'Night, Scott, see you in the morning, I'll wake you up.'

'Dave, we're gonna win this race tomorrow,' he cuts in.

'I hope so. I really hope so,' I say, lingering for a few moments. 'Night.' I close the door behind me.

James:
Saturday 2 November 15.34, Putney Embankment

It didn't initially feel like a triumph. My coxless four of Matze, Hugo, Nate and I thought we had a decent if not great row when we'd crossed the line at Putney. Now I'm picking up a burger with Hugo and Wayne from one of the stalls that pop up for the day, the drizzle forcing everyone beneath the gazebos. The Smith parents and gran are here too, umbrellas at the ready, to meet Ben first, then walk fifty metres down the bank to their other son, Matt. It's nice to see them; Lord knows how many times they drove me to school with Matt or picked us up from rowing.

Waiting for fried onions for our burgers, Wayne says he didn't think their row was great either and Tim was pretty unhappy with it. Not a huge surprise as Tim is an absolute perfectionist. The coxed four of Tim, Wayne, Busch and Groves, with Steph, last year's Goldie cox, had become known as the Four of Doom over the last few weeks, renowned for its general aura of unhappiness and frustration. Despite the name, though, they are always fast. And so it had proved today.

Both our fours have won their divisions, beating Oxford's boats by decent margins and the rest of Britain into the bargain. Our 'third' four went almost unsettlingly fast, finishing just behind Oxford's coxless four, and third in the country. New Aussie Kris Coventry, known in relaxed Australian fashion as KC, Ben Clare, TJ and JA had been formidable. Overall definitely 'Cambridge Victor', as someone said, parodying the movie *Gladiator*.

For me it's a rare easing of tension. For once I feel free. Free of the relentless everyday questioning – are we doing enough to win? How fast are they? Is this whole year going to be wasted? It's a great feeling, even if it can only last a day. Tonight we'll party but tomorrow morning we're back in training, side by side in eights, while Oxford are having the day off. I wonder what the ultra-competitive Scott Frandsen will make of that.

David:

Saturday 2 November 16:02, Westminster School Boathouse, Putney, London

Christ!

The damn Cambridge coxed four beat us by five seconds! I stand there a little stunned; partly from the defeat, and partly from just how fast these Cambridge guys are. The comments after the race were correct. Oxford did not perform well. Acer's instinct, that we let them slip away in the second half of the race, was right.

I push my way back through the crowd that has amassed around the results board at Westminster School Boathouse before emerging on to the empty balcony. I stand for a few moments looking at the river, our battle ground next April.

'Plenty more work to do,' says Acer, appearing next to me. He pats me on the back glumly before wandering off in the direction of the minibus.

I go over the times again in my head. We lost, and lost badly. It's not good, whichever way you cut it.

'Shit, their coxless four even beat ours by nine seconds!' I say under my breath, reaffirming what a large margin our other top crew of Matt Smith, Matt Daggett, Bas Dixon and John Adams had lost by. What the hell are we going to do? What can we do to get back on track?

James:

Thursday 7 November 06:27, Cambridge

My feeble bike light glimmers on a large black puddle in the cold pre-dawn and I swerve out into the middle of the road, almost getting hit by an early morning commuter. The car pulls past with windscreen wipers going and the windows mostly steamed up.

'Bastard!' I swear under my breath. The driver's snug and warm in there. Out in the cyclists' darkness it's still raining. There's been a miserable, constant, understated downpour for what seems like the last month. How is that even possible? Surely the sky can't hold that much water? Someone at training said we're already on for the wettest November on record. It's very believable. Leaving a sleeping, warm, near-naked Sam in my single bed this morning, and heading out into the darkness and icy rain, was the hardest thing in the world. It seems inhumane. The happy glow from the Fours Head has already evaporated.

The bike tyres fire a continuous spray of rainwater on to the back of my soggy jeans, the mudguards somehow redundant. We are in a liquid world. When we get to Goldie boat club for training, there'll be a brief respite from the dampness while we change into our training gear, but once a few weights have been lifted or a couple of minutes done on the ergometer, sweat will soak us. Then it's into the shower and our damp clothes for breakfast and lectures. The views from the drive to Ely after lunch will be obscured by rain against the windscreen and condensation covering the windows. A wipe with a damp sleeve will reveal a glimpse of a muddy brown vista before the condensation edits out the outside world again. When we are rowing, the rain penetrates no matter how many 'waterproof' layers are worn. A splash of river water from the oar of the man in front doesn't cause the normal grimace as we are perpetually soaked through.

When I get to the boat club I glance into the erg room on my way to the changing room. Wayne and Matze are already on the erg warming up. God, they are such intense trainers. Matze apparently gets up at 5.30 a.m. so he has time for his full stretching regime and doesn't have to rush breakfast.

In the changing room, Hugo is regaling those present with Buschbacher's recent activities. There is normally plenty to say on the matter. Ladies seem to like him. And he likes the ladies.

'So it's the Guy Fawkes night fireworks on Midsummer Common and we – that's me, Bungle and some of the other guys – are watching from the St Catharine's boathouse and we're all getting showered with burning embers. Busch is there enjoying himself with his arm round some girl . . .'

'As usual,' says Wooge.

Hugo continues, 'Yep. Then the crowd in front of Busch parts and a really pissed-off-looking girl storms up to him and says, "I thought you said you were busy!" He looks at both girls then turns to the really angry one and says, "Er. I *am* busy." '

David:

Thursday 7 November 17:30, Wallingford

The bus pulls away from Wallingford. I rummage in my bag and bring out a folded piece of paper. It's an email from our president, Matt, which he sent yesterday. I begin to scan it once again:

> We are not a club that makes excuses. The results at the Fours Head are not an ideal way to begin our racing season against Cambridge; however, they are not disastrous. We have done a lot of talking about being elite athletes, it is now time to step up, and take on the responsibility of acting like them.
>
> We will have a Fours Head debrief and goal-setting meeting tomorrow night straight after rowing. I would like everybody to think hard about what they are doing this for, so when you arrive everybody has an honest answer to the question, what is the goal of your training with the OUBC?
>
> This is where we come together and get that edge, fight for that inch, and do it every session.
>
> Matt

As we drive through Newnham Courtney, on our route back to Oxford, we pass the second-hand car dealership. The mannequin on the forecourt, permanently dressed in a Hawaiian shirt, electronically waves his arm up and down in salute. I see far more of him than I see of Maria. So far training this year has been solid, measured and disciplined; sticking to the training splits and heart rates we have been given, keeping it steady. Now it is time to really push on, and with each session we need to start clawing back at Cambridge's lead. We can't be left behind. I can miss no more training outings for academic work; no more just going through the motions. We are going to have to put everything on the line. Matt Daggett won't love the suggestion of missing his MBA classes. We have only five more hard weeks until our short Christmas break.

The minibus pulls into the Iffley Road car park. We walk over to the gym. Inside, we sit down on mats, boxes and the odd chair. Sheets of paper are handed round, as if this is the receiver's board meeting for a failing company.

Fours Head Results comparison:
Average race times of top two boats

Year	OUBC	CUBC
2000:	18m.55s	18m.40s

CUBC win by 15 seconds

| 2001: | 19m.08s | 19m.01s |

CUBC win by 7 seconds

| 2002: | 19m.30s | 19m.20s |

CUBC win by 10 seconds

Matt, Sean and Derek stand at the front, ready to address the workers.

'Right, guys,' starts Matt, 'we all know why we're here. The results at the weekend did not go as planned. As you can see on the sheet I've handed out, we have a gap of ten seconds between us and Cambridge. It's a big margin but not an impossible one to make up. Tonight we're here to discuss our goals and what we're going to do to beat Cambridge next April, because if we don't change something we're going to lose.'

Doing all this for nothing; the bleakness of a Boat Race defeat. I can only imagine the hollowness and emptiness. The group of twenty or so of us sit daunted and disheartened. We knew there was a mountain to climb ahead of us but now the route has been re-written and it's even steeper and higher than before.

Sean takes over from Matt: 'I would like to make a few points. We clearly need to keep pushing the training to make the necessary improvements. Also I have revised the training schedule and put in some harder weeks till Christmas. Technically we still have a long way to go until we're rowing the correct way. We are generally missing too much water around the front end of the stroke so by the time our legs are working we've lost a third of the drive. Physiologically, the testing tells us we have to produce at least twenty more watts of power per man if we're going to have a chance.

'We have to face it: physically there is no question that Cambridge are more powerful than us.'

James:

Friday 8 November 18:52, St Chad's, Cambridge

I'm not looking forward to this. I've been putting off this call for hours.

'Hello?' Sam sounds a little down.

'Hey, babe.'

'Hey!' She brightens. 'I've just booked this really nice Italian for tomorrow night. I discovered it with my parents. I think you'll really like it. I've been to M&S too and . . .'

'Er, Sam,' I interrupt.

'What?' she replies, suddenly suspicious.

'I can't make it this weekend,' I blurt out.

'But . . .'

'I'm really sorry,' I interject. 'I'm just so behind. I've got three essays to do for Monday and I'm behind with supervision work.'

'We've had this planned for weeks.'

'I know . . .'

'You can study up here. And on the train.'

'It won't work. I need to be in the library.'

'But you haven't been up here once yet. It's been months! And I thought you said this is one of the only chances you have to come up because you've got Sunday and Monday off for once.' She sounds really upset.

'It is. I know, I'm really, really sorry. I'm just so far behind. And we're seeing each other next week, aren't we?'

'If I drive to your door. And even then you're at that bloody ergo competition all of Sunday.'

Her tears are painful to listen to. She sounds devastated. I feel like the world is falling in.

'It'll be different after the race,' I tell her.

James:

Sunday 17 November 11:30, National Indoor Arena, Birmingham

Today is the twenty-second anniversary of my birth. Almost a quarter-century on the planet so far. I should be celebrating. Sam has driven down from Nottingham specially. After my dropping out last week I ordered a big bunch of flowers from a florist, but they wouldn't deliver to Sam's address. Her kind flatmate Penny took pity on me and Sam after I'd spoken to her, and she collected the flowers and installed them in Sam's tiny room as a surprise.

Last night we went for dinner at an Italian restaurant overlooking the Cam, with me on the mineral water, carefully monitoring the amount of protein and fat in my order. Hardly Mr Romantic.

Now I'm in Birmingham, in the arena that used to house *Gladiators*, while Sam hangs out in Cambridge with my flatmate Andy.

Instead of partying I'm watching each of my friends punish themselves in turn. It's like a scene from rowing Hades. Over a hundred ergometers line the arena floor in five or six rows with athletes pulling desperately at the machines, while supporters and competitors fill the banked seating, watching and cheering. A vast screen stands behind the machines and indicates the relative positions of the competitors with computer-simulated boats. This is the annual National Indoor Rowing Championships, where 3,000 come each year to race over the standard two-kilometre distance and measure themselves against the best in Britain and their own personal bests. The fastest men in the world complete the distance in around 5 minutes 50 seconds. The best in our squad are looking for 6 minutes, the lighter or less experienced 6 minutes 20 seconds. No matter how long it takes, the outcome is the same. Blinding pain. Hearts will be racing at over 200 beats a minute, bodies full of lactic acid. There is nowhere to hide out there, no crewmates to blame or commiserate with. There is no opportunity to take it easy and catch your breath, as there is in side-by-side rowing races if you can develop a commanding lead. It's just you and your score. A good result here and you can really stake your claim on a seat. Robin and the coaches will study the results closely to help with selection and gauge our training for the coming months.

Oxford are here too, stalking sternly around the stands. Their defeat at the Fours Head has made them all prickly and they seem to have crew-issue scowls. David is even more distant than a few weeks ago back at home. No birthday wishes from him. Sean seems to instil hatred for the opposition in his teams, and Dave is falling under the spell, willingly brainwashed.

Wooge and I sit in the front row of the stands with Goldie coaches Donald and Rob. Wooge is grumpy. He had a cold earlier in the week and decided, with Robin's blessing, to miss the test. I asked him about it and he mumbled a few disconsolate words, something about not being ready. He is here to support and to lead as president. I think he's feeling the pressure.

I'm putting myself under pressure too today. My post-collar bone comeback score of 6.15 was closer to the Goldie standard than a typical Blue Boat score. I need to prove I'm really back, that I'm fit. I want Robin pencilling me firmly into his plans for the boat and to beat the Oxford guys into the bargain. First, I have the luxury of watching others test, as my under-23 race is one of the last of the day. Dave will race in it too.

Wayne and our Aussie Kris Coventry are the first to race, sitting on ergs side by side, with Matze in the row behind. KC looks impressive. We all agree he appears even more lean than normal, with veins bulging in arms and legs. He stares manically at the readout on his machine as he drives to the finish. Wayne, alongside, doesn't seem to be having a good test and in the stand we grimace to each other as he clamps his eyes shut in an attempt to block out the pain and finishes with short stabbing strokes. Wooge, the coaches and I cheer enthusiastically, trying to mitigate his agony. Matze and KC finish in 6.10, with Wayne a few seconds behind on 6.16, a little way off his best.

A few divisions later we get to enjoy watching cox Jim battle it out on the back row. He's dwarfed by those on either side of him but he still battles gamely. Despite going a luminous shade of red and clearly being totally shot in the last 500 metres he finishes in 8.02. He may be half our weight but he's not twice as slow. It's pretty heroic.

Then it's young TJ's turn in the under-18s. Most of his category are still schoolboys, apart from the floppy-haired Sam Parker, who is a fresher at Oxford. For Sam and Tom there's no one else in this race. They eye each other before the start. On the 'GO!' TJ is off into a controlled long rhythm, looking technically perfect. The splits aren't fantastic but he looks so composed. Parker is pulling away, with a determined push. Sam and Tom raced together in Britain's top junior crew, the coxless four, just a few months ago at the Junior World Championships in Lithuania. They'd been in the gold medal position but had faltered in the final hundred metres and had to settle for silver. There were questions about what had happened and both Sam and TJ are obviously desperate to prove the last-minute failure hadn't been their doing.

As we watch and cheer the minutes tick by and Tom starts to notch it up while Parker begins to struggle. A few commentators with micro-phones stalk amongst the machines, noting courageous charges and interesting battles. One of the commentators is my old teacher and coach, Martin Cross, who won Olympic gold in 1984 with Steve Redgrave, charging through the mist of Lake Casitas in Los Angeles to pip the Americans. He loves this Oxford/Cambridge match-up and his commentary reaches fever pitch as TJ passes Parker in the closing metres in a perfectly judged race. Wooge and I raise our eyebrows at each other. There's a contender for the Blue Boat here.

Now it's my turn. Dave and I curtly nod to each other on the warm-up machines. I must beat him and Oxford's top bowsider Robin Bourne-Taylor.

On the arena floor I find my race machine, alongside Oxford's Scott Frandsen. He's going to regret pushing past me in my own home – accident or not. Nate's to my left. He looks pale. We clasp hands.

'For Cambridge,' I say. Groves is a few more ergs along and his dark eyebrows are furrowed deeply. He looks angry.

I pull a few final practice bursts. My limbs feel heavy; adrenalin is doing its work. I'm ready.

Then the voice of Barry Davies echoes round the vast arena. 'And away we go! Cambridge nearer the camera, Oxford on the far Surrey side.' I don't need to look round to know they've started to play the video of the Boat Race six months ago on the big screen.

Great. After a minute the images on screen cut to midway through the race and the voice-over continues.

'Cambridge's technique is perhaps coming into its own now. Cam-bridge have their nose ahead.' The camera pans to our light blue boat moving ahead of Oxford on the outside of their Hammersmith bend.

The footage cuts to the finish. 'Cambridge are in real trouble on strokeside but it's still up for grabs. From here on in it's a straight sprint!' shouts Barry Davies on the voice-over.

Matt Pinsent, realising Cambridge are in trouble, says, 'One of the Cambridge men is absolutely spent!'

And Barry continues, 'It's one of the great races of all time here. Just look how close this is. Oxford are inching in front!'

I hate this.

'You cannot imagine how tired they are now,' Matt Pinsent chimes in pitifully.

I can, Matt, I can.

Then Barry, taking over for the final yards: 'The seven oarsmen of Cambridge are trying to hold off the Oxford charge but now they're coming to the finishing line. Oxford are going to win the Boat Race! They've done it. What happened in the Cambridge boat?' Then the screams of Oxford as they realise they've won. Then they cut the feed.

The compère takes up the microphone. 'Can Cambridge avenge themselves today? Let's find out. Competitors pick up the handles. Attention. Go!'

The remaining metres fall to zero on the machine and I slump over, panting, a half second after Nate. Satisfyingly, it takes Frandsen a few more strokes to finish. Still breathing hard, I look over my shoulder. Dave is still going, eyes shut and teeth gritted. Good. I watch his little computer boat on the big screen as it bobs in 8 seconds after me, in 6 minutes 16 seconds. Excellent. I see Groves finished in 6.02, by far the fastest of any of us. Bourne-Taylor was behind me and Nate. Again, good.

Crossy, the commentator, walks over to me and grins. 'James Livingston, of Cambridge. Well done, a good score. How do you feel? Did you get what you were looking for?'

'Thanks, Martin. I'm pretty happy. It's not far off what I was looking for.' I'd been aiming for 6.05 but couldn't find the right rhythm early on. The damn 2002 race kept playing itself in my head. Martin nods at me to continue. '6.08 will do. And it's always nice to put one over your little brother, isn't it?' I smile, turning to look over at Dave and wink at him. But he doesn't see me, he's laid out prostrate next to his machine.

David:
Sunday 17 November 15:21, National Indoor Arena, Birmingham

The arena roof spins around me, the lactic acid sears my entire body as if to punish me for my disappointing test score. My limbs are splayed wherever they fell from the machine.

'Dave, Dave. You OK, mate?'

I don't open my eyes but it sounds like James. My chest still heaves up and down furiously.

'Dave? Have some water.' I feel a bottle at my mouth and I open my clenched eyes, accepting some of the liquid.

'I'm fine,' I choke. I try to mask my grimace and the pain. I don't want to show him my vulnerability.

'Come on then, best walk it off.' He helps me up and we stagger out of the arena into the cold November air. I stumble to the metal railings that skirt the arena.

'I'll be fine. Leave me here,' I insist, facing away from him, leaning on the cold rails. Without their support I'd be on the floor again. A few silent moments later James walks off to the cool-down area.

James:
Sunday 17 November 15:39, National Indoor Arena, Birmingham

Half an hour later I'm in the stands with the remaining Cambridge team, rustling through my bag for a dry T-shirt. Robin approaches Groves, who's sitting a few seats further down, looking as though he's chewing a wasp.

'I know what you're going to say, Alex,' says Robin, with his palms up.

Groves launches in. 'It was shit. I just couldn't find a rhythm. It didn't feel right.' Groves is desperate for his first Blue and, despite pulling the best score of the Cambridge camp by a margin, he is sure he could have done better. As a junior international he was renowned for his freakish physiology. When doing step tests, short pieces of progressively higher wattage on the rowing machine, the levels of lactic acid in his blood actually decreased, to the shock of our team physiologist. It was only when Groves was almost flat out that the lactate actually increased and even then it was only to a couple of millimoles, when for most people it would be ten times that. He hadn't managed to capture his huge potential in his first two years at Cambridge, partly due to developing two bulging discs in his back in 2001 which almost ended his career and could have left him in permanent chronic pain.

A tap on my shoulder distracts me.

'Happy birthday!' say Mum and Dad as I turn to them, smiling. 'We've brought you your cards. Gran says well done.'

'Thanks! Have you seen Dave?'

Mum looks sheepish. 'He hasn't really spoken to us. He's upset with his result.'

We chat happily for a few minutes more before my phone beeps with a text message. It reads, 'Where are u? Beer waiting in minibus! DB.' Looking round, I see that everyone else has left.

'Mum, Dad, I've got to run. Thanks for coming up.' We hug and then I dash back to the van. As I climb into the back there's a chorus of 'At last!' and 'Finally, Bungle.' Dan Barry, one of the new guys in our squad, who along with Busch, the squad clown, is our self-appointed social secretary, passes me a four-pack of cold Fosters.

'Happy birthday, Bungle!'

Halfway through my second can, as we turn on to the A45, I realise my mistake. I'm already drunk, at least two hours from Cambridge and need the loo badly in a bus full of guys impatient to get home. I reach into my bag for my empty water bottle. What a birthday this is turning out to be.

Chapter 5
Two Houses Both Alike in Dignity

David:

Friday 22 November 14:23, The M4, near Oxford

Our minibus sits stationary in the motorway traffic of the M4. Acer manages to drive another few feet forward before putting on the brakes and coming to yet another standstill. The flash of red brake lights frustrates me. There's barely enough time in my day as it is, without unexpected delays. We won't be at Eton College's Dorney Lake rowing course for another half an hour at least. My essay on 'The future challenges for the survival of deep-sea ecosystems' for tomorrow's tutorial will have to be a rushed job tonight. Despite my concerns about deep-sea fishermen devastating populations of the orange roughy and the concurrent destruction of deep-sea ecosystems, my immediate priority is getting a good, sizeable dinner and some sleep.

An article about BT in the student newspaper had just about kept us entertained on our commute thus far. It described his impressive rowing achievements for Oxford and Great Britain. The female journalist was obviously quite enamoured with BT, so much so that one line read, 'Women want him and men want to be him', which had caused huge rounds of piss-taking.

'Boys! Look what's coming from the other bus,' shouts Acer excitedly, peering at his rear-view mirror. Turning round, I can make out the figure of a big, naked, very ginger guy running along the M4 towards us, in nothing but a pair of dark brown deck shoes.

Seconds later Mark Vickers pulls open the minibus side door and bundles in, jumping on to poor, defenceless Henry, who sits in the window seat.

'Urrr, mate, get off!' he shouts in outrage as Vickers's dangly bits crush up against him. The whole bus is in stitches of laughter. Henry shoves Vickers off, who then perches on the edge of the seat by the door before reaching over and locking it.

'Here comes another one!' shouts Acer.

This time it's a naked Sam Parker who runs along the tarmac road. He arrives at the bus, expecting the door to pull open. It doesn't budge. He tries again, giving us looks of beseeching desperation which only serve to make it funnier for us inside. As if by magic, the traffic pulls off in front of us. Acer restarts the engine and moves the bus forward. We gain speed; it seems as if the jam has dissolved. Sam jogs alongside us, passing cars in the nearside lane of traffic, which remain at a standstill.

Between snorts of mirth, Henry points to a girl in one of the stationary cars. Her head is in her hands, shaking with laughter at the sight of a naked man running along the motorway. She'd probably be even more surprised to find out he's one of the nicest, most polite boys she could ever hope to meet. He'd be 'bloody sorry' about this behaviour.

Seeing we're laughing too hard to unlock the door, Sam falls back to the other minibus waiting behind. Initially they won't let him in either, but after a few seconds they relent; their door swings open and he piles in. We're finally on our way again.

David:

Sunday 24 November 07:37, Dorney Lake, Eton

The man-made lake stretching out in front of us reflects the dull and lifeless winter sky. A gust of wind whistles across the exposed surface, chilling us still further. This soulless place is our temporary rowing home as our Wallingford base has been badly flooded by the near-constant rain of the past two months.

Given the depressing weather, endless commuting and the drudgery of training, morale is predictably low. The squad is tired, cold and hungry. And while the adversity and strains of training day in, day out have begun to bond us, internal competition for the eight seats is constantly on our minds.

Henry stands shivering on the edge of the group, his arms crossed to conserve warmth. He's only recently come back to training after breaking his wrist in a bike accident earlier this season. Bill Fedyna (one of our six Americans), started training with us around the time Henry got injured and, as a former lightweight World Champion, is certainly a threat to his seat.

With the season well underway Blue Boat candidates are rising to the surface. At the moment, BT and Macca look to have taken two bowside seats. Daggett, John, Henry and Bill will fight for the other two seats on that side.

Far more relevant to me is my competition on strokeside. Matt and Bas, the two former Blues, are almost certain of a place and Scott too is likely to be named in the crew, given his impressive performances on water and on the machines. That leaves me fighting with Hutchy and Sam Parker for the last precious place. My anxiety about making it has helped me train hard, but deep down I'm still not sure I'll ever be good enough to be a Blue. Hutchy might be chosen for his phenomenal power, which compared to Cambridge we lack this year, or Parker for his general athletic ability and boat-moving skill. Both are very worthy adversaries and I fear them.

In the small peoples' world I think Acer has all but got his position sewn up. Megan, a five-foot-tall Princeton alumna, and Will Young, a friend of mine from the junior GB squad, will wrestle for Isis.

As I look around it's obvious that we're the only boat club training here today. No one else is crazy enough: it is arctic out here. Enviously, I think of Sally, who I left studying in the warm college library.

The dark blue coaching car pulls up. Out stumble the coaching staff wrapped in layer upon layer of clothing, resembling Michelin men. Sean unfolds a piece of paper from his pocket and begins to read crew lists of two eights. As he does so it dawns on those of us who have gone through this before that these crews are more meaningful than normal. These are Trial Eights crews.

Just before Christmas OUBC race two notionally equal boats over the Boat Race course. Cambridge of course have a similar race too. Trial Eights is the only time we race side by side in eights over the four and a quarter miles of the course, except for the Boat Race itself, and as such is a major event in the season. Athletes new to Oxford are able to appreciate first hand just how much longer four and a quarter miles is than the international regatta standard of two kilometres; returning squad members are reminded of the mental endurance required. Coxes can practice their race tactics and their lines into the bends. The coaches use the Trial Eights to try combinations of oarsmen and look for weakness. The press use the Trial Eights to see how the universities are shaping up and to tip the future contenders. The six or so oarsmen who are not selected for the race will look on enviously, knowing they're going to have to step up their game to be in with a shout of a row on Boat Race day.

'Looks like we've got Trial Eights crews,' Henry says quietly, confirming my thoughts.

'And we've got the internationals in our crew,' I reply smugly. The power and strength of Macca, Daggett, Hutch and Scott should come in handy in a race situation. While they are not known for their fine technique, the crews produced by the American universities achieve astonishing speeds, largely through a combination of brute strength and ferocious race aggression.

'Scott's crew are in *OUBC1*, please, Matt's are in the *Sleeping Elephant*,' instructs Jonny, Sean's coaching assistant. I lean towards Henry. 'We've got the newer boat, then. Another good omen!'

The yellow boat, *Sleeping Elephant*, was used by the 2000 Oxford Blue Boat. The name apparently came from the movie *When We Were Kings*, the documentary about Mohammed Ali, a hero whose resilience resonated with the OUBC.

A few paces over towards the boat rack I overhear Steve, a college rower from Magdalen who wants to step up to the big time this year, talking to Sean. 'Sean, my name wasn't read out,' he says, somewhat concerned. It's a bad sign. This is probably the end of the road for Steve and we'll start tomorrow's training with 24, rather than 25 athletes. Poor bastard, he'll go back to college with nothing to show for his efforts over the last three months apart from a pile of overdue work to catch up on and the odd piece of dark-blue rowing kit. Sean must have forgotten to give him the news before he got on the bus to Eton.

We complete the warm-up and line up next to the other crew at the top of the lake. 'Hurry up and turn around,' Sean's voice booms across the water, his megaphone peeping out of a slit in the car window on the bank, so as not to let out their precious hot air.

'OK, let's row down together, rating 18 to 20. We'll be taking times.'

A race, in other words.

'Tuppen, take a stroke,' Acer instructs. The puddles flow under my blade, slewing the boat straight in the buoyed racing lane. 'Bow pair, row it up.' The strokes draw us level with the other crew. I'm confident we can beat these guys.

'Get ready,' Sean shouts. 'Attention, Go' he says flatly.

We draw off the first few strokes. Out of the corner of my eye I can tell we're already slightly ahead of the other crew.

'That's good boys, long strokes, holding in the finish,' Acer tells us.

I try to draw my oar handle up a little higher and point my toes at the finish of the stroke in the hope of getting a bit more length.

'YEAH! That's it, boys, now we're moving away.'

'Both crews, come down to rate . . . NOW!' demands Sean. Neither crew is following the specified training rate.

'Ok guys, we're at 24, we need to let the boat run four strokes per minute, ready, GO.' Acer's call makes us take more time between each pull on the oar, slowing us down. But it's not what we want to do as the crew next to us is beginning to eke out a lead with their higher stroke rate.

'We're through 500 metres, boys, in 1 minute and 40 seconds. Crisp, sharp, crisp, sharp.' Macca and Scott's oars cut into the water faster at the front of our slides, gripping the water more effectively.

'Yeah, let's go, ten strokes now,' I say between my gritted teeth.

We begin to take a few more strokes per minute, and start clawing back the slight lead the other crew has on us. 'Moving back,' Henry shouts from a few seats behind me. The thrill of competition pumps us with adrenalin and our rate stroke rises even more. We're way above Sean's specified training tempo now.

'Bring the rate down, both crews! Acer, your crew's at 26, Megan, yours is at 27, take it down NOW!' Sean yells with irritation.

The coxes obediently relay the instruction, but neither crew is listening. We know we're not training at the right levels but we're not taking our stroke rate down until the other crew does. What are we doing this for if not to win?

James:

Wooge lowers his mobile. 'Bakes is going to be 15 minutes late.' Half the squad, which is now reduced to about 24 in total, is assembled at Goldie Boathouse waiting for Rob Baker, our boatman, who is driving the second minibus and towing the trailer of boats.

'Pub?' Groves offers. There is general agreement and we stroll up the road. There is a tangible buzz amongst the guys. Term ends today and we're off to train for the weekend on Windermere in the Lake District. This is Robin's new idea; he's a keen sailor and has often sailed on Windermere and thought that it could make an excellent training venue. Essays and reports have been done and supervisions completed. Academically we can take a breath now. Most of us have mountains of project work, set holiday essays or just plain catching up to do but it can wait. It's a relief. Academic and social pressures and the cumulative sleep deprivation from early morning training have reduced most of us to zombies. I fell asleep having my hair cut yesterday.

Winter is definitely upon us. We get back from Ely in darkness and dawn doesn't come until halfway through our morning gym sessions. Still, adversity has brought us together; even though most of us met only two months ago, many of the new friendships feel lifelong.

Girlfriends have been given notice of the trip to the Lakes and they are not happy. Rowing is yet again stealing their men. One of last year's Goldie crew is particularly in the dog-house as it's his girlfriend's birthday.

As I hand him his pint he explains, 'She really wasn't pleased when I said, "Sorry, I can't make your twenty-first birthday party, I'm off to the Lake District rowing."'

After a pint-perfect interval, Bakes arrives and we tumble into the bus. When we reach the motorway Jim opens his shiny Apple laptop and those in the back of the bus crowd round to watch *North by Northwest*. Midway through, the ex-Goldie man's phone beeps a message. I see his face drop as he picks it up. He looks up, sighs and, seeing I've noticed his reaction, passes me the phone.

It reads: 'Just tell me how long I have to come second to rowing for and I'll see if I can do it.'

After a brief consultation the bus consensus is to reply: 'Four months. Thanks.'

Sensibly he doesn't take our advice.

It's a common problem. Juggling training, testing, selection, tutors, supervisions, essays, exams, job interviews, mates and a girlfriend is just too many balls to keep in the air and inevitably one or two fall to the floor with a bang. The trick is not to let the ball on the floor distract you from keeping the rest airborne.

A couple of years ago one of our Blue Boat rowers was being interviewed by *The Times* on the demands of the sport, when he talked about his priorities.

'Ah yes,' said the journalist, 'no point letting the degree go to waste if you're at Cambridge.'

'No, no, no. You misunderstand. Rowing comes first, then the degree, then the girlfriend.' Needless to say he didn't have to worry about his third priority after she read the article.

For me the trip to the Lakes offers the chance to get out of the dog-house for a change. I've organised a lift to Nottingham with our physio Gill, whose other half handily lives there. After we've finished at Windermere, and for the first time since the season started, I'm going to turn up on Sam's doorstep in 'Grotty Notty'.

Impatient with how long the trip is taking, Bakes pulls the minibus and trailer full of boats into the fast lane to overtake two identically paced lorries. The minibus engine screams as we crawl past them. Suddenly a police car appears from nowhere.

'Er, Bakes,' someone shouts from the back. He checks his mirror.

'Oh shit,' he says. Poor Bakes, things like this shouldn't happen to such a nice guy. Unlike the rest of the coaching team he's very much 'one of the boys', being almost our age, laid back and not one of those responsible for making the final crew selection.

Bakes slows and pulls back behind the lorries. The cop car flashes its sirens and indicates to pull over. We pull into the hard shoulder and stop. Bakes hangs his head. The bus is silent as the police officer walks up and asks Bakes to follow him back to their car. Someone shouts, 'Free Bakes!' as he opens the door to leave.

'Yeah, thanks guys,' he manages to smile.

Eventually, after much sweet-talking, we get on the road again and five hours later we finally pull into Ambleside youth hostel in darkness.

James:
Saturday 30 November 07:30, Lake Windermere

Next morning brings little cheer. The view from the window is a study in grey. Windermere and the hills are shrouded in cloud. We rig two eights, attaching the riggers and sliding seats that were removed for transportation, everyone wrapped in waterproofs and woolly hats. The coaches' ten-foot-long yellow catamaran is lowered on to the water. It's known as the 'launch of doom' as it produces wash big enough to ruin a rowing session if you're stuck behind it and its weight makes it a pain to release and retrieve from the water, particularly at the end of a session when all you want to do is go home.

Finally we get afloat on the biggest lake on Britain. I'm in the eight with Wooge sitting at stroke. We paddle out of the marina, with its many little sailing boats berthed for the winter, and cruise off at an easy 20 strokes per minute. Despite the mist the scenery change is welcome after the sensory deprivation of the raised grassy banks at Ely. The gentle wooded hills, the expanse of lake; to our left the shadow of dark, rugged mountains through the cloud. As we clock up the miles, mist rolls further down the hills and we can only just make out the bank with fingers of grey drifting between the ranks of evergreens. We stop to do some technical exercises and there are disgruntled mumblings from some of the foreigners about the Brits having hyped-up the supposed incredible scenery only for the British weather to let everyone down. I can't disagree.

After several miles of rowing an island materialises ahead and we row past and around it to meet the other eight and coaches, who are wrapped up like deep-sea fishermen.

Robin's megaphone crackles, 'Right, boys, side by side for the ten kilometres back to the dock. Max rate 24. If one eight gets a length, notch the rate down two until you're level again. No funny business.' We set off, each eight pushing hard to dominate the other and the yellow boats cut speedily through the grey water. Robin cruises parallel to each eight, coaching each oarsman in turn. Nothing escapes his gaze – hands on the oar handle too wide apart, shoulders not relaxed enough on the recovery, knees tilted incorrectly. He uses synonyms and metaphors to try to get the messages across to us in different ways.

'Ben, a little slow at the catch. Just drop the blade in. Yes, imagine you're posting a letter in the letter box.'

'Hugo, a little more patience on the recovery. Control the body weight into the front. Imagine you're coming into land on an aircraft carrier, you're ready to land with the lightest touch.'

Satisfied for a moment he lowers the megaphone and confers with Donald and Bakes. In two weeks we will race our Trial Eights over the Boat Race course in Putney, in front of the press. Oxford will be watching too. The closer the race, the more lung-busting and painful the event, the happier the coaches: they get to see how their athletes react under maximum stress and pressure and so can predict how they'll perform on the big day.

Coxes Jim and Ellie are hunched like prize jockeys, demanding more from their crews each stroke and using every possible tactic to give their crew an advantage. Their skills and steering ability are under scrutiny too; it's really between them for the Blue Boat driving seat, despite last year's Goldie cox Steph also having a good go. It's the American raciness and energy of Jim against the calmness and Tideway steering experience of Ellie.

James:

Saturday 30 November 13:01, Lake Windermere

As I finish lunch I realise I've left a waterproof in the boat so I take my leave of Wayne and Ellie, who are busily discussing the design of our new Trial Eights race suits. Wooge, ever the fashionista, has been pushing for more Prada-style black.

I head into the older, darker part of the house. In the main living room, full of old comfortable settees and boxes of Scrabble, there's a mother watching her two kids playing by the bay window. I hear the door open behind me.

'James.' I recognise Robin's voice instantly. He smiles and guides me towards the window. 'You haven't met my family, have you?' He introduces me to his wife and kids. They seem lovely and very normal. I'm so surprised to meet them, their names kind of wash over me. I've known for years Robin had a young family but it's kind of like meeting Santa Claus – I was always told they existed but subconsciously never quite believed it. To us it always seems as if Robin has no life beyond the race.

James:
Sunday 1 December 07:40, Lake Windermere

The smell and humidity in our room is something else this morning as we each dig out dry kit for the morning row. The still sopping wet and sweaty clothing from yesterday's three sessions, two rows and a run into the hills, hangs from every available nook. At breakfast several guys arrive thickly wrapped in civilian clothing rather than rowing gear and report various illnesses to Robin.

Andrew Shannon, a strong and promising oarsman from Scotland, looks grey-green and certainly won't be rowing for a few days. Buschbacher also looks ill, with dark, sunken eyes.

'Robin's found the only place in the world wetter than Ely,' moans Busch, picking at his breakfast and looking out of the window at the rain.

David:
Saturday 7 December 06:35, Oxford

The alarm wakes me but I can't bring myself to leave the beautiful girl lying next to me in my warm, cosy bed. I'm struck again by the selfishness of my rowing – and the difficulty it's causing our relationship. No free weekends, no time to do anything spontaneous, always some sort of rowing commitment. Maria and I wouldn't have a relationship unless she came to Oxford. I haven't even been able to see her student halls in Bristol yet. It is hard for me to explain the draw of rowing to her. The never-ending search for the perfect stroke. The joy of the crew becoming more than just the sum of its parts. My desire, above all else – to make the Blue Boat.

Finally, I find the will to get up and leave her.

'Sleep well, baby,' I whisper as I close my bedroom door behind me. By the time I arrive at the Iffley Road gym, the guys have already started on the rowing machines. Another hour of solitary for me this morning.

James:

Saturday 7 December 21:39, Cambridge

The queue of Playboy bunnies is quite indecent. Most of them are shivering with the December cold. They're queuing for the Playboy Mansion cocktails, which the CUBC are putting on in Cambridge to raise funds. Organising this has been part of my vice-presidential duties for the last couple of weeks.

'Groves, Wayne, you've got this covered, haven't you?' I confirm, as they each stamp another bunny's hand.

'No worries, man,' says Wayne. Groves just grins at me. He's resplendent in aviator sunglasses, reflective yellow waistcoat and a black T-shirt which reads 'Dip me in honey and throw me to the lesbians' in luminous yellow letters. He picked up the T-shirt on our trip to New Zealand, where one of the local boat clubs was sponsored by a nearby lap-dancing club. An interesting tie-up.

Inside the modern venue Ben Smith, JA and cheerful Aussie Breck Lord are manning the bar, topless apart from collar, cuffs, bow tie and baby oil. Young TJ, Aussie KC, Busch and Nate are also in Chippen-dales garb, Nate with additional furry handcuffs and chains. The boys with six-pack abs are making use of them.

Everything seems under control. Busch is resident DJ, the drinks are flowing and people are dancing. Looking again, I see that there is one issue – a preponderance of women, something I never thought would be a problem. We are full to bursting with 'blue tac', girls who target Blues and university sportsmen for romantic liaisons. It is astonishing what the sight of a blue blazer can do to many a sensible, well-adjusted girl. At last year's Boat Race Ball a non-rowing mate of the then president Tom Stallard was lamenting the lack of available girls. 'They're only after guys with the blazers, mate, no one else exists,' he'd said.

'Give this a whirl,' said Tom, who passed over his coveted Blue's blazer, the thick woollen Cambridge blue jacket denoting a rowing Blue. Other Blues sports at Cambridge, like rugby and football, also have blazers but theirs show the crests of their respective clubs on the front pocket. The rowing blazer isn't emblazoned with a crest, in honour of the fact that rowing was the 'original blue', the first of the Oxford/ Cambridge varsity match-ups.

Within fifteen minutes Tom's friend, now wearing the blazer, was sighted dancing with a rather attractive brunette. After another fifteen minutes he was noted leaving the ballroom with her. Twenty minutes after that they returned looking rather dishevelled. As Tom's friend walked past Tom, he returned the blazer with thanks. The girl on his arm looked horrified as she realised the blazer fitted Tom much better and went with his Blues bow tie. She stood gasping for a second before storming off.

If anything this effect is even more exaggerated the year after an Olympics, when rowing internationals are common in the Oxford and Cambridge squads. The girls who target Olympic medallists rather than university oarsmen have earned the moniker 'metal detectors'.

Yes, the room is awash with bunnies. It looks like a lot of guys have stayed away. Things are not buzzing quite as much as they could, so Ellie and I load two super-soaker water pistols with vodka and start administering medicinal shots to the throng. In return one girl from my college posts a standing invitation to her bedroom, which I politely decline.

Half an hour later, I overhear another girl asking Hugo where Buschbacher is: 'I'm his girlfriend from Harvard.' Knotting his eyebrows, he points out Busch, now behind the bar, and the girl heads up to meet him. They start canoodling and I wander over to Hugo and Wayne, who have met in conference, glancing regularly at the active couple.

'So that's Busch's girlfriend from Harvard?' I ask them.

Wayne, who spent four years at Harvard with Busch, studies her once more and concludes, 'I have never seen that girl before in my life.'

David:

Sunday 15 December 16:37, Trial Eights Hammersmith

In front of me Daggett hangs his head despondently, which exposes Hutchy's curly afro at six. Daggett's normal Harvard self-assurance seems to have evaporated.

The imposing green steel structure of Hammersmith Bridge looms behind us. Automatically, I look to the second lamp-post from the Surrey bank, which is recognised as the best marker of the racing line for the bend. Just minutes ago, we'd been racing our Trial Eights under the bridge and Acer had called for an almighty push.

'Yeah, boys, and we're coming back!' he'd screamed in response to our efforts. I'd ominously noticed Acer hadn't told us the margin of their lead. I craned my head round in desperation, to see if we had any chance of a victory. I was left aghast. They were miles ahead, at least three boat lengths and early into the race. The training pieces between the crews suggested the Trial Eights would be close. Instead, we were so far behind I knew there was no hope. We'd rowed out the remaining eleven minutes deflated, knowing we would cross the finish line decisively beaten. Those minutes felt like an eternity.

The press launch that has followed the race takes the opportunity to speed past as we've pulled to a stop on our way back up to the boat house. We sit unhappily bobbing in its wake. I'd hoped tomorrow's headlines would say 'Safety first', a play on our two light-hearted crew names, 'Health' and 'Safety'. Sadly for me, 'Health' had beaten 'Safety' decisively, and with two such disparate crews tomorrow's papers will probably suggest we're going to get crushed by Cambridge. What's more worrying is they may be right.

The eight sits quietly, all of us doubting ourselves. This is my first bitter taste of loss over the championship course. I'd won both my Trial Eights and Isis race last year. Now I'm dejected and empty, my confidence shot to pieces. How had the other crew gone so fast? The combination of the tenacious Matt and BT in the stern of the other eight had proved more devastating than feared. Even having the strength of the internationals in our eight hadn't provided us with a victory. My chance at making the Blue Boat is slipping away.

The rival eight steams up behind us, their body language radiating pride, the synchronous noise of the feathering of the blades amplified as they row under the arch of the bridge. They stop their advance just behind us.

The smile of their cox Megan is plain to see.

'Fuck, Megan, wipe that smile off your face,' Scott bellows from our boat. Megan doesn't reply but the smile turns to a scowl.

Scott's shout is brutal and aggressive but not completely unexpected. It has become squad legend that when he lost a game of Risk, he stormed off complaining of 'unfair alliances' and that it was 'bullshit'. His passion and drive to win at everything is evident and he can't wait to prove any doubters wrong. He takes defeat harder than anyone else I've met. No wonder he took Megan's smile as a taunt. I'm different. My way of dealing with failure is to lock up the hurt inside, become more insular and blame myself for the poor result.

'Guys, let's get moving,' Acer calls. 'All eight ready, go.' We lope off slowly like a wounded animal, working our way back to Putney through the bouncy, awful river conditions. We navigate through the flotilla of sailing boats that's appeared, many tacking just in time to miss a collision with our shell. The wind is on my back and against the incoming tide, which whips up the water into white horses. Every so often the boat lurches uncomfortably from side to side, partly because of the choppy water conditions but also due to our poor rowing technique. My knuckles and fingers, already bloodied and bruised, slam into the boat once again. When the boat next rocks over on to my side my rowing Tourette's gets the better of me and I let out a 'What the fuck?!'

Back on dry land I steady myself with a few deep breaths and tell myself all is not lost yet. I must pick myself up, go back to the drawing board and return stronger. Now Michaelmas term's finished, we leave for Davos, Switzerland, the day after tomorrow for our cross-country skiing camp. Then we're free to go home for a few days at Christmas before we head off to Mequinenza, Spain for a rowing camp at the start of the New Year. That's where the main crew selection will take place.

James:

Thursday 19 December 22:22, The Bucks Club, Piccadilly, London

Finally we've made it: Trial Eights' dinner. The whole team has been nearing the point of complete exhaustion and now we've reached the Christmas break. Eleven days of bliss. No 6 a.m. alarms. No lectures. Christmas pudding, family and sleep. OK, so Robin's given us a training programme but we get to choose when we do the sessions and there's even a couple of days off scheduled. Our results and progress so far are excellent and if we keep this up we'll have a great chance against Oxford, and I can finally fulfil my dream.

Despite a fairly lengthy speech from one of the old boys, the atmosphere is boisterous in the Bucks Club. Everyone, even today's losers, are brimming with happiness and positivity. After dinner the port is passed around and then the Secret Santa presents are handed out, each of us having been assigned another member of the team to buy a Christmas present for. Chris Le Neve Foster, a new triallist, the year below me at St Catharine's, passes Tim a poorly wrapped package, which he opens. Tim grins and immediately dons the white naval captain's hat that emerges. One of the waiters casts a disapproving look over the gifts as he clears the tables, particularly JA's two large bottles of Hobgoblin ale. JA promptly slugs them both down.

Breck, another new triallist from St Catharine's, gives Wayne his package. Wayne looks slightly weary as he opens the parcel. In our monthly fat tests, conducted by our physio Gill taking calliper measurements of skin folds on five parts of the body, Wayne has been consistently amongst the 'fattest', although in the real world he's very slim, with just 13.3 per cent body fat. The jibes about his fat percentage have been endless, trying his good humour and patience. The parcel opens to reveal bars of Slim Fast and a calorie counting book. Across the table Matze is showing his beagle calendar to a laughing Hugo. Poor sweet Matze. A few weeks ago he had been talking to Breck in the back of the bus about the veterinary exams he'd taken when qualifying in Germany and he matter of factly mentioned a practical exam in which he was required to take a sperm sample from a beagle. Breck had burst into laughter and since then Mazte had put up with a lot of dog-lover digs. In fact our Trial Eights had almost been named 'Dr Matze' and 'The Jolly Beagle'.

On the next table a now rather drunk JA hands Ellie a pot plant. The crowd at the table is a little quiet. No one understands the joke. There must be a joke, surely?

'Don't you get it?' JA slurs. 'What you've missed all term. Seven inches of Basil!' Ellie blushes and giggles and everyone else laughs. It's a reference to her Oxford boyfriend, Bas Dixon, who is out cross-country skiing with Dave in Davos. She's been keeping her Oxford link very quiet, particularly to Robin and the coaches, and when chatting about how things are going in the back of the minibus he's normally been labelled as 'Fred'. If Ellie retains her cox's seat in the Blue Boat, fighting off Jim's challenge, then she'll face Bas on Boat Race day.

David:

Friday 20 December 13:21, Davos, Switzerland

My gait aggravated by incredibly sore inner thigh muscles, I stumble into one of the neat little Alpine shops on Davos high street. The postcard rack has a number of shots of the picturesque, snow-covered town. Noticeably there are no postcards of cross-country skiers exerting excruciating effort, which would be much more appropriate in the circumstances. So far this has been more boot camp than holiday. No matter how much our Swiss instructor coaches us, rhythmically repeating 'zee pushing and zee gliding . . . zee pushing and zee gliding' while elegantly skimming across the snow, most of us are still very novice. Apart from Scott, that is, who grew up on ice skates in Canada.

I select a few of the more appealing cards to send to Gran, Maria and the parents and then browse the selection of English newspapers. There are bits and pieces about Canada ratifying the Kyoto Protocol and the USA's biggest trade deficit in history. I flick to the back pages; it looks like it's all football as usual. Then I turn another page and a headline grabs me: 'The Boat Race: Oxford Seek to Build on Success'.

The article begins by talking about last season's Boat Race as the 'Race of the Century'. I doubt that would provide much consolation for James. The stalemate between the clubs is highlighted, with both refusing to be on a 'losing streak'. Such is the way with the Boat Race, successive victories or successive losses. After Oxford's winning run from 1976 to 1992, only interrupted by the Cambridge victory in 1986, Cambridge had won seven races on the trot until the 2000 race. Cambridge then won the controversial 2001 race before losing the 2002 epic. Now it seems both sides are confident and are producing great crews. As the article points out, each year is a 'clean slate' with a new bunch of oarsmen, keen to achieve their Blue.

As I carry on reading through the article, a quote from Sean jumps out at me: 'One definite fact is that we don't have that many options to choose from. It will be a very competitive squad. Lots of people will be looking to make the Blue Boat, but that's a reflection on the fact that there aren't a lot of really outstanding people who would automatically be in it.'

He's right. We don't have our usual quotient of brash, arrogant internationals, who've all but measured themselves up for their dark blue blazer on arrival. The backbone of the squad for this race is a bunch of young, hungry undergraduates. It seems to give the squad a different feeling from last season – there's more humility about it.

Our Trial Eight's defeat is described as a 'crushing ten lengths' with my crew 'looking visibly demoralised'. No shit. It was an embarrassment. I never want to feel that ashamed again.

Sean's interview continues: 'I guess Cambridge are a little bit ahead of us, looking at results from the Fours Head, the indoor championships and the national trials. We're not bluffing or pretending. We've seen the results and we know we're behind and we know we don't have any more aces to pull out of the sleeve. This is what we've got.'

I fold the newspaper and put it back on the rack. At least in Davos we're away from the river, where Sean is an ever-watching, unrelenting judge, mentally making notes against your name with every stroke. Each bad stroke pushes me further away from my goal. After the Trial Eights defeat I'm going to have an uphill struggle.

David:

Sunday 22 December 22:42, Davos, Switzerland

I hold the door for a teammate who staggers off arm-in-arm with a girl. He's already leaving the club with her and we've only just arrived.

'That's some piece of fast work,' says Brian, sloping up to me, clutching a bottle of Jack Daniel's.

'Right, let's step this up a notch,' I say grabbing the bottle and taking a swig. The alcohol tastes bitter-sweet in my mouth. This is our last group night out before we meet for training camp in the New Year. We walk off back into the bar, where Vickers and Scott are sitting round a tree trunk with two locals. One of the locals picks up a hammer and with the V-shaped end used for pulling out nails, slams it down at a nail in the middle of the trunk. He misses. The small crowd of mostly Oxford oarsmen roars.

'Watch this,' says Vickers. He raises the hammer and brings it down to land a partial strike on another nail, pushing it in some way further. It looks like Vickers and Scott are winning.

The other Swiss lifts up the hammer and strikes it straight on the nail, pushing it almost completely into the trunk. Bull's eye! His mate reaches over and gives him a high five. 'That is ow it eez done, my friends,' he shouts across at Vickers and Scott. Turning to the dance floor, I survey the scene and take the occasional swig from my alcopop. The rounds of beers in Bar X, further into town, have taken their toll and we're all pretty lubricated. None more so than Parker, Montana Butsch and Bill, who have already set up their stall on the dance floor, head and shoulders taller than the rest and with much sillier dancing. Montana is twirling a girl around enthusiastically.

Back at the lumberjack game, one of the local opposition has driven the nail all the way in, finishing the game with an almighty blow. Vickers and Scott look seriously pissed off. The Swiss start shouting something about a bet. Vickers seems to acknowledge the defeat, albeit begrudgingly, and goes off to get them a round of beers.

Minutes later, the game forgotten, we are all on the dance floor. John Adams clutches his leg to play air guitar as Guns N' Roses' 'Sweet Child of Mine' blasts out, with me on the air drums. Meanwhile I notice a local hassling Scott, pushing him around. Suddenly fists fly across the dance floor, the darkness and strobe lighting shadowing their flight. Those nearest dive in to restrain the two guys, with me getting in between them, my long arms separating them. He'd picked the wrong man to bully. Scott would never back down.

'Let's get out of here,' I say to Henry, who's come over to see what the commotion is all about. We yank Montana away from his local Fräulein, rudely interrupting him mid-snog, and heave ourselves out into the sobering night air.

We carefully climb up the ice-covered road towards the sports centre, our home for the week. The snow reminds me of Christmas and the fact that I've done no Christmas shopping.

I'm looking forward to some time at home, seeing more of Maria and not thinking about training or work, or the stresses of the selection process. Although I'm not sure how I'm going to react to living in close quarters with James again. It'll be strange, given my developing hatred for the light blues.

James:

Monday 23 December 17:45, Strawberry Hill, Twickenham

'Welcome home, Dave.' Dad hugs my brother. Dave drops his bulging black kit bag in the hall of our family home. He is covered, from ear warmers to tracksuit bottoms, in the dark blue of Oxford. Next in line is Mum, who kisses him on the cheek. Then it's my turn to greet him.

'Hi.'

'Hi.' And we shake hands, then half hug.

Our hackles are still up. He feels like the enemy.

James:

Tuesday 24 December 21:12, Teddington

The rum punch is as powerful as ever at the Smiths' traditional Christmas Eve drinks, reminding everyone of their father's Jamaican heritage. The Smiths live about half a mile from the Livingston family home; we're practically neighbours, and have been for fifteen years. Being back in their house, where Dave and I attended many happy teenage parties, band practices and video nights, has thawed the Oxford/Cambridge rivalry, although in the living room next door where our parents and their friends natter, all the talk is of the four brothers in the kitchen. Matt, Ben, Dave and I are laughing and drinking with other Hampton school friends, whose regular piss-taking brings us out of our Oxbridge camps. The talk is of old girlfriends and old times, sometimes referring to photos on the wall of our Hampton eight and Matt's junior GB coxed four that pulled a Junior World Championship gold from nowhere. Noticing how focussed Matt looks in the photo I'm reminded that that is when our paths diverged; a month or two after it was taken, he was at Oxford.

'That's still up as well then, Smithy.' I raise a glass towards a school photo of Matt at age eight or so, high up next to a cupboard. He sports a brilliant sweep-over haircut exposing an ample forehead. There's not an inkling of the intense competitor that he's become.

'Yes,' he laughs, 'Mum won't take it down.'

After another rum punch I head upstairs to use the facilities. On the landing I can't miss another montage which knocks all the Christmas cheer and light-heartedness out of me. The two photos in the frame show Matt's Oxford eight mid-stroke in this year's Boat Race, all grimaces and bared teeth, and a formal photo of them in their Blues blazers. The calligraphy reads, 'Oxford, winners of the 2002 Boat Race'. My stomach drops. If Dave and I do go head to head this year, there can be no gloating pictures of the event put up by the winner to pollute part of our childhood home for one of us for ever.

David:

Wednesday 25 December 11:12, Surrey

Driving past Box Hill, late as usual, my phone beeps a message in the back of the car. We're halfway to our cousin's house in Worthing for Christmas lunch.

'John Adams got engaged!' I grin. The parents and James give a little cheer and I reply with congratulations from the whole family.

My hair is still wet from the shower after this morning's training cycle ride in Richmond Park with Ben Smith. James's hair is dry; Matt and James had shaken last night on not training on Christmas Day. Meanwhile Ben and I had decided to meet at 7:30 this morning at the end of his road. It was a bright and fresh morning and my Santa's hat made it feel a bit more special. We cycled to Richmond Park and then did laps, tiring our legs. I chose to take the British decathlete, Daley Thompson's, never-say-die attitude. When asked how he stayed ahead of his rivals, most particularly Jürgen Hingsen, he said: 'It's quite easy, really. I train harder than he does. I know, for example, that he will not be training on Christmas Day, so I make sure I do. One day's extra training might just be the difference between coming first and second.' In fact Thompson used to train twice on Christmas Day, just in case his competitors decided to match him. Maybe that's what kept him fractionally ahead. Unlike Thompson, though, I only did one session, knowing my competition rather better: he's sitting next to me in the car.

After one lap Ben and I stopped to have a swig from our water bottles. A man walked past our bikes with his dog and said, 'Good luck in the race this year.' Ben and I were so surprised we only managed to reply with a sheepish 'Thanks!' I guess my dark blue Oxford long-sleeve T-shirt must have been a giveaway. Even though Ben is in the Cambridge rowing squad, I don't feel the same sense of competition with him. From what I've heard he's not in contention for the main crew. Plus, of course, he's not my older brother.

I've watched James's training over the Christmas break with interest, and I know he's been watching mine. I've even surreptitiously noted James's scores on the family rowing machine by cunning use of the memory button.

A Porsche overtakes us in the fast lane. 'Awesome,' I mutter. Mum and Dad have told me that 'Porsche' was the very first word I ever spoke. James's first word, in contrast, was 'pink'. As I'm always happy to remind him.

David:
Thursday 26 December 17:10, Strawberry Hill, Twickenham

I stomp up the wooden stairs leaving James and Dad in the living room playing the board game Risk. After Mum had got slaughtered early on, and retired to the kitchen cheerily, James and Dad had turned on me. I fought with all my armies but the dice went against me and soon I'd lost. Rage built up inside me like some uncontrollable force. I hate losing to James, particularly in front of my parents. It makes me feel unworthy.

Sitting on my bed sulking, I feel like a child again. When we were younger James and I would often fight. My temper tantrums were the result of desperation to win; to prove myself against him. Maybe it was natural competition between brothers.

Lying down I reminisce back to one particular fight between us in the kitchen when I was seven. I can't even remember what started it. He hit me harder and harder, while my returning thumps were ineffectual, and impotent rage built in me. The pain made my eyes well but I would not show my pain to him. I blinked away the tears. As I stumbled back from his blows I noticed a long silver kitchen knife on the counter to my side. Impulsively I grabbed it and, quite hysterical by now, pointed it towards James. He backed away. I enjoyed this change of fortunes, the hunted becoming the hunter, and I lunged at him with it for effect. He turned and ran off, out of the kitchen and down the hall. I took up the chase. James ran left into the living room, which joins the kitchen through another door. Realising I would never catch him I threw the seven-inch knife at him. It ricocheted off the wall and bounced onto the floor. We were both left shaken. Did I really want to hurt him this much? I think I aimed for the wall but I couldn't be sure.

James:
Sunday 29 December 07:42, Hampton

The dawn rain continues. The water runs from my hair down my face and I can taste yesterday's hair wax and bile driven up by the previous night's drinking. Matt Smith is in front of me, at stroke, Dave behind me, and Ben Smith steers at bow in our brotherly coxless four. We've borrowed a boat from Hampton School and now we're out on the river where we started our rowing careers, back when we were on the same side.

I wish I'd had a few more hours' sleep. I was out till late in London partying with a couple of St Catz guys, which I regret more with each stroke. The boat is flying along, fuelled by our egos. Each of us is displaying our own strength and how far we've come in our university's systems.

David and Matt's punchy strokes shout 'Oxford, Oxford, Oxford'. Ben's and my longer, smoother strokes, 'Caaaambridge, Caaaambridge.'

It's a relief to be off the rowing machine. I did an uncomfortable 70 minutes on the family erg on Boxing Day, my pulse racing higher than normal, which I put down to Christmas lunch. Thankfully my score was better than Dave's; I've been subtly checking his scores over the break.

After my Boxing Day erg we played a family game of Risk. Dad and I slaughtered Dave early on, which left him in a foul mood. He stormed off, muttering under his breath, echoing the young tantrums of yester-year. Naturally we never the finished the game. Before I headed out Dave and I watched *Predator*, which perked him up, and we happily quoted it to one another. As I left we gripped right arms in an air clinch, like an arm wrestle but without the table.

'What's wrong, Cambridge got you pushing too many pencils?' Dave asked as we leaned our weight on each other, trying to get superiority. There was deadlock before the clinch was broken.

Now there's deadlock again as Cambridge on bowside and Oxford on strokeside try to pull the boat around, but it runs straight as an arrow. At each turn we catch our breath quietly and there isn't the usual extensive technical analysis and discussion. No one wants to give anything away.

Matt drops us home after we finish our miles on the river. Before I get out, I turn to my old friend.

'Well, see you at the Boat Race Ball, then.'

'Yep, see you there,' he replies and we shake hands. As Dave and I walk up the steps to our front door I reflect how nice it will be to have both my best friend and my brother back after this next four months of bitter struggle.

David:

Monday 30 December 17:35, Somerset House, London

Two huge Christmas trees stand in front of the illuminated Somerset House. My speed across the ice increases to almost jogging pace. I have a sudden wobble and almost fall backwards but my tight grip of Maria's hand helps me to steady myself. She breaks into a smile at my poor coordination. Two kids half my height skate past us backwards and come to a sharp halt at the edge of the rink. I envy their low centre of gravity.

The ice gives us complete freedom. Right now we're like any normal couple. My alter ego, my other life, isn't holding us back. It's a change from quiet nights in at Oxford and me subjecting her to my cooking. Despite being given Delia's *How to Cook* by my parents after starting university I'm still hopeless in the kitchen. 'Tortellini surprise' is my signature dish. The surprise being it's tortellini again.

James:

Tuesday 31 December 21:12, Oxfordshire

'Cheers!' and everyone round the table downs their shot.

'Wow, that's really good,' nods Sam, surprised. There is a chorus of agreement. Busch starts making another round, pouring vodka and sugar into the bowl, then squeezing in some lemons. In an out-of-character display of organisation, this being the man who'd slept through his own 21st birthday party, Groves is hosting a New Year's party at his home near Oxford, or more accurately the nicely converted barn adjacent to his parents' house. It's purely CUBC and girlfriends. Wayne and Jim are back from Christmas in Canada and the USA, Busch has stayed with the McGarel-Groveses throughout the Christmas break, Lukas and Swaino, both from previous CUBC vintages, have come up with their girl-friends. Another round of drinks is poured.

'Right, New Year's resolutions,' shouts Jim. 'Bungle?'

'Er . . .' I slur.

'To be seven seat?' suggests the indefatigable Aussie Lukas.

'To stroke the damn boat! No. I don't care. Just to win.'

'To move downtown,' says Lukas's girlfriend Amy.

'To study at least 14 hours a week,' laughs Lukas, who's finding his law practice course less challenging than he thought he might.

We turn to Groves, who sits on the sofa with his girlfriend. 'I want to stop pulling mingers and . . .' His girlfriend's jaw drops and Groves realises what he's said. 'No, no I don't mean you – or other girls . . .' There's a chorus of laughter. She looks heavenward.

The night descends into thumping music and games. Jim introduces one that has everyone trying to bounce coins into glasses, whooping and screaming at the forfeits. Then, as a finale, come the flaming sambucas.

Part III

'Good day. We are privileged to live another day in this magnificent world. Today you will be tested.'

From *Assault on Lake Casitas* by Brad Alan Lewis

Chapter 6
Internal Struggles

2003

James:
Thursday 2 January 08:25, Banyoles, Spain

There's barely a ripple on the placid blue lake this morning. The reeds lining the water and the trees behind are perfectly still. In the middle distance green hills crest above the trees; beyond are hazy, grey, bald mountains and further off still are the first snowy peaks of the Pyrenees. We stroll along a sandy path lined by bare trees with white peeling bark, heading for the boathouse 500 metres from our hotel for a morning row. Everyone seems to have got a digital camera from Santa and like kids with new favourite toys Wayne, Matze and I are all busily trying to take the perfect photo of the view, comparing and commenting on each other's screens.

'Heads up,' shouts Wooge behind us and the American football, which is now a permanent part of the squad, whistles overhead into Nate's waiting arms, his flip-flops spraying sand as he comes to a stop.

Ben Smith wanders past chatting to KC, looking so laid back he's practically horizontal. He's wearing a hand-knitted woolly hat with tassels and a luminous orange shell-suit top that I remember from school. Dave's got a similar top; their Hampton four bought the loudest charity shop shell-suits they could find. KC wears the only marginally less hideous orange shirt of his Aussie Rules football team.

'How's the serenity?' I ask Kris in my best Aussie, as he passes, quoting from the Australian cult movie *The Castle*.

'You know what I like about you, Bungle? You're an ideas man,' Kris replies in quote talk. He looks a lot more at home wearing sunglasses, T-shirt and cap than the many layers he's had to buy to survive Ely in winter.

It's great being back together and in the relative winter warmth of Spain, able to wear a T-shirt and shorts without risking the loss of extremities. I feel for those we've left behind in England, like the Scotsman Andrew Shannon, who's been out with glandular fever ever since our trip to the Lake District, and the giant Ben Clare, who has developed some sort of respiratory problem. Neither can train for the moment. It might be the end of their road.

Our light-hearted banter on the way along the sandy path belies the underlying tensions. In a few days' time this lake will see us pitted against each other in final selection for the Blue Boat and Goldie. We've each come with something to prove, our own personal goals.

When we return to Cambridge in ten days' time some of us will be immensely disappointed, with our year's hopes and dreams in tatters. What's worse, it will be our friends who have taken those dreams away from us. For now, though, it's nice just to be in the sunshine.

David:

Thursday 2 January 15:23, Mequinenza, Spain

The wide expanse of calm, inviting, dark blue water of the Ebro River winds its way through the valley of Zaragoza, boxed in by bare, steep hills on either side. The vista from the left-hand side of the coach gives the newbies their first taste of what we'll be training on for the next ten days. Of our waking hours we'll spend more time out on the river than on dry land, beating the hell out of each other, being put through endless training pieces. By the end of the camp the coaches will have determined the rank of the oarsmen using 'seat racing'; the unforgiving method of pitting individual against individual. The coaches race two boats side by side and then swap one oarsman for another between them, and rerun the race, giving them a relative measure of who moves the boats fastest. By the time they've finished, the friendships we've developed as a squad will be frayed. There are only eight seats in the Blue Boat and eight in Isis; you either make it or you don't. I feel the familiar nerves in the pit of my stomach at the very thought of it. I can do it, I must do it if I want to race Cambridge – and James.

The New Year only started two days ago; the 'holidays', if you could call them that, are over, and everyone knows it's serious now. By the end of the camp we'll all but have the boats selected and within four months and three days those 18 people will be sitting on the start line by the University Stone. The time will pass in a flash.

As we enter the sleepy town of Mequinenza, the water disappears behind pale stone houses. The bus comes to a halt outside the familiar Hostal Rodes, the end point of our transfer from Barcelona airport. The shabby building is the only hotel in this small town in northern Spain. Hostal Rodes will be our home from home for the next ten days: the only place we eat, sleep and exist, away from the boathouse, gym and the water.

Oxford University used to go on training camp in Seville, where we'd raced earlier this year in a pre-season friendly. The weather there is hot and sunny and the local area is vibrant and fun – too much fun, apparently. Sean changed Oxford's training camp venue to Mequinenza in 2000 not only because of the training advantages of the expanse of calm water, but also we suspect because there was no danger of wayward athletes actually going out at night or enjoying themselves. There is nowhere else to go and nothing else to do here. Stepping out of the bus we notice that the street resembles some kind of Spaghetti Western film when the villains ride into town. There's not a single person around; doors creak open and shut in the gentle breeze. I half expect tumble-weed to blow across the road.

I grab my kit bag out of the belly of the coach. It's bulked out by the four lever arch files of biology notes, my training diary, energy drinks and 'Slim Fast' shakes. In contrast to most 'Slim Fast' drinkers, who have one for breakfast, one for lunch and a healthy dinner, I drink them as a snack after training, on top of five meals a day. If people want to slim fast they should try rowing twice a day.

As yet, there's no sign of the coaching staff, who are staying in the villa down the road. None of us has seen it but I bet it's nicer than Hostal Rodes. The rowing coaches left in the 'rig', trailering the boats on New Year's Day. At roughly the same time as they reached the ferry port in Dover, I'd woken up in a dilapidated stately home; a 26-bedroom Georgian house owned by a school friend of Maria's, after a drunken New Year's Eve party in Truro, Cornwall. Yet even though I'd trained on New Year's Eve, my sense of guilt kicked in over breakfast. I was itching to get back on the rowing machine. I could not leave my usual routine behind. Yes, it was great to see Maria, but I needed to keep my fitness levels up over the 'holidays'.

Matt emerges from the small doorway, jangling and laden with keys, a clipboard in hand like some kind of Mequinenza tour guide. 'OK, guys, dump your stuff in your rooms and we'll meet down at the boathouse to rig in thirty minutes. For those who don't know the boathouse, it is over the road and to the right. The guys who've been here before will show you.'

Matt looks at his clipboard and selects a key from his collection. 'Henry, Tuppen, Bas, 305,' he says.

They walk towards Smithy. 'Here you go.' Smithy tosses the key at Henry, who manages to catch the poor throw.

'Also, I almost forgot, no head starts on the beard growing, a mandatory shave for those who aren't clean shaven.'

Vickers is already proud of his promising ginger growth. 'Smithy, the rules state that growth is from New Year onwards!' he protests, throwing his arms in the air. 'I don't make the rules, I just enforce them!'

Matt chuckles. 'OK, fine.' He knows it's a losing battle arguing with Vickers.

'Acer, you've got a single,' Matt continues. Acer has a 30,000 word thesis due three weeks before the Boat Race. 'Livingbone and Parker.' I reach over and grab the key before he can throw it. Sam follows me inside into the dimly lit corridor, the tiled walls leading to a set of stairs. 'Dining room's in there,' I say, pointing towards the open door to our left, halfway along the corridor.

Climbing the stairs, I realise that things could get very awkward between Sam and I. Along with Hutch, he's my most direct competition; one of us will leave savagely disappointed with not having made the crew. Selfishly I hope that while I was sweating at home on the rowing machine, desperately trying to squeeze more fitness into my body, they were on their second helping of Christmas pudding. Somehow I doubt it.

As we climb the stairs the sound of modern Spanish music gets louder. A power ballad wails down the third-floor corridor as I fumble with the room key in the gloom.

'I see they've found the Spanish music channel,' I say, turning to Sam. I hum along with the chorus. The remnants of Spanish GCSE mean I can understand the words for 'my heart'. The room is small and basic.

Opening the shutter to look out of the window, I see the path leading down to the body of water, winding past a statue of the Virgin Mary in prayer. The view of the massive flooded valley is breathtaking. The early evening sun cuts the crisp air and the water shimmers with the prospect of racing. It's good to finally be here, ready to fight for our places.

James:

Friday 3 January 18:25, Banyoles, Spain

The Germans sit quietly in Australasia, unable to escape across the Penang Straits while the massed American armies continue their offensive across the Kamchatka Peninsula. We're playing the training camp favourite board game, Risk.

'Come on,' Jim says as he rolls the dice. Two sixes and a five.

'Pants,' says Andy Smith.

'Sorry, Moth,' Jim smiles. While the unlucky Andy pulls his last men out of Russia, Wayne looks up at the photos displayed along the wall of the Mirallac Hotel bar. There's a picture of every Cambridge squad since 1999 standing in front of the hotel in mufti.

'Check out that one,' I say, nodding towards the 2001 photo. Wayne, Andy, Jim, Breck and Matze turn to study it.

'Yeah, what about it?' says Jim.

'Look at Dunn.' Rick Dunn, last year's stroke, grins down at us. His smile is particularly broad and slightly smug. Wayne breaks into laughter, followed slowly by everyone else.

'Nice,' says Wayne. One felt for the manager of the Mirallac, who had proudly put up the photo in pride of place in his bar. He'd obviously missed the fact that certain parts of Dunn's anatomy were discreetly hanging from his tracksuit bottoms in the centre of the picture.

At the next table Hugo and TJ are locked over the chessboard. It looks like Hugo is winning. Young TJ is deep in thought, as he seems to spend much of his time – quiet and thoughtful.

'Bungle!' Jim pulls me back to the game impatiently, his competitive instinct surfacing. It's my turn to roll. Playing Risk again brings back memories of Christmas and our family game just a few days ago.

It feels like a different life now I'm back with the boys. Dave was just my little brother while we were rolling dice but now we're each back with our opposing factions. I wonder what Dave and Oxford are doing now?

James:
Tuesday 7 January 13:01, Banyoles, Spain

The door to Wayne and Groves's room is ajar as I creep quietly along the carpeted corridor, heading for the room I'm sharing with Jim. I glance inside and see Wayne in his racing kit, stretching a hamstring, eyes focussed on some far distant point beyond the ceiling. By contrast I can see from the feet and ankles dangling over the end of the midget-sized Spanish bed that Groves lies flat out, either asleep or plugged in to his big headphones and house music. Robin announced at lunch we're seat racing again this afternoon. We're each dealing with the pressure in our own way.

Over the last couple of days Robin has whittled down the number of potential challengers for the seats in the Blue Boat through relentless racing of the middle of the squad. On strokeside Busch beat Dan Barry but then lost to Nate. On bowside, Andy Smith lost badly to JA, who then unexpectedly had his dream snatched by Ben Smith in a major upset. So this afternoon Nate and Ben are the contenders for the last seats. The question is, who are they going to knock out?

A seat is mine to lose. Yesterday I was swapped with Groves and managed a five-second victory in some medium tempo work. I pray it has secured my place. Oddly it feels like the stakes have been raised further again. I've got further to fall now. It's still conceivable that Mum and Dad will be proudly cheering on their younger son in the Oxford Blue Boat while older brother plugs away disconsolately in the reserves, again. 'Hasn't Dave done well?' the family will say and there'll be much sympathetic nodding. 'And James, too, of course, good for him too.' The dread of failure and most of all the fear of my kid brother calmly beating me at my chosen endeavour is beginning to consume me.

I also wonder how Wooge is doing. He and Hugo were almost coached to death yesterday in a pair which didn't go well. They did innumerable circles of the lake, one balancing the boat while the other perfected his stroke under Donald's eye. They returned to the dock in darkness, well after everyone else had got back to the hotel. Not good for their confidence levels.

In our room Jim flicks speedily between TV channels, ending up with Spanish *Eurosport*, which shows a snowy biathlon with intent-looking Scandinavians in lycra body suits whooshing round a pine forest on their skis. Unable to settle, I head to the bathroom and drip more antibiotic drops into my right eye. Over the last few days an unpleasant white pustule has grown on the inside of my eyelid. At night, as I try to sleep, it feels like a large chunk of grit is permanently stuck in my eye. I peel back the eyelid. It's still there. Grim.

Back in the bedroom, I check my phone for any texts from Sam but there have been none since last night. I need something to take my mind off the impending racing.

'Jim, please tell me more about the American Civil War,' I request, as I force myself to lie down. He starts where we left off last night. Outside the sky darkens.

David:

Tuesday 7 January 14:30, Mequinenza, Spain

'DOWN,' shouts Sean, the megaphone carrying his voice loudly over the water. The din of coxes shouting and of blades rolling in their gates comes to a stop. As the three boats float across the water, borne on the momentum of previous strokes, the only sound is water trickling under the shell and my panting as my body desperately tries to take in as much oxygen as possible. I can taste blood in my lungs, the first piece of intense training in a while bursting fragile capillaries. I feel small and insignificant on the huge expanse of water, surrounded by the steep valley sides. As we peer across we see that we've finished the race half a boat length down on Megan's four with Acer's boat two boat lengths in front. I'm pissed off we lost but it's not a bad start, given I'm in what on paper appears to be the weakest crew.

'Bring the boats together,' Sean instructs calmly. By contrast I'm anything but calm. I think back to what I wrote in my training diary: 'I know I can do this. I must have white hot concentration, focus on technique, keep my hands moving at the finish of the stroke and follow the others. Win this.'

'Two strokes ready, go,' calls Will, our tiny cox. We roll up our slides, lift our hands to put our blades in the still water and pull away. 'Easy there, down,' he calls: We stop rowing and let the oars lie flat, skimming over the surface of the water, and pull up parallel to the two other boats.

Sean comes up alongside in his launch. Lifting his megaphone, he yells, 'Swap . . . Livingston and Hutchinson.' Taking two more strokes, we interlock oars with the other crew. Sitting adjacent to Hutch, my direct competition for this seat race, I unstrap my feet, ready to climb across. This is my chance to prove I deserve a seat in the Blue Boat. For God's sake don't fuck this up, my own personal devil on my shoulder reminds me. I'm not sure if I could cope with losing this race. I take a deep breath; the extra oxygen calms me and clears my head of negative thoughts. I can win this race; be confident.

'Have a good one, Dave,' Bill says, turning to face me from the seat in front. I throw across my water bottle and the long-sleeve top I'd taken off after the warm-up and clamber awkwardly past Hutch into the other boat. One wrong step and my foot would go through the delicate honeycomb of the £15,000 racing shell. Hutch and I exchange no words as I slot into my seat behind Henry, and he takes his place behind Bill. The two boats are pushed apart.

'How was the last race?' I ask, still adjusting my foot plate, hoping they were disappointed with the last one and had something left to give in the next one.

'It was OK, not great, I guess,' says Smithy from stroke, taking responsibility for the performance.

'You'll be great,' John says from behind me. He sounds as composed as ever. This is a great crew: Smithy, Henry and John are all phenomenal athletes.

The low-rate strokes back up to the start give me a few minutes to recover physically and ponder the few technical points I want and need to focus on for the piece. As long as I'm more than half a length ahead at the end of the race it'll mean I've sped up this boat relative to the other and I've beaten Hutch. I'm going to need a great row; physically, Hutch is a beast who set rowing machine records as an undergraduate back at George Washington University. He's a determined guy; his goal is the same as mine. When I glanced at him he barely looked tired from the last race.

We're back at the start sooner than I'd like. We drift for a few moments. I look skyward; whatever will happen, will happen. Just go for it; one stroke at a time.

'Let's go hard in this one,' I say, nervously searching for words that will encourage the crew to put in a few more ounces of effort in this race.

'Yup,' Henry replies, simply nodding, knowing that he could be swapped in the next race.

'OK, all crews get level,' Sean calls through his megaphone. The coxes bark at their crews, we slowly get into fair alignment. The coaches want us to be level, but I want us to be more 'level' than the other two crews.

'Two strokes to build the speed, then we take it up on the second Go call,' reiterates Megan.

'We took a big push on three minutes last time; let's do it again,' Smithy declares.

'Sounds good,' I reply. 'Let's make it count,' I say under my breath, half talking to my legs, as I shake them up and down. We come forward into the ready position for racing. My pulse speeds as fear rushes through my body. This is it.

Sean stands up in the launch, raising his megaphone. 'Attention, GO!' he calls. I lever the oar through the water with all the physical effort I can muster. 'GO!' calls Sean again, signalling they have started timing the piece from that point. A few strokes in and it's so far so good; we have rocketed off the line, we're level with the top crew and a seat up on the other one. 'Bring the rate down to 34.'

Our stroke rate comes down, the rhythm feels powerful; the boat is running well for us between strokes. Smithy is doing a great job at stroke. I'm off to a good start, although it's early days. I reach out a little further round my rigger to try to row longer, more effective strokes.

Acer's crew, led by Bas at stroke, with the same crew as I'd been in at the Fours Head, has begun to stretch out a lead but only a third of a length. Slowly we are moving away from Hutch's boat, although it's only inches per stroke. 'Two minutes gone, sit up, sit up,' calls Megan. I sit up from my lower back, checking my posture, levering my back to accelerate the oar through the water, that little bit faster. Yeah; that's good, we're still moving away.

In front of me Henry and Smithy row in almost perfect synchrony, quickly getting hold of the water at the front of the stroke and letting the shell float underneath us on the recovery.

'Right, boys, that's three minutes,' she calls.

'Let's go,' shouts Smithy. I push my legs down harder; the lactate is stinging; the poison pains my legs. The eight pistons working harder begin to increase the speed of the shell.

'Yeah,' calls John. We're moving away. I can now see Hutch to my right, tearing at each stroke with animal aggression as he tries to put more power on to the oar.

'One . . . two . . . three . . . four . . . five . . .' I count to myself. I can barely focus on anything. My body tells me to stop.

'Moovvviinngg,' screams Megan. We still haven't been dropped by Bas's crew; he's level with me.

Hutch's crew fall back still further, their full boat shell is visible to us now. I'm going to win this race if only I can hold on for a couple more minutes.

Megan's screams begin to blur into one. 'We're coming back on Bas's boat, yes, we can do it.' I glance to my right; the top boat is still only a third of a boat length ahead.

'Last fifteen seconds.'

'Down!' Sean yells finally. My eyes roll into the back of my head. I reach for the side of the boat to support my tired body, on the boundary between consciousness and unconsciousness.

I wince with the lactate, which still builds even after we've stopped; I can't seem to get enough oxygen into my lungs. My senses and the control of my racing pulse slowly start to return.

'Yes, yes, yes,' I mutter under my breath. I've taken my chance. I've beaten Hutch by a decisive margin. There's a long way to go yet but I've put myself in a good position to be in the Blue Boat.

The coaching launch moves up behind the flotilla of crews. 'Switch, Morris and Daggett,' Sean dictates. His face is unreadable; I'd love to see the comments on his clipboard.

The boats come together again. Henry is to race the Harvard jock Matt, who'd won the coveted Ladies' Plate at Henley last summer with James's new friends Hugo, Wayne and Jim. Henry's broken wrist had set him back earlier in the season. Now he, like me, has his chance to prove whether he can make the step up from Isis to the Blue Boat. There'll be lots more swaps and racing today. I wouldn't be surprised if I race Sam Parker as well.

Henry clambers out of the boat into the seat in front of Hutch. 'Have a good one,' I say to him, repeating the simple words of encouragement Bill said to me minutes earlier.

James:
Tuesday 7 January 16:25, Banyoles, Spain

'Down!' shouts Ellie, from the finish line, and both fours collapse, panting. The icy sleet keeps pouring down relentlessly from the purple clouds hanging over the lake, covering the decking of the boats and filling the footwells as the boats drift to a stop.

Robin's motor-launch, which has been following the two racing fours for the 1,500-metre race, powers down 20 metres away. Robin and Donald are wrapped from head to toe in their Gill all-weather gear. Donald's waterproofs in particular are straining to contain the luminous orange down puffer jacket on top of his generous frame.

Slowly the panting and gasping in both boats becomes more controlled. The ice starts to collect on our heads and shoulders. The lake is so changeable. Two days ago we were floating serenely through morning mist, rowing in the clouds on a millpond surface. Yesterday blue sky and sunshine warmed us and prompted T-shirts off for some winter tanning. Now we're freezing or drowning or both. There is no shelter.

I reach for my cap in the footwell but leave it when I see it's swimming in two inches of icy water. Matze behind me starts shivering despite our recent exertions. A few minutes pass. Is it my turn to be swapped? How did I perform in that race; was it the best I could do? If I get swapped will be it be good enough? Maybe Robin's going to do the sensible thing and tell us to go in and get warm – after all, we've done four races in these ridiculous conditions already. We've had Hugo vs. Ben Smith, Matze vs. TJ, KC vs. Wooge. Surely no more; half of us will be out for weeks, half dead, after this.

Matze's teeth begin to chatter. 'Come on,' he says miserably. The cold, and the desperation to fathom Robin's mind, are getting to us. I sweep the ice out of my hair. Is he going to swap me? Is my seat safe? I'm still gripped with fear of failure. This has to be Cambridge's turn to win. I need to be in that boat.

A three-second margin is seen as a solid win in a seat race but many of the results will be a second or less, which means every inch counts. Robin has the results of the winter's performances to go on, with ergo scores and pairs racing results, but seat racing is the biggest single factor in selection. Man to man, face to face.

It's theoretically possible for athletes to throw a race for a guy they don't want to be in their boat by not putting in 100 per cent effort, but it's an immature and short-sighted thing to do. For one thing, the coaches keep the order of swaps totally secret so you never know if it's your race next. If you slack, trying to throw another man's race, then it could be that you're killing your own chance. Of course, if the athletes did try to manipulate the seat racing results then when it gets to Boat Race time it's very unlikely that the fastest combination will have been selected and that's a sure way to lose.

Looking at the haggard but determined faces around me I know that we're free of that kind of scheming. Everyone just wants to do their best and make Cambridge as fast as possible on the day. Sure, there are guys that I'd prefer to row with but the honourable and sensible thing to do is to put personal preferences aside and let quality show.

'Come on!' Tim shouts across from the other boat to the launch, voicing our thoughts. More moments pass.

'Aaahhh,' yells Matze, shaking himself to try to ward off the shivering. His face is contorted with pain. He's an ex-lightweight with a smaller frame than most of us, and I guess the cold gets to him most. Behind him I can see Wayne is also feeling the chill; even his unfairly renowned fat percentage seems unable to insulate him.

A couple of moments later the megaphone is raised. 'Nate and TJ.' Robin's muffled voice crackles through his balaclava, pitting our talented young fresher against the determined Yale man with something to prove. I'm flooded with relief and disappointment simultaneously. My turn is yet to come.

Dark-haired young Tom looks solemn and fragile as he prepares to battle Nate. He's barely out of school. Now he's more than holding his own against the seasoned internationals, having just drawn with Matze.

When only a couple of feet of water separates us, he stands, holding on to the gunwales of our boat, and reaches a leg to the other craft.

While Nate and TJ pirouette around each other carefully, I look over to the bank. Through the sleet, thirty metres away, I can just make out Ellie and Jim huddled on the bank, puffed up like pigeons in what looks like all the clothes they own. Jim raises a gloved hand in salute. He's obviously having a good time too.

TJ and Nate quietly pass each other their spare clothing and water bottles sitting in their footwells, each making sure they're not carrying any of the other's excess kit. A half empty water bottle or a soaked T-shirt is just another kilo of weight to carry down the course.

Then we push away from each other and it's just four of us again. Nate starts adjusting his foot stretcher to fit his height while Matze and Wayne turn the boat around and begin rowing us back to the buoy in the middle of the lake that denotes the start for our session of seat racing. I wrap my arms around my knees to give Matze room to row, and more importantly, to keep warm.

'Damn,' exclaims Nate, exasperated with his foot stretcher, 'Can someone pass the wrench?' The bow pair stop for Matze to pass me the ten-millimetre spanner, which I turn back to pass on to Nate. He finishes moving his shoes before turning his attention to the metal rigger to his right. As he clumsily tries to lock the tool round a loose nut I notice the tips of his long fingers are ghostly white. I look down to my own, wrapped around the oar handle and pressed into my chest. Also white and wrinkled, numb too.

The splash of the spanner dropping into the water makes me look up. 'Damn!' Nate turns to us. 'Got any more?'

''Fraid not, man, the other one got dunked too,' Wayne replies.

Nate tightens the nut as much as possible with his icy fingers, and then turns to us with a steely look in his eyes, his short blond hair soaked and flecked with ice. 'Let's go, guys. This is it.' He taps the sideboard of the boat loudly a few times to emphasise that he's going to go all the way. This is his shot at the Blue Boat, his chance to put the Yale defeats behind him.

We paddle down to the start, tweaking our technique to get the most speed from each other. I notice that the church on the promontory halfway down the lake looks Gothic and menacing. 'I'm with you, Yale,' I reassure Nate. I remind myself of my major performance attributes, an exercise our squad psychologist has worked on with each of us. As instructed I have carefully tracked in my training diary the development of key technical, physical and mental capabilities I believe I need to win. Now I must exploit them.

We arrive at the orange starting buoy after some bursts of race pace, as much to warm ourselves as to practise in the new combination, and then we frantically bail the icy water from the footwells using empty water bottles, soaked T-shirts and our hands. None of us wants extra weight slowing us down. We have to wait a few moments more for the other crew to arrive. By the time they do my arms are numb to the elbow, my feet are cracking with pain and my head feels like it's in a vice.

' "What doesn't kill us . . ." ' Wayne reminds us from the bows as we line up against them.

James:
Tuesday 7 January 20:45, Banyoles, Spain

Knowing we'd all rapidly tire of the hotel's standard dinner – there are only so many dishes the kitchen could produce in the industrial quantities required – Robin booked out Banyoles's only pizzeria a few days ago. Now the diminutive staff are looking on goggle-eyed as each of us, bar the coxes, tackles a family-sized pizza. Despite constant ferrying of garlic bread, coke and beer our combined hunger and thirst are near impossible to satiate.

The horror of the ice storm is behind us. We raced five times in the end and I wasn't swapped, which was at once frustrating and a relief. I'm in. I'm sure of it. After the fifth piece when Robin's megaphone announced, 'That's it, boys,' we rowed to the bank almost as quickly as we'd been racing, threw the boats in the shed and ran back to the hotel. Then, of course, the hotel's antiquated boiler couldn't take the demand for hot water so most of us simply changed into dry kit and got into bed under all the covers we could find. The screams from those who managed to run a hot bath made me glad I was warming up more slowly.

In the restaurant the comfort food, e-numbers and caffeine have produced a relatively buoyant mood. There's a general relief that racing is over but a few, like Nate, are notably quiet and disappointed.

At my end of the table talk somehow turns to the number of conquests, notches on the belt. There's a surprising range. One of our number announces he is in the hundreds. We gasp in disbelief but this is rapidly independently verified by a housemate.

'Hundreds? Wow! How do you find the time?' Matze asks, looking shocked. To rack up that total by your early twenties, whilst in training, requires some serious presence of mind and presumably broad taste. In contrast, Matze has been going out with his girlfriend since schooldays.

Most of the rest are in the high single figures, with one targeting Ellie for his tenth. It'll never happen, she's way too classy.

James:

Wednesday 8 January 16:04, Banyoles, Spain

Ben carefully eyes the old stone church before setting his pencil to paper and sketching with free-flowing strokes. He wears a long-sleeve golden-yellow shirt with Hampton emblazoned on the back, which makes me wonder where I've put mine. Seeing the easy-going Ben doing any form of 'work' feels slightly wrong.

Robin has granted us an afternoon off after yesterday's trials and we've driven the minibuses to a picturesque nearby town, complete with a Roman bridge and cobbles. In the summer it's probably full of tourists but right now we're the only visitors in the square. The resurgent sunshine helps the group's relaxed mood.

'Nice shorts/hat combo there, Moth,' JA comments as the willowy Andy Smith sits down at our wicker table with his coffee. His electric-blue board shorts with black lightning-effect clash impressively with his luminous red beanie. Poor JA. Another year of Goldie looks likely after his Blue Boat dream was slain by Ben.

'Wow, yeah, very summery,' I add, pulling down my sunglasses from the top of my head.

'Don't listen to them, Moth. I think you look hot,' says Ellie, coming to Andy's defence. As ever El's been getting a lot of attention from everyone, being one of the few girls. Laughter breaks out at the next table of Hugo, Dan Barry and Nate.

'I bet I do fit,' Nate says as he gets up and walks to the tiny red bus set against the stone wall at the edge of the tables. The machine looks as if it's meant to entertain toddlers. He squeezes into the seat, wedging his head, legs and arms under the roof. Busch feeds the machine a couple of euros.

Nothing happens. Then he notices the plug at the wall and flicks it. The little bus starts playing the tune 'The wheels on the bus' as the lights begin flashing and the bus starts rolling up and down.

'Yeah!' shouts Nate, whooping like he's on a Grand National winner. He's trying to cheer himself up. TJ beat him yesterday so it looks as though it's Goldie for Nate too. Having said that, TJ beat or drew with everyone he raced. Coach Donald now refers to TJ as 'the dark destroyer'. We all knew he was good but none of us quite expected this.

'Smile,' says Matze, arriving at our table. He wears a tight lilac polo shirt. Very European. 'That beard is looking nice, Bungle; I think you could be in with a chance.' Me and Andy pose stupidly for a photo. The annual CUBC beard-growing contest is on in earnest. Away from girlfriends, tutors and job interviews, it's the perfect time to experiment with facial hair that you'd never get the chance to grow otherwise.

'I don't know. I think you may have started sculpting too early,' says Wayne, who pulls a 'west side gesture' with his hand and pouts for Matze's camera. Wayne's developed a good, general, bristly growth, which complements his baldness quite well, adding further gravitas. In contrast I've trimmed my stubble into a handlebar moustache that links across to straggly lamb chops. Very tasteful.

When we get back to the Mirallac, an hour or two later, I bump into Robin in the lobby. He looks unhappy.

'You missed the interview. That's unacceptable.' Damn, now I remember. A reporter is out to do a piece on our Spanish preparations and after interviewing Robin and Tim had asked to talk to me about my brother. Robin had mentioned it but I'd promptly forgotten and jumped into the minibus to town. I offer my apologies and then head to the 'quiet' room, the hotel's underused second dining room, to finish my essay on 'Strategic alliances in the airline industry'. Andy Smith, KC and Ellie are in there already. Andy's writing up his experimental psychology research while Ellie does some 'land economy'. I still haven't quite worked out what that is. KC is writing his thesis for his chemistry PhD, something about squeezing plastics under high pressure. He's quirky and eccentric; a member of his college choir for example, an atypical pastime for a competitive sportsman. He's smart, too, at Cambridge on a full scholarship from the Bill Gates Foundation.

I struggle to concentrate on my essay and turn to fill in my coxing questionnaire, being careful to make sure Ellie cannot see my entries.

Tim has circulated a spreadsheet to all athletes to assess the team's views on the coxes' technical, personal and leadership characteristics. There are four great coxes left but it's still between Jim and Ellie for the Blue Boat. I know where the Harvard boys' loyalties lie but I think the overall decision will still be tight. To complicate matters I think Jim may have a bit of a crush on Ellie and he thinks Ellie and I are sweet on one another, misinterpreting the closeness we have developed as the only survivors of our boat last year.

After I finish the questionnaire I find myself staring at the ceiling, flicking my pen between my fingers, on autopilot. Would I be facing Dave? I couldn't let myself consider it before – my focus has been on winning my seat in the Blue Boat – but now it is a distinct possibility.

That night I text Dave, ostensibly to wish him good luck and let him know that I'm probably in, but really to find out whether he's made it. I follow that with a text to Sam, who replies almost immediately with news of her return to Nottingham. Her text ends with a string of kisses. It's lovely to communicate with her; she reminds me there is life outside the pressure cooker of the squad and there is life beyond rowing.

David:

Wednesday 8 January 22:15, Mequinenza, Spain

My phone beeps from under my bed, signalling the arrival of a text message. Putting down my class notes, happy to find any excuse to avoid revision, I reach under my bed, searching, until I find it. It's probably Maria. I sent her a text earlier just to let her know things are going well so far.

Opening the message, I see it's from James. It reads, 'How are things going with you? I think I'm OK. Good luck. James.'

By OK he'll mean that he's made their top crew. I'm pleased for him. He deserves it, given his dedication and obvious desire for another shot at victory. He'd have been devastated not to make the boat; despite the cover story of wanting to do a management degree, he's basically only back to win the Boat Race. It's his fourth and last attempt.

I'd like to call him to congratulate him. But now we're out of the holidays and into training mode, our relationship is conducted only through sparse messages, even cagier than before — a normal conversation is out of the question.

I start on a reply; 'Hey. Well done! Seat racing went well, looks like I'm going to make it too!'

I stop, delete my draft and start again; 'Hey. Well done. Looks OK for me so far.' I tap in and hit the send button. Normally I'd let him know that I'm in the boat too but I don't want to give my chances the kiss of death. I was in the boat at this point last year only to be dropped later. Now it looks more likely than ever I will actually race him in the Boat Race. On 6 April he'll be the enemy.

David:
Thursday 9 January 15:55, Mequinenza, Spain

The boat hums along underneath us; there are no sounds save for the splashing of eight oars into the water at the front of each stroke. Acer's silent and there isn't the usual drone of Sean's coaching launch. He's fallen back, letting us have the last few minutes of rowing to ourselves just to think.

Each stroke leaves eight vortexes, our only signature on the water, propelling us towards the Mequinenza landing dock. I'm excited to be sitting in the four seat, the position in an eight normally reserved for the workhorse with less technical finesse than the rest of the boat. It's a welcome change for me as I've most often been placed at six or stroke.

The thrill of being in the first outing of the provisional Blue Boat has everyone hyper alert, trying to convince Sean that he should finalise crew selection and announce the crew today. If the crew does stay like this I'll be racing with Henry, John, and Acer from our winning Isis crew last year, Matt, BT and Bas, experienced winning Blues, and Macca and Scott, two of the new international arrivals. It's a line-up of relatively young undergraduates, an increasing rarity in modern Boat Races, which now tend to be full of older, postgraduate internationals. I'm not yet twenty years old. Similarly Henry, Bas and John all arrived last year, as wet-behind-the-ears schoolboys.

Somewhere round the corner the provisional Isis boat is out training, no doubt filled with the disparate and difficult mixture of happy and very disgruntled oarsmen. I have no doubt that in time they'll develop a fantastic crew spirit given the calibre of the guys – Hutch, Tuppen, Sam Parker, Bill, Reevo and Vickers – some of the toughest competitors and dedicated crewmates you could hope for. Most miserable is the spare four, the four oarsmen who made neither crew. We passed them going in the other direction on our way back from the 20-kilometre turning point by the 'chemical weapons factory' some time ago. It looks as if Montana and Brian, two of the American guys, will fill the two spots in the spare pair, whilst the other two will be binned before the Boat Race. The spare pair will remain the unsung heroes of the squad, training all year just to have an unofficial race with the Cambridge spare pair a few days before Boat Race day. They don't even get half Blues.

Acer sweeps us round the large bend in the Ebro River, signifying the last two kilometres. Sit up and spin the hands I repeat to myself, the technical points that Sean has had me working on during the camp.

'Yeah, boys, the rhythm feels good, keep up the concentration for the final few minutes to home,' Acer says in his normal acute tone. Acer once let slip that his name meant 'fierce, keen and eager' in Latin. It's a surprisingly appropriate description of him. Sweat drips into my eyes, stinging and blurring my vision. Save for the crew and the deep blue water, my blurry panorama is of the high, barren hills fading further away into the distance with each passing stroke. We pass under the road bridge, the noise of eight turning oar locks echoing.

'Let's sharpen up the catch timing on bowside.' Acer is working on what he can see from his view in the coxing seat. 'That one was better. Yep, looking good, boys.' Acer's instructions are confident and technically precise, exactly what we'll need this year if we're to overcome Cambridge.

It is a rare feeling of joy when a boat goes as well as this. We're making order out of disorder. It feels as though all eight rowers are part of one big machine.

The rowing becomes Zen. I half shut my eyes, skimming over the water, floating, flying even. The countless strokes have calmed my mind; my body feels as though it's moving in a natural rhythm, gripping the water with the oar handle as an extension of my arms and the foot plate connecting me to the boat. The boat and I are one. There are seven other moving parts yet I feel like I'm rowing on my own. The flow moves my legs up and down, without the normal tension in my muscles.

They are always moving, never stopping. It is bliss; a pure, simple feeling of harmony.

'Next stroke, easy there,' Acer calls. We stop at quarter slide, our oars off the water. With our momentum we glide across the millpond-like water towards the dock. Turning round in his bow seat, John jumps out on to the wooden boat raft. Bas simultaneously reaches out, holding the boat. I unhook my shoes, undo my oar lock and step out on to the dock with my oar. It feels much heavier and more unwieldy on land than on the water.

I walk alongside Henry up the steep, rusted steel ramp connecting the pontoon and the dock. I pat him on the back. 'Good start,' I offer.

'Yeah, very solid,' he replies. 'We've got a long way to go yet, though.'

'Too right,' I reply, 'too right.'

The seat racing has been a stressful experience for both the squad and the coaches, but we've almost finalised the nine good men and true who will be facing Cambridge in April. There's less than four months left to turn us from a promising bunch of athletes into a truly spectacular eight. It'll take as much physical and mental devotion as we've put into making the boat, if not more. We have no idea how fast the Cambridge eight will be, but, given the results of the Fours Head of the River and the ergo championships, we're up against it. From now on in we're training against an unknown force, a light blue ghost. I can't make out the faces in the Cambridge eight, except for one – James, who stares back at me with his dark brown eyes.

James:
Thursday 9 January 17:34, Banyoles, Spain

Thunk, thunk, thunk. The eight pounds along with intent. This afternoon Robin has put out two crews which he has labelled 'A' and 'B'. I'm in the middle of the boat following Matze, Groves and TJ, who are setting a powerful, determined rhythm. Behind me Wooge, Wayne, KC and Hugo provide our front-wheel drive. The levels of professionalism, adrenalin and focus have pushed up another notch. Donald and Robin's launch has sat alongside us all outing, but they're pretty quiet, no doubt analysing and discussing the order of the crew.

Robin shouts 500-metre split times at us on occasion. We're moving fast.

The 'B' crew pass in the opposite direction, followed by Rob's coaching launch, an aura of melancholy hanging in the air. Last year at the same point in the season one of the guys in the 'B' crew had insisted midway through the depressed outing that they needed to cheer themselves up, with the result that they all whipped off their kit and rowed along in the sunshine, the way nature intended. Ellie, in the coxing seat, kept her clothes on and suffered the view, which must have been memorable. The strokeman, Ewan Robson, was a pasty white Yorkshireman with a tendency to splay his legs apart at the catch.

Gradually the hills around the lake fade to grey, and by the time we pull into the dock darkness has fallen. We're unusually quiet as we get out of the boat. There's an appreciation from each of us that, bar disaster, this is going to be the Blue Boat. It's up to us to defend Cambridge's name.

When we get to dinner in the hotel later, the 'B' crew is already seated at one table, eating and joking, and we fill up the adjacent one. The change in team dynamic is tangible. All the guys on the other table are wishing they were on ours.

Chapter 7
Heart and Nerve and Sinew

James:
Wednesday 15 January 18:51, St Chad's, Cambridge

My flatmate Andy Done and I set up a human chain to unpack the mountain of shopping bags that have just been delivered to our upper-floor flat. Four-packs of beans, ten huge boxes of cereal and dozens of jars of sauces are passed from the floor to me and on to the shelves or cupboards. The sauces are key to our culinary variety. Dinners are a rotation of 'Simply Sausages', 'Chicken Tonight' and, Sam's favourite in my repertoire, spaghetti bolognese with the obligatory Dolmio sauce. The cupboards and shelves are filled to bursting and I start heaping stuff on top of the fridge then finally the floor.

'I think we might have overdone it' Andy says.

'I think you may be right.'

Lent term officially started yesterday and contrary to the spirit of Lent, we've decided to stock up. With all my training I go through boxes of cereal and packets of Jaffa Cakes like most other students go through pints of lager. Poor Andy is constantly amazed by how quickly the food vanishes. As an emergency measure last term we started getting economy malt loaf, piling them up like bricks, to stall me from getting through the rest of the supplies. It didn't work. Unsurprisingly at 10p a throw, they had a gummy, sticky consistency and lacked any real taste. They weren't a patch on Soreen.

As Andy arranges the groceries on top of the small fridge, several cans of Heinz thump on to the floor and we both wince, hoping not to incur the wrath of Dr Chiswick, world expert in invertebrates, who lives below. He knows us – he taught me last year – but he takes a dim view of student disturbances to his research into snails of the European inter-tidal mudflats.

Academically I've moved on from biology and this new term means new lecture courses. I have the joy of organisational design, corporate strategy and advanced economics for the next eight weeks. Naturally I missed economics this afternoon because of rowing, which means I'll probably never go at all. Better never to show your face than go once, get noticed and then be obviously absent. To a few lecturers I was unknown, just letters on a page.

One of Dad's cronies at St John's, Francis, did not go to a single lecture, supervision or seminar – not one – in three years. He was far too busy haunting students from the college battlements or going to Great Yarmouth with his girlfriend. He learned his languages at his own pace. In May term of his final year, two weeks before his final exams, he bumped into his tutor in the university library, who recognised him from the welcome sherry and cheese party in his first week of Cambridge three years earlier.

'Francis. Good to see you. What are you up to these days?' the amiable old tutor enquired.

'Well, reading up for final exams, sir.' Francis stated matter-of-factly.

'What? Finals? You're still here? You can't be! You can't! No, Francis, it's too late! It's just too late!' Francis wished him good day and took his leave before the tutor's brain could re-boot. He passed OK and went on to be a television presenter and run his own TV production company. Like all his Cambridge stories the retelling left Dad misty-eyed and grinning, the love of his student days shining out brightly. Dave looked uncomfortable during these recollections.

Dad would inevitably continue, 'Yes, that was Francis. Typical Francis. I'll never forget the day I met Sainsbury. Knocks on my door my first day up, asks me if he can use my waste bin and promptly throws up in it!'

While I'd never had the 'Sainsbury experience' I could see echoes of the Francis story in Groves. No lectures. No supervisions. Ellie was regularly passing him her previous year's land economy notes in the back of the minibus to help Groves concoct his one essay a term, without which his supervisor would have sent him down.

Both my flatmate Andy and I are a little more conscientious, if not paragons of virtue. My complete James Bond video collection is doing Andy's project on signal processing no favours at all. After lunch today I left him watching *Octopussy* and headed to rowing, only to return to find him midway through *Diamonds Are Forever*, acoustic guitar on his knee. It gave me a bad case of non-rowing jealousy.

James:

Wednesday 15 January 21:59, St Catharine's bar, Cambridge

In the intimacy of St Catharine's bar Chesney Hawks blares while most of my college gyrate on the dance floor. 'This is my one and only hit', the students sing mockingly as he croons. I can't help smiling but Andy Smith sitting across from me remains downcast. The first college bop of term, the opportunity for everyone to catch up after the holidays. Sam is at the bar chatting to Andy's girlfriend Belita, a Catz girl that Andy met through the CUBC as she trialled as a cox earlier in the year, lasting until mid-November. That might be the only good thing the CUBC does for him this year.

'Things haven't gone well at all, Bungle,' he confides across the table. 'It's not like last year. I'm really not enjoying it.' Andy's normally smiling face is drawn thin and he looks utterly helpless. 'I know I'll be in the spare pair.' The worst place to be. Unless something drastic changes, his awful prediction will be right. When Robin announced the crews each day he was generally not in either the A or B eight. There is no escape for Andy that I can see – he wouldn't give up; he'd never leave his friends when they needed him – but I don't envy him. The spare pair is a critical boat for Goldie, as regularly in training they have to lend their top guys to sub in when one of the Blue Boat is sick or away with some critical academic commitment. I try to cheer him up, give him hope, but in his current, realistic frame of mind it's difficult. Seeing the much-loved, sweet Moth sad is terrible.

'Moth, mate, the second year always feels like you're not improving. It's just because you're beginning to reach the plateau, the improvements are more gradual. Sometimes you have to take a step back to go forward.' I can see he's not convinced. 'It's not going to be like last year. I remember when you turned up, the wide-eyed streak of piss from the Caius second eight.' I was grinning at the recollection. Andy had been hugely inexperienced and had legs and arms like pipe cleaners. Half a smile creeps on to his face but his eyes remain sad. 'No one, not even you, thought you were going to last beyond the first week. But you just improved so fast. At Banyoles you couldn't do anything wrong and you booked your seat in Goldie.' His improvement had been meteoric.

'That feels like a long time ago now,' he says. We're quiet for a moment as S Club 7 take over from Chesney and on the part of the bar designated as the dance floor everyone starts 'reaching for the stars'. To complete Andy's unhappiness yesterday he overtook Wayne in the monthly fat test to become the 'fattest' amongst us. I don't think a joke about that will help. Wayne had undoubtedly carefully planned his weight loss over Christmas, knowing everyone else would be tucking into turkey and chocolate oranges.

Andy and I cut our discussion short as Sam and Belita return to our table through the throng, with plastic glasses full of red liquid.

'Fire engines,' Sam sighs, smiling wanly at the drinks. 'John the barman wouldn't let me order gin and tonics on my first time back to the bar for a while.' The 'fire engine' is the unofficial college drink as it mirrors the college colours. Its popularity certainly isn't due to its taste: after three and a half years I still don't know what's in it.

'Cheers,' I say and we touch our plastic glasses together, which feels a little pointless without the nice chink of glass. Andy and I sup our cokes, needing the caffeine to keep us awake.

It was in this corner of the bar that Sam and I first met, a little over three years ago. We'd only been at university three days, a frenzy of trying to make friends, putting up what you hoped were the right sort of posters in your room, buying textbooks and a million other things. All conversations started in the traditional fresher way: What course are you doing? What A levels did you do? Which school were you at? Which corridor are you on?

Three days in came the Freshers' Bop, the first party of the term, an opportunity for us freshers to meet the rest of our year group and for the seniors to pass judgment on us. I was standing at the bar talking to a couple of new friends when up walked a beautiful blonde girl with a dazzling smile. One of my new friends introduced us and we instantly hit it off.

This came as something of a shock. I'd spent the last five years at an all-boys school and with a bad haircut, which meant my experience of bubbly conversations with attractive girls was relatively limited. But Sam and I moved from the bar to the tables where we're now sitting with Andy and Belita, discovering more and more common ground as the conversation went on.

I remember thinking that if this is what university is like then I think I'm going to enjoy it. When Sam went to get more drinks, our new friend Simo, the college chef, a sociable character who played football for the college team, leaned across to me, winked conspiratorially and said, 'I think she likes you,' before spotting a friend on the other side of the bar in urgent need of his conversation just as Sam returned. Then she asked me to dance.

'Right,' says Sam after another sip of her fire engine, 'enough of this rowing chat. You two crazy kids need a dance.' As if on cue, *Grease*'s 'Greased Lightning' kicks off. Thankfully I'm well practised at dancing sober.

David:
Friday 17 January 22:12, Oxford Town Hall

'Hi, your names please?' Lawrence asks the gaggle of girls standing in front of the trestle table.

'Josephine Park and two guests,' replies the petite blonde, who is wearing a short, black cocktail dress. Behind them there is still a lengthy queue and yet more black-tie-wearing students are coming up the stone staircase of Oxford Town Hall to join it. Lawrence scrolls down the lengthy guest list.

'OK, that's fine, go on through to the party,' he says, crossing her name off.

'Can I stamp your hands, please?' I request, my stamp raised and ready. They present their dainty, feminine hands and one by one I take theirs in mine and press the thick, black stamp of 'Cardinals Cocktails' on to their skin to show their entry fee is paid and they're free to come and go as they please. 'Enjoy the party.' I open the doors to the raucous town hall.

'Thank you,' says Josephine's friend, smiling up at me. She totters in, following her friends. Those high heels must be killing her but she looks fantastic, like some sort of Homeric goddess with her gold ball gown hanging silkily off her shoulders. Wow, I love being a Cardinal. Our cocktail events are widely known as some of the best parties in Oxford and all the best-looking girls in town emerge from their various colleges for the event. But for me it will be an evening of sobriety with an early morning outing at Wallingford tomorrow.

With a last lingering glance I let the doors close and begin the handstamping again. Soon I'm relieved of my duties by one of the older Cardinals. I don't know his name but the gold bow tie embroidered with a black CC is unmistakable.

Although the Cardinals share the name of senior members of the Roman Catholic Church the similiarities end there. We are a drinking and social fraternity, named after Cardinal Wolsey, the founder of Cardinal's college in 1524 which later became known as Christ Church. Each year a few more Christ Church men are picked to join the club, recruited from friends, sports teams or the college bar. Entry seems based on being deemed a 'good lad' and perhaps a little on drinking prowess but not on which school you went to, although we do have our share of Old Etonians. Each term the Cardinals run a huge cocktail event in the town hall, open to all members of the university. Hundreds turn up. They're attracted partly by the venue, partly by the reputation but mostly because it is another excuse to drink. The profits are put to excellent use, funding a massive dinner for the Cardinals at the end of each term at one of the nicest restaurants in Oxford. Being an all-male club there are always whisperings of strip clubs after the dinners, although this is generally bravado and rarely followed through. For me that dinner is something to look forward to after the Boat Race is over – a glimmer of life beyond it.

The ballroom is a cacophony of noise with hundreds of students packed in, drinking and chatting drunkenly. It's just possible to make out the university jazz band playing on the stage at the far end of the hall. This attendance is great news for our dinner later this term: perhaps the profits will stretch to the embroidered gold silk dressing gowns we have been talking about? Or maybe we can go down to London for a night and conclude our evening at Stringfellows night club? After all, he is an honorary Cardinal.

I was initiated into the Cardinals in the traditional way, last summer term. Three other freshers and I found invites in our pigeonholes in the closing week of term. The Cardinals' crest was embossed at the top. It read simply, 'Tom Quad, 9 p.m., Wednesday'.

The four of us gathered under the bell tower of Old Tom in the main quad at the allotted time. A minute later the Cardinals emerged, all in black tie. The Head Cardinal walked up to us while the rest dispersed round the quad, some holding shopping bags.

'It is a race, gentlemen. You get round as fast as possible,' he said nodding to the quad's corners. 'Follow the instructions at each station. Oh and obviously this needs to be done naked.' We looked at each other, then shrugged and disrobed before taking our marks, sprinter style.

'Go!'

We sprinted to the first corner. 'Ten press-ups!' I pumped them out, the flagstones cold on my hands, feet and nethers. 'Now these.' Pints of lager were shoved into our hands.

'Come on, quickly!' We downed the liquid before sprinting to the next corner of the quad, towards the Peckwater library.

'Twenty star jumps!' Wow. What a sight: four naked boys doing star jumps! As we finished, bottles of Smirnoff Ice were pushed into our hands. I downed mine in one again. My stomach churned, not enjoying the volume and mix of alcohol and exercise.

We ran to the next corner, past the twelfth-century cathedral. Another ten press-ups. I was in second place.

'Enjoy these, boys.'

'Oh no.' A can of Newcastle Brown ale. I'd never liked bitter. In my urgency to finish it, half of the can ended up across my chest. Now I felt really terrible.

Two quiet PhD girls almost dropped their folders as we ran past and offered them polite, breathless 'hi's' on our way to the final corner. Twenty star jumps again. As I finished them, a Cardinal from the year above thrust a glass of port into my hand. Again, down in one. The sweetness of the port tasted great in comparison to the bitter.

Once clothes were back on, we were handed gold silk bow ties, the badge that will label us as Cardinals at all future events.

Tonight I wear my bow tie with pride. I've earned it. I make my way through the throng of people to the first bar area, where Filipo and Stu are desperately trying to man the overrun bar. Beyond them I notice Josephine taking some drinks away from the bar over to her friends. I wish Maria was here; training has put our relationship on hold yet again. We haven't seen each other since New Year.

'Can you mix up some more Seabreeze?' Filipo asks over his shoulder as I duck under the wooden bar shelf. He is frantically dipping a jug into a black, plastic rubbish bin full of a red liquid before pouring it out to those waiting at the bar.

'Yup, sure can.'

I grab our 'cocktail menu'. Seabreeze, right, that's two parts grapefruit juice, two of cranberry and one of vodka. The other two options on the menu are gin and tonic and vodka and orange – 'Cocktails' is quite a loose term when it comes to our parties. But who cares when for £15 a head you can drink as much as you want? I scrabble for some scissors to open the cartons of grapefruit juice but without success, so I rip them open by hand before squeezing the contents quickly into an almost empty bin. As I pour the juice, attempting to hide the cheap carton from the girls in ball dresses and guys in black tie, I reflect that some high society spiked with student debauchery is the perfect respite from the loneliness of the erg.

James:

Wednesday 22 January 19:05, St Chad's, Cambridge

I just can't take it any more. The training is destroying all of us, not helped by supervisors baying for blood. An hour and a half on the erg this morning. It is hell, every time. Fingers lock around the machine handle in a painful claw, hamstrings pinch, eyes sting with sweat, legs ache, backs crunch. All the while the machine stares back, taunting, the seconds ticking down imperceptibly. At points I shut my eyes and wish the time away but when I open them again only a few seconds have passed. I start counting out ten strokes at a time. The white wall in front of me is the only stimulation: our stereo is broken, like most of us. Young TJ, on the machine next to me, looks grey and haggard and constantly shifts his weight around on the seat in discomfort.

Time on the machine cuts like a blade now we are so fatigued. Einstein tried to explain his theory of relativity with the metaphor, 'Put your hand on a hot stove for a minute, and it seems like an hour. Sit with a pretty girl for an hour, and it seems like a minute.' Sit on a rowing machine for 90 minutes staring at a wall and it feels like a lifetime.

This week is the hardest Robin has ever set. More miles, more intensity than ever before. This afternoon we battled in our pairs, against each other and against the miles. Back between the raised grassy banks on the dull, arrow straightness of the Ely stretch, the warmth of the Spanish lake a few weeks ago seems like a dream.

We slogged along, lame, hands and calves bleeding, until finally we turned our backs on the pylons. The rain then joined the wind in battering us, until finally Matze's relentless rhythm got us home. In the bus we all forced down our food without pleasure. The fatigue has killed our hunger and our taste buds. We are just machines that need to be fuelled.

Now, standing in the relative warmth of my kitchen I resentfully hang up my mountain of washing. It piles up so rapidly, particularly now that for the second session of the day we are wrapped up like mummies against the chill rain. Even when I'm not rowing the obsession dominates my life, eating, washing or sleeping.

James:
Thursday 23 January 11:45, Cambridge

I wheel slowly down to Catz and find a card and package in my pigeonhole from Sammy, a close friend who rowed at the CUBC for the previous three years and is now working in the City. We'd won and lost together hundreds of times. In particular we'd both been seared by the shame of the defeat in 2000, the end of Cambridge's seven-year winning run. Tintin is on the front of the card, a reference to my designer quiff.

'Bango, thought it was about the right time you read this. Hope Spain went well, expect you handed out some fury in the seat racing. No prisoners this year, crush the dark blues into submission and inspire the new guys.'

I open the package. I know it's a book; Sammy and I had got into trading books we found particularly meaningful. He'd sent me *Banco*, the follow-up to Henri Charrière's amazing story of retribution and repentance, *Papillon*. I'd responded with *The Long Walk* by Slawomir Rawicz, the tale of a Polish soldier sent to a Siberian gulag during the Second World War, who escapes with five comrades. Over many months they flee south, across the Gobi Desert and over the Himalayas to India. Both are true stories of forbearance and survival; I hope I can survive my struggle.

Inside the package is a copy of *The Catcher in the Rye*. The handwritten inscription reads:

All men die but not all men truly live!
Happy New Year,
Sammy

James:
Tuesday 28 January 10:52, Goldie Boathouse, Cambridge

As they reach the last minute of their torture we stop warming up or stretching and move over to the doors where we find ourselves horribly glued to the glass panels. We stare, eyes wide. The second and last five-kilometre erg test of our season. Sixteen minutes or so of pain. A last-ditch attempt for those who've lost seat races to pull something out of the bag. A final opportunity to underperform and be dropped for those in the provisional Blue Boat line-up that Robin's been putting out. It feels like the sharks are circling. Any sign of weakness and your seat could be snatched away from you.

I stand next to Nate, who has his headphones on, and looks particularly intent. This could be his last shot at knocking KC out. Through the glass our friends sweat and pull at the machines, eyes resolutely on the readout, until the last metre ticks away and they fall prostrate, chests heaving, with tortured expressions etched on their faces. Robin and the coaches prod at the fallens' ear lobes with needles to get a lactate reading. It's like watching the execution before yours, knowing that the noose is going to be round your neck next.

I walk into the changing room and notice for the first time a thin oval brass plaque on top of the changing room door. It reads 'We have the whitest and stiffest dickeys in the trade'. My fourth year and only now do I see it.

The fear of the five-kilometre test makes you see things differently. A crewmate a couple of years older than me who'd joined the army after university and then successfully completed selection for the SAS said that of all the horrible things he'd had to endure nothing was ever as bad as a five-kilometre erg test. The test pushes you so far that it isn't unheard of to lose control of bodily functions. The year before I joined one guy, desperate to keep his seat in the Blue Boat, had 'lost control' in the latter stages but kept going, spreading the mess along the floor. The next poor unfortunate on the machine was told to 'clean that shit up'.

'What is it?' he asked, not believing what he saw.

'Well it's shit, isn't it.' What a horrible moment.

As the last of the five fall from their machines we return to the warm-up machines. One by one they join us as they stumble through the dividing doors and collapse on the stretching mats, covering them in films of sweat.

We pat them on the shoulders and nod well done. There isn't much talk from either those who've just tested, who are too exhausted, or from those who are about to take their turn. We're all in our own worlds, too concerned with what faces us. The opposition is your own body's limitations. When will your legs scream no more? When will your lungs beg for mercy? Psychologically will your mind be strong enough to keep pushing on or will it break? Do you want this enough?

I remind myself of my race plan and my technical focuses at each point. I'm splitting the race psychologically into three blocks – the first two kilometres, the middle kilometre and the final two.

The quiet amongst the athletes is a far cry from last night's light-hearted 'pasta party' hosted by Hugo at his house near the Hawks Club. Nate was there, cap on backwards, Hugo of course, the chatty Dan Barry, Matze and Wayne in one of his smart polo shirts, as always looking the most presentable of us. We got through mountains of pasta and tomato sauce and the latest squad gossip. But today, even though we're all together, we are on our own. It's just the machine versus you.

David:
Wednesday 29 January 19:45, Christ Church, Oxford

'Voilà', I say, placing the plate of potato and pasta in front of her, a rower's carbohydrate dream. 'They say the first taste is with zee eye,' I suggest in my best French accent. In reality the sprig of mint does nothing to disguise the poor preparation. Sally takes her first bite. I stand over her expectantly, wearing her chef's apron.

She chews for a minute and swallows. Then she asks, 'Did you cook these potatoes?'

'Of course I cooked them, I fried them.'

'Did you boil them first?'

'Well. No, I fried them.' She raises her eyebrows. 'You have to boil them first before you fry them?' I look incredulous. 'Really?' I take one from my plate and arc it into the air and catch it in my open mouth. Burnt on the outside, rock hard on the inside.

'Shit. I can't believe I got even this wrong,' I say, quite disappointed.

'It's OK, the pasta's pretty much cooked to perfection,' she says smiling at me. Her spag bols, lecture notes and real-life perspective have got me through much of this year. She is, all in all, very understanding. It is good to have her around, one of my few non-rowing friends.

I dig into my plate, avoiding the hard potato bits where possible. 'You know the guys still can't believe there is nothing going on between us,' I say between mouthfuls.

'I guess they see me with you more than Maria.'

'True, true,' I nod.

The honest truth is that, attractive as Sally is, and though she looks out for me and keeps me on the rails and nags me when I need it, kissing her would be like kissing a sister.

James:
Saturday 1 February 14:00, Ely

The icy gravel crunches underfoot as we walk up the drive in our blazers and ties, exhaling clouds of frosted breath. On this one occasion it's a relief the woollen Blues blazers are almost an inch thick. Legend has it that Mallory wore his version on the first ascent of Everest; even then he was probably on the verge of overheating.

Bakes, our youthful assistant coach, leads along the path and buzzes at the door. He turns to us while he waits for it to open. 'Now, whatever you do, boys, don't fucking swear.' He grins.

He turns back to face the resigned countenance of the Bishop of Ely, standing in the open door.

'Oh. Bishop. Good afternoon,' he stammers. We desperately try to stifle our laughter as the bishop quietly welcomes each of us into his lodgings, overshadowed by his vast cathedral, the 'ship of the fens'. He's

invited the squad for tea, as he does each year, to cement the town's
relationship with the CUBC. There have been non-stop 'meet the bish'
jokes for the last week or so.

We mill around his reception room, trying to look respectable. It's all
dark wooden floors and ornate framed old oils of previous bishops,
staring on with expressions ranging from stern to positively disgruntled.
The more establishment-friendly guys, like Wayne, me and Wooge,
chat to the bishop and his associates while Groves and Busch look
slightly uncomfortable in the background. Everyone is much impressed
by the quality of the bishops's Bang and Olufsen speakers.

Nate and KC are noticeably quiet. In our row earlier we did four by
1,500 metres at race tempo, swapping the two of them between the
eight, the as yet unconfirmed Blue Boat, and a pair. The coaches
watched eagle-eyed with stopwatches. We all know Robin is looking to
place the last piece of the jigsaw that is the final crew. KC had just edged
out Nate on the five-kilometre test but I couldn't tell you who was faster
on the water; it felt good with both of them. Robin has not published
the times. Nate has been on edge for the last few weeks; normally light-
hearted and one of Buschbacher's partners in crime, now he is solemn
and quiet. His personal drive to put the Yale losses behind him by racing
and winning in the Cambridge Blue Boat is loading the pressure upon
him. Now he is staring up at a picture of Jesus hung on the wall, as if
wanting answers or divine inspiration.

In the old days the church used to be the next port of call for ex-
CUBC rowers. Students from the first Boat Race in 1829 included the
future Bishops of New Zealand and St Andrews, the Deans of Lincoln,
Ely and Ripon and a Prebendary of York. Nowadays most ex-squad
guys head into the City as lawyers, bankers or consultants. How times
change.

In the far corner of the room, the bish's catering lady peels
clingfilm from the plates of nibbles and causes a slow-motion
stampede as we each disengage from our various conversations
and move quickly but politely to the honeyed sausages and perfect
triangle sandwiches.

As I stretch for a glass of apple juice an errant sausage roll leaps from
my stacked paper plate and plops squarely into the tomato soup.

'Oh Christ,' I mutter, depositing my plate and beginning to fish
around with a plastic fork. I manage to lift out the now disintegrating roll

but it slips off again and dives back once more into the soup, splashing a few drops on to my blazer.

'Bollocks,' I whisper, deciding to leave the scene of the crime. I turn to find the bishop is standing silently behind me, holding his empty soup bowl.

James:
Wednesday 5 February 19:05, Goldie Boathouse, Cambridge

In hushed silence we sit together in the Captains' Room of Goldie Boathouse. The hand-painted gold names of the previous Blues gleam down at us. The room is much emptier, much quieter than when we started on this journey. Fifty or so hopeful triallists reduced to twenty; many have fallen. Poor Ben Clare, the silent strong man, lost to a lengthy chest infection. Sam Minors, the Hampton schoolboy who'd been in the bronze-winning world's eight with TJ and my brother Dave, crippled by an injury to the discs in his back. Then of course all those that Robin has binned.

Tim announced at the morning session that following the afternoon row there would be a meeting at the boathouse. We all knew what this meant. The crew announcement. This evening we find out who will fight Oxford on 6 April. I'm sitting alongside Matze, TJ, Wayne and Hugo; I would be proud to call them crewmates.

Suddenly the sporadic conversation drops to nothing as the Cambridge blue door opens and Nate and Busch walk through, both silent, their eyes set to the floor. It's standard practice to bring in the one or two oarsmen who were closest but just missed out on the Blue Boat and tell them the news early, to allow them time to collect themselves.

Robin and Wooge follow them. Wooge walks to the front.

'As you know, tonight we will announce the crews that will represent Cambridge against Oxford on 6 April. We have all come a long way but our greatest effort is still ahead of us. While we will now train in selected crews remember that we are still one squad and we all need to support each other to succeed.' He says some more inspiring words about us having to push on now and build two of the best Cambridge crews ever. Finally, he comes to the nub of the matter.

'The 2003 Cambridge Blue Boat that will face Oxford in the 149th

Boat Race is made up of: Jim O'Martian, Alex McGarel-Groves, Kris Coventry, James Livingston, Hugo Mallinson, Tom James, Matthias Kleinz, Wayne Pommen and myself.'

I've made it. Thank God. I catch TJ's eye next to me and wink at him; he can barely contain a smile. There are no outward public displays of celebration; we are too aware of those sitting next to us, devastated, their dream crushed.

Tim Wooge continues, 'Selection for Goldie is not yet complete but we anticipate we will confirm selection in the next two weeks. The crews need to remain private until the official announcement to the press in a few weeks' time. Those with family connections,' he says, looking at Ben and me, 'please be mindful. Now let's push on, we have a job to do.'

After he concludes we all stand and start shaking hands with those around us. There are heartfelt handshakes between those selected. Those that haven't made it offer quiet congratulations to those that have, with the stiffest of stiff upper lips. Ellie and Nate are particularly badly hit. Behind their eyes the heartbreak is easily read. Poor Ellie, she won't get to right the wrongs of last year.

As I head out of Goldie into the cool, fresh air, a weight feels lifted from my shoulders. I will get another chance to help put Cambridge back where it belongs. Before I jump on my bike I text Sam, Mum and Dad the good news. I'm over the moon.

James:

Thursday 6 February 06:05, St Chad's, Cambridge

Munching cereal, feeling invigorated even at six in the morning by yesterday's fantastic news, I flick on my computer to check out the BBC news website. I'm surprised to see an email in my inbox addressed to all the newly confirmed members of the Blue Boat.

6 February 2003 2:57 a.m.
Subject: from Robin
Thanks for attending tonight's meeting and very warm congratulations on securing your seats for the Boat Race. You have all worked hard and have forged a great spirit in the Club this year. Well done. This is, of course, only the beginning.

You deserve to celebrate but also bear in mind the feelings of the ones who have aspired to a seat who have not managed to win one. I would like to have another (hopefully short) meeting tomorrow to just set the tone for the coming weeks. It is now up to us to become a great crew and there is much work to go in before that will happen. So a brief meeting would get a few thoughts out in the open and help us to press on with our progress. Can we make 15 mins after Ely?

Robin

2.57 a.m.! Robin was obviously as excited as the rest of the crew.

After the usual cold, dark cycle to the boathouse I prepare myself for the morning ergo, setting myself up alongside Hugo. Nate takes the machine to our left. He has a determined look in his eye as he plugs himself into his walkman, sets the machine for the required 70 minutes and starts to crank away at a pace most Olympic oarsmen would be hard pressed to keep up with. He's going to prove to himself he's still got the hardness and physiology he was renowned for at Yale. His self-belief has taken a battering with yesterday's announcement and months of intensive coaching, required to change his style from the agricultural Yale technique to the Cambridge model. His attack on this piece is a big 'screw you' to the coaches.

Ten minutes in, he's still going like a machine, while Hugo and I cruise at the more controlled pace Robin has outlined in his training programme, carefully analysing our technique in the mirrors set out in front and to the side of us.

All of a sudden Robin appears behind us, looking flustered.

'Nate, what are you doing?' he questions. Nate keeps going doggedly. 'Nate! Stop,' Robin demands, louder this time. With great reluctance Nate comes to a halt and takes out his earphones, downcast. Robin is incredulous. 'This is a recovery day. Your body has got to recover after the weekend. It's not sensible. Just stick to your target splits.' Nate doesn't say anything and looks broken. His last attempt foiled. The coach has just berated him for pulling too hard. Practically unheard of. He climbs off the machine and stalks off to the changing rooms.

Hugo and I are on our 57th minute and dawn has broken outside when Nate returns to the machine with a resigned look on his features. Busch is also struggling to deal with Robin's selection decision and is absent this morning. I hope both of these strong Americans can adjust to the idea of rowing in Goldie and drive the crew forward; they'll be critical to its success.

David:
Saturday 8 February 05:05, Christ Church, Oxford

I groan as I prop myself up on one elbow and press the left button on my heart rate monitor watch. It lights up. 5.05. Oh God.

I pull off the duvet cover, exposing myself to the harshness of the cold air, and swing my legs on to the carpet before stumbling to my feet and over to the door. I reach out into the darkness for the light switch.

Ping! The light floods into my eyes, forcing me out of sleep mode. I walk over to the corner of my bedroom on a fruitless search for clean clothes and training kit. The dank smell of sweaty lycra seeps out of my washing basket in the corner of the room, so I settle for retrieving my worn jeans from where I tossed them last night. Crunch! My head hits one of the eaves. 'Shit.' I rub my head and let out a deep sigh of unhappiness. The bloody eaves, beautifully antiquated as they may be, are not designed for all six foot seven inches of me and especially not this early.

Back in the centre of the room I ratchet up my blind to check on the weather conditions, but it is hard to make anything out in the moon-light. The weather has proved challenging so far this year. Our normal home stretch in Wallingford has been severely flooded. Last week, instead of going to Dorney Lake, our temporary home, Sean decided that we should spend two sessions a day in the gym on the indoor rowing machines. I understood Sean's decision, though. Physiologically we still need to find more watts of power to be able to come even close to competing with Cambridge in the aerobic stakes.

Two or more hours a day of sweat on the machines has left me in a state of constant lethargy as my glycogen supply, the fuel for my muscles, is severely depleted. On the worst days I wonder why I choose to row, rather than another less arduous sport; I can see why rowing was reserved as a punishment for Roman galley slaves.

I know now – Mum told me – that James is in the Blue Boat. Here, we're still awaiting the official announcement. So far I've held on to my place in the notional line-up but my seat still doesn't feel secure. Last year Sean showed no remorse in dropping me at the last minute, and he'll do the same again if I'm not pulling my weight.

My short bike ride down to the gym leaves me damp and sweaty, with numb fingers and ears. Bike locked up, I jump in the back of the bus. 'Morning guys,' I mumble, taking the back row of seats for myself and my kit bag. A few others stir from their slumber to mutter 'Hi' or 'morning'. Scott on the row in front of me has covered his face with his Cal Berkeley sweatshirt. As a Canadian, I can't imagine he is too happy about trekking all the way to Boston, Lincolnshire, the most soul-destroying place in Britain, for the Great Britain rowing trials. He can't escape because Sean, and no doubt Robin Williams too, have persuaded the selectors to let our foreigners race the five-kilometre time trial in pairs so they can use it as part of crew selection.

Today is an important day. It's our last chance to race Cambridge before the Boat Race itself. Our last chance to see if our changes are working.

I've been dreading going back to Boston ever since the first set of trials earlier this season. I know James will be there as he harbours ambitions of one day making the Olympic team, following in the footsteps of our role models the Searle brothers and Martin Cross, who we'd rowed with from time to time at school.

My fitful sleep is interrupted as we lurch over a bump, my head slumping on to the cold minibus window. As I lift up my hat and wipe away the condensation with my sleeve, we swing past another roundabout and past yet another McDonald's. Ronald McDonald's big, plastic, happy face is too much to take this early. I roll my hat back down over my eyes to try to get some more rest before racing.

James:

Saturday 8 February 17:43, Boston, Lincolnshire

The time trial format and the backwater ditch of a course combined to make today's race pretty unexciting. Dave and I had acknowledged one another with only a nod across the crowded safety briefing before taking to the water. Now we're on the way back to our respective universities. In the front of the minibus Bakes's phone rings. He turns down the radio and clamps it to his ear. Everyone goes quiet. This must be the results:

'Fifth – Frandsen, Bourne-Taylor. McGarel-Groves and Coventry, seventh. Eighth – Smith, Morris. Tenth – Livingston . . .' my head goes up, Matze and I did OK if we're this high up the list. Annoying to lose to Matt but not a disaster. '. . . Livingston, Adams.' Christ, he means Dave. Matze and I are two places behind in twelfth. It feels like a body blow. Little brother beat me. Have Oxford turned the tables on us?

David:
Sunday 9 February 10:07, Christ Church, Oxford

On the way to All Bar One my hangover builds. The after-effect of drinking Foster's laced with foot sweat from Reevo's shoe – an unpleasant drinking penalty levied due to my spilling Matt's pint. With today's rare day off training we'd taken our last chance to have team drinks.

By the time I arrive, the ten or so guys are already sitting around one of the long wooden tables. Without delay I place my order for a full English breakfast and a pint of orange juice.

'Hey, man,' I take a seat next to the well-built Isis oarsman Nick Tuppen. Along the table things are quiet. The guys seem decidedly sombre, even glum; it's probably their hangovers. 'How was the club? Any good stories?' I enquire.

'You weren't there?' Tuppen says between mouthfuls of breakfast.

'I was already falling asleep before we left the bar.' I'd got to the back of the long queue for the club before sloping off home.

He puts down his cutlery and looks more serious. 'So you don't know about Matt?'

'No. What is it?' I break into a smile, expecting an amusing drunken story.

'Montana got attacked on the dance floor by a group of Colombians. Luckily the bouncers kicked them out after a few punches were thrown. Later on Matt left the club alone to go and see Laura. He ran straight into them at Magdalen Bridge. Knowing he was one of us, they beat him till he fell to the floor and then kicked him while he lay there.'

'Christ, is he OK?'

'Luckily Scott found him and managed to get him out of there. He was pretty messed up, bleeding heavily from his face. An ambulance took him to A & E where he got patched up early this morning.'

'Is he badly injured?' I ask. My breakfast has arrived but remains untouched.

'I'm not sure.' Tuppen's expression is grave.

I slam my closed fist down on the table. I wish I'd been there to help my friend.

David:

Tuesday 11 February 07:05, Iffley Road gym, Oxford

The Blue Boat gathers quietly in the coaches' lair in the back room of the gym. An almost unrecognisable Matt stands with the coaches and Sam Parker. His nose is horribly swollen and bent; he looks like a defeated boxer. Yet more worrying is the fact that his right arm is in a sling and his hand is heavily taped. Tuppen didn't mention this – at this late stage an injury to his arm could rule him out of the race. Without Matt, our leader and strokeman, we surely don't stand a chance against the indomitable Cambridge.

Bas rushes in a couple of minutes late, closing the door behind us. Now we're all here, Matt stands up to speak.

'Guys, for those of you who don't know what happened on Sunday night, I got beaten up outside Clementines night club. That's in the past now, there's nothing I can do to change it.' His voice is full of disappointment, and steely resolve. 'In terms of my injuries, I've broken a bone in my hand. This will take me out of the boat for the next few weeks. So I guess this is it, we have ten guys here that will make up the Oxford Blue Boat. We have seven and a half weeks to turn this into the tightest, fastest, best-prepared eight that Oxford has ever seen. I will get better before the race, and I'll do everything I can to get back in the boat as soon as possible. In the meantime, Parker will come in as a replacement from Isis, and I'll do the work-outs on the bike.'

Looking at shaven-headed Sam standing next to Sean I can't help but be unnerved. He is still my competition, and this could give him another chance at making the boat.

Sean and Derek take their turns, saying a few words each, but despite the fighting talk the mood is depressed. As the others shuffle out for the morning ergo I wait a few moments for Matt in the corridor.

'Hey, I just want to say I'm sorry I wasn't there to get your back.'

'What's done is done,' Matt replies, tight-lipped. He wants to put the whole experience behind him.

'What did doc say about your nose?' I ask. He hasn't mentioned it. 'Is it broken?'

'No, doc says it isn't.'

'Good. Well, get better soon,' I say, feeling suddenly stuck for words. As I turn to leave for my morning rowing-machine session Matt says, 'We can still do this, Dave. We can still win.'

I'm beginning to have my doubts.

David:

Tuesday 11 February 23:27, Christ Church, Oxford

My fingers hover over the keyboard. I'm up late, desperately trying to wrap up this essay with some form of conclusion so I can get it in for this week's tutorial. It's already one day late. I scroll the mouse up and hit word count. It is 1,727 words long; surely that's near enough to 2,000 words? A new email message alert pops up in the corner of the computer screen. It's from Bill Fedyna, titled 'Serious, non rowing related'. I open the message.

Guys,

I'm not even sure why I'm emailing this message out. Being academically busy and with (as you all know) rowing getting more intense, I had a little lapse and started thinking about life.

A quick note: Just so all of you know, the main reason I applied to grad schools was because immediately after 11 Sept., I wondered what the point of things was and realised how life is too short and how I should do now the things I always wanted to do.

Attached is a link (bottom of email) to a PowerPoint show about the attack on the World Trade Center. There are many pictures and some commentary about the aftermath of the disaster. I bet I've never even made it halfway through the presentation. On one of the slides, there is a picture of World Trade Center 7 in ruins (there were 7 buildings in the WTC plaza – no. 7 was 47 storeys and also fell down with the Twin Towers). And in front of the ruins is a vendor's cart. His name was Hassa and he was the same guy I talked to every morning on my way to work. Every morning for nearly one and a half years I got off the subway, he'd see me, and he'd have my four cinnamon raisin bagels waiting for me. We'd have a quick morning chat and I'd be off. He was located on a small alleyway behind WTC 7 that few people walked on. I took the route because I could jog faster to work and not be seen doing it.

I guess I hadn't made it through the presentation up to this slide before. And seeing the cart, I know it is his. It is in the exact location where he would have been. And I must say, I did one heck of a double take when I saw this picture. For your info, the building I worked in is next to the ones being hosed down. I always wondered what happened to him and for the next year of work, I kept going to different vendor guys trying to find him. Seeing that cart again gave me a jolt and made me really think about why I am here right now.

It's not about whether I can model the photosynthetic growth of roses or the drilling of oil wells or the pricing of options better than the next guy, but rather it's about all of you, i.e. people & friends & loved ones: how you/they are the most important things and how we should cherish all the time we have here together.

Now I hope you're not reading this, thinking the old, crazy dude on the squad is trying to preach here. I was just so struck by that picture that it reminded me of a few things and I really wanted to share them with you.

There's so much more I want to say, yet I've already said way too much.

Maybe the most applicable thing right now is for all of us to treasure all of our time here (and our millions of hours rowing) and to bond greater as a team. After this past weekend, I think we all are more cognisant of what it means to be a part of a team (Smithy probably feels it more than most) and we can use this to push harder and achieve more.

I hope I didn't offend anyone, annoy anyone, waste anyone's time, or overstep my bounds. I just had to share these things that are jumping around in my head.

See ya all bright and early for a few 15-minute pieces.

Bill

I open the attachment. The cart sits in front of the ruins, just as he said. Bill's right; we should treasure our time as part of this team. Over the last six months these guys have become my family, a sense of brotherhood having grown among us. It's so strong that I now feel closer to my teammates than to James. I just hope I can make them proud when we race together for Oxford.

James:
Friday 14 February 18:34, St Chad's, Cambridge

'Happy Valentine's Day, babe,' I say to Sam as I pull the cake out of the cupboard. 'May I present, da da da daaa. The love cake.'

'Oh sweetie, that looks lovely.' She seems surprised and slightly concerned. The sponge cake glistens with white icing studded with strawberries, blueberries and raspberries. I find a knife and cut us both slices.

'Cream?' I ask.

'Yes, thanks.'

Sam takes up her fork, bites into it and makes encouraging 'mmmmm' noises. I watch her eat half of her slice with a smile before I bite into my generous portion and realise it's not properly cooked. The sponge hasn't risen properly. I'm deflated, like the cake. Thankfully, Sam is emphatic that it really is the thought that counts.

Her present to me, a remote control version of the Aston Martin from the latest James Bond, which I've gone on about ever since seeing the movie, is more of a success.

David:
Saturday 15 February 11:43, Christ Church, Oxford

I open my training diary and start scribbling. I want to record this.

Though Matt hasn't yet returned from injury, Sean has finally confirmed the Blue Boat. Acer, Matt, Henry, BT, Scott, Macca, Bas, John and I have made the crew with the caveat 'if we need to change the line-up we will'. I'm ecstatic to be in the Blue Boat for the 149th Oxford–

Cambridge Boat Race and to seal it I had a quiet celebratory pint with Henry at the college bar last night.

Slowly I'm overcoming my constant anxiety that I might be dropped and I'm focussing on the main challenge: beating Cambridge.

Not only am I rowing with a bunch of great rowers but great friends too. We have developed an amazing passion and intensity since the Fours Head. At the crew meeting Scott dubbed it 'Factor X'; it's our drive to excellence. It's not about size and strength. It's that intangible mental difference between winning and losing. It's about refusing to stop, when your body is screaming at you to give in. It's refusing to lose. Take Matt or Scott: they're not big but they have the mental and technical ability to win races against bigger, stronger guys when they shouldn't be able to. I want our crew to be remembered for our drive and passion, for our 'Factor X', but most importantly for winning on 6 April.

Boston showed that the tide has turned for us. We beat Cambridge and I beat James. My belief that we were improving has turned into something more concrete. We have objective proof that all our changes and the increased intensity since the Fours Head are working. The group's been training as if every day is our last.

Now we have to make sure we're ready for anything: bad wind and water conditions, unfair stream, blade clashing. I know that escaping the vicissitudes of the weather and water is impossible and this makes the Boat Race completely unpredictable, but we have to be good enough to win even on a bad day. We must leave no stone unturned in pursuit of victory. From washing the boat shell after outings, adding vortex edges to our blades so they grip the water a little better, buying bike lights and jumping fewer red lights in case of injury, to drinking the sickly Slim Fast shakes after training. Every last detail; everything for those inches.

Chapter 8
Fixtures and Fittings

James:
Sunday 16 February 11:30, Ely Boathouse

Robin stops the video player. We all sit in silence. He's just showed us clips of the greatest Cambridge crews of recent years. They are all Olympic final standard.

'These crews won, not because they were stronger, but because their superior technique allowed them to maximise the efficiency of their work. As you saw, Oxford sometimes led them for the first half of the race but in the third and fourth mile Cambridge's technique allowed them to move on and win. This year we probably have a slight physiological advantage over Oxford but as you saw in Boston they're absolutely determined and move boats fast.'

He hands round some sheets of paper. The title reads 'The Philosophy of our Technique'. Robin continues, 'Developing a superb high cruising speed is our first goal. We need the least deceleration possible between strokes. The boat has no brakes. It will only check and sink if we make it do so. You weigh 90 kilos on average and between you each has to carry a 20-kilo share of the boat and cox. We must use our mass to propel the hull forward during the drive, and slow it down as little as possible as you come forward for the next stroke.'

He takes us through the rest of his technical plan up to Boat Race day. Each week has a theme, each outing a goal. The aim is to be the best technical crew ever produced.

'In one week we race at the Head of the Trent. Oxford won't be there but there'll be some good university and club crews to test ourselves against. The key objective of the race is to perfect your cruising pace.'

David:

Thursday 20 February 13:03, Christ Church, Oxford

'Hey, great to meet you, Hazel.' I hold out my hand, into which hers disappears. 'My Dad and I love to watch *Ski Sunday*. Such a great programme. I can't believe the Herminator has come back from that awful motorbike accident.' In truth I hadn't watched an episode in some time but I'd read about Herman Maier's comeback Super-G victory in Kitzbuhel.

'Thank you, David, he's an amazing character.' Her light Scottish accent and friendly demeanour put me at ease.

'Right, I'll show you to my digs, then. Follow me.' Hazel Irvine, the BBC sports presenter and her dorky-looking camera crew shuffle along behind as we stroll across Christ Church's Peckwater Quad. 'Permission is all sorted by the way; I cleared with the college authorities.' She's here today to film a day in the life of a Boat Race rower and, no doubt, to ask me about how I feel about racing James. Since the Trial Eights the press and media have begun to take an interest in us. After all, it's the first time two brothers have raced one another in over a hundred years. I find it quite strange that people are interested in what is a personal story.

'David, how tall are you?'

'About six foot seven inches,' I reply. It isn't an unusual question for someone who's just met me; I'm towering over her. 'It helps when it comes to rowing as it gives me extra leverage in the boat. I don't know how James manages, being only six foot five!' She hadn't even mentioned James but already I'm benchmarking myself against him.

'Wahey, big man!' I spot Stu popping his head back inside his college room from his vantage point on the second floor. I give him a salute of acknowledgement. Lazy git's still wearing his dressing gown and it's lunchtime.

'Right in here.' I punch in the numbers into the security key pad and beckon them into my college staircase. I notice my nervousness. I'm keen to give the right impression on film and not give anything away to the Cambridge coaches, who will probably see the footage pre-race. 'It's right at the top.' I point up the staircase, holding the door open for the camera crew, who carry large bags and cameras.

'Typical student, I see,' says Hazel, noting the washing-up piled high in the sink outside my room. 'We need to get a shot of that, please.' The camera crew stop and start to set up.

'It's not usually like that,' I mutter unconvincingly, my cheeks reddening with embarrassment. Hazel gives me a wry look. 'Well, maybe some of the time.' Entering my 'set' we surprise my flatmate, who jumps to attention from reading on the sofa. 'This is my flatmate, Henry Hammerbeck. Hamm, these folk are from the BBC.'

'Hi,' he offers, bemused by the intrusion of a presenter and camera into his living room. I should have warned the poor guy. He stands there awkwardly for a few seconds before walking off into his room.

'Let's get a shot of this,' Hazel calls to the cameramen. They come over and set up the tripod. The enormous lens focusses in on our DVD collection. At the top of the pile is *True Blue*, the film of Dan Topolski's book on the Oxford Boat Race Mutiny of 1987. It is pretty sad that I have a rowing film as one of the few DVDs that I own, yet in my eyes it is a classic.

'This is my bedroom,' I say, pushing open the door. Lucky I tidied a bit before they arrived as Hazel, ever the journalist, is looking for juicy details to base a story around.

She reads my Mohammed Ali poster on the wall. Ali's in his boxing trunks, primed ready to throw a punch. 'The training is done behind all the lights, far away, before the fight', reads the text. Ali is one of my sporting heroes: he seemed to be the epitome of the professional athlete. That's pretty much the only decoration in the basic room, which is full of clothes, biology notes, a computer, a bookshelf full of sports biographies and some dumbbell weights furtively stacked in the corner.

'Let's get a shot of you working at your desk. We'll make it look like night time,' she says. 'Dan, can you block out the light please?' She addresses the cameraman's assistant. He delves into one of his attached bags and goes to work on the window with some black paper and tape. 'We can get the shot from here.' She stands in the corner of the room. 'Dave, if you sit at your desk and do some work,' she suggests.

'Ok, great,' I reply, opening my biology notes and reading them. Every few moments will help me in the exams later this year.

'Action,' calls the cameraman. The red light on the lens pops on, the boom sits out of sight just above my head. There's not much sound to get here. I flick through some notes on coral ecosystems. 'OK, we're done,' he says.

'How do you fit on that?' asks Hazel, pointing to the college standard-issue bed, which looks smaller than a standard single bed, probably to scare off the prospect of guests.

'With difficulty.' She's right, my feet hang off the end, my toes exposed.

'By the way,' I ask, trying hard to sound casual, 'when are you going up to see James?'

'We'll be in Cambridge next Thursday. We're seeing Tim and James then,' she replies.

Hazel will know more about how my brother is getting on than I do. Things between James and I haven't been normal since Christmas Day. The last time I exchanged contact with him was on the water at the GB trials in Boston, where a nod at the start had been enough to acknowledge each other's presence. The closer we're getting to race day, the less we actually feel like brothers.

James:
Sunday 23 February 14:02, Head of the Trent, Nottingham

Jim waves his arms wildly and screams at the Oxford Brookes crew in front. 'Move right, you idiot. Move! No, the other way!'

'Come and have a go, then, Cambridge!' one of the Oxford Brookes crew yells back at us. We're firing along the River Trent, passing Nottingham Forest Football Ground, with the Brookes crew swerving in front of us, blocking our path. The call is a red rag to a bull. We've been here before, with Stanford blocking our path at the Head of the Charles last October, losing us the scalps of Harvard and Wisconsin. This time it's not going to slow us down.

Jim shouts, 'You heard him, boys, let's go through them in fifteen strokes. Ready, boys, go!' Wooge takes us up a gear and we charge. We're almost on top of them before their cox pulls away hard then realises he's over-compensated, and cuts back again, causing our blades to clash, carbon fibre striking carbon fibre. There are curt exchanges of colourful language and challenges from both crews before TJ silences them by knocking the Brookes five man's oar clean out of his hand, splaying him backwards. While his oar drags parallel to the boat, spraying water, a useless brake, we pass speedily. As our stern passes their bow Jim cuts in front of them, washing them down. They get a taste of their own medicine as we row away and shoot under a large green industrial bridge, which means we're into the last mile of the race.

'OK, boys, take it home, up two. Go!' Jim demands. Robin had instructed us that we were not to break 34 strokes a minute until this point, so the newly formed crew could develop a strong base rhythm and the high cruising speed that we need. Now we are off the leash but after the excitement of the crash it is hard to raise the tempo.

After the final bend we cross the line, frustrated, and pull to a stop.

'Cambridge, you can't stop there, move on!' a grumpy umpire rants through his megaphone. Groves replies with some choice phrases before we shout him down and row on to avoid disqualification.

An hour later, the boat slotted back on to the trailer, Robin debriefs us under a cloudy sky. We won, which is a relief; anything but a victory would have been catastrophic. Happily we also set a new course record and were 30 seconds ahead of our nearest rival. Goldie were 53 seconds back, which is pretty concerning for them but we've done what we set out to do.

The mood brightens further as KC hands round T-shirts sent specially from Oz. They read, 'Cambridge loves Hard Yakka'. We'd seen him wearing a few 'Hard Yakka' tops earlier in the season and thought the brand was entertainingly Australian. We put them on and pose for a photo to be sent back with a thank you. On closer scrutiny of the digital camera shot in the bus home Hugo spots that Wayne is surreptitiously standing on tiptoe in our line-up so as not to look too short. And so the abuse begins.

David:

Friday 28 February 20:02, Putney

I follow Maria into the packed gastro pub. It's the first time we've been able to get together for a Valentine's dinner. She's muted today, lacking her usual infectious enthusiasm. She doesn't seem happy to see me.

I order drinks at the bar, a white wine for her and my usual diet coke, before taking a seat opposite her. Outside, rain begins to pour down. Headlights of passing traffic illuminate the falling drops. For once I'm not getting wet. The mid-thirties couple on the table next to us lean in to kiss.

After a bit of small talk she comes out with what's on her mind. 'Dave, I'm just not sure whether this relationship is going to work out,' she says. 'I've barely seen you since I started at university. You haven't been down to Bristol yet. Not once! I come up to Oxford the whole time.' Her voice rises in exasperation. My heart sinks. What the hell have I done? I've never seen her as upset before.

'Maria,' I start, but she cuts in.

'You never want to come up to see me, even when you're not bloody rowing. You get time off on Mondays and you don't make any effort to come and see me.' She pauses. 'Do you even like me?' she says finally. Tears begin to roll down her cheeks. The couple next to us look over awkwardly.

I lean across the table and take her hands in mine. 'Maria, I'm so sorry. Of course I like you, in fact I love spending time with you. I think you're just great.' She begins to look a little cheered. 'I've been totally crap, an idiot of a boyfriend.' She manages a small giggle through her tears. 'I've been caught up in my rowing bubble, desperate to row for Oxford and win the Boat Race.'

'Is it all worth it?' she questions. 'You might not win.'

'I've got to do it, Maria. I need to try. To prove something to myself.' I don't mention how much I am motivated by the prospect of beating James. 'I really want us to be together but please give me time. In two months this race is over. If you give me another chance I promise that I won't let you down again.' I squeeze her hands in mine.

It takes a few moments for her to decide. 'Bloody rowing,' she says, a rueful smile returning to her face. I lean across the table to kiss her. 'I didn't understand quite how much it meant to you.'

'Everything,' I reply softly.

I sit silently looking at Maria, at a loss to know how to proceed. Seeing her upset has made me realise I have completely fallen for her. How could I have let her down quite so badly? I don't want to sacrifice her for a race, my girlfriend whom I love, but I'm committed to see it through.

Am I completely defined by my rowing?

My real life is on hold until I finish this race, but my biggest fear is that I'll have nothing to come back to.

David:

Rivulets of sweat drip off Matt's forehead, his hunched body pedals hard on the stationary bike. I've finished my two 15-minute pieces on the ergo but he's stayed on the bike for a bit longer. This afternoon Matt's rowing with us today for the first time since his injury. He's been given the go-ahead by the consultant. I'm so glad he's back. Matt is such a natural strokeman. He rows with the flow of the boat, as opposed to forcing it. He infuses his crews with metronomic perseverance, and an ability to push themselves harder than they thought possible.

When Matt saw the consultant last week it turned out that his nose was broken in the attack and would need to be reset by rebreaking it back into place. It was a simple enough procedure, said the doctor; he could even do it on the spot. But the general anaesthetic would take him out of training for ten days, the doctor told him.

'Do it without an anaesthetic then,' Matt replied. 'I don't want to miss any more training.'

'Are you sure?' the consultant replied, throwing a quizzical look at his medical students sitting in the corner of the bay. 'Matt, this is going to hurt, particularly now it's partially set in the wrong position.'

'Yes, I'm sure,' he insisted.

'Fine. It's your call.' The doctor left to fetch a towel which he put against Matt's nose. He beckoned to one of the students to hold Matt's head. 'Are you ready?'

'Yes,' said Matt. The doctor placed his open palm against Matt's nose and then withdrew it a few inches.

'Crack!' went Matt's nose. Matt almost passed out with the pain but it was done. Afterwards he joined us for a crew lunch with his still-bleeding nose.

When I look at it today, it already looks straighter despite the swelling, and I'm sure it will be back to normal soon. I'm more worried about his hand; I hope he can row with the injury. We've just over four weeks till the race.

James:

Wednesday 5 March 06:55, Goldie Boathouse, Cambridge

'One hundred. Halfway there. That's it, Matze. Down Chiswick Eyot, pushing Oxford away,' I encourage my red-faced friend, who sits trapped in our leg press machine, forcing the huge metal discs up to straighten his legs before lowering them for another repetition. Sweat rains down his face. There's 120 kilos sitting piled on the contraption, which looks like a torture implement from the Spanish Inquisition: a pile of metal on 45-degree angled runners looking as if it could slide down to crush a man.

'One hundred and fifty done. Fifty to go. Barnes Bridge and home,' I offer as enthusiastically as possible. His eyes are now clamped shut as he passes through pain barrier after pain barrier. Still he keeps going. Now there are only four weeks to the big day we are doing our last few weightlifting sessions, a special regime that Robin has devised. I'm sure these ultra-high repetition weights sessions are physiologically good for us but probably more important is the psychological benefit. Watching each of us going through the fire unbroken, supported by the rest of the crew, is a powerful bonding experience. Agonised groans and explosions of breath all around are met with encouraging words. Whether the accent is Canadian, Australian, American, German or English, we are one.

David:

Saturday 8 March 15:50, Dorney Lake, Eton

'Hold,' calls Acer. His shout filters deep into my brain and tells me to push harder on the foot plate.

'HOLD . . .' he repeats louder.

'HOLD, GO!' he bellows. We're sprinting for the finishing line. Our stroke rate comes up and up.

'YEAH, let's go,' comes from one of the others behind me. Now we're really flying, we're taking as many strokes as we can. I spin my hands and try to keep up with Henry and Matt in front of me.

'Red buoys,' calls Acer, 'last 100 metres!' The lactate surges through my body. Last few, keep up with Henry.

'Down,' Acer calls, as we cross Dorney Lake's finishing line. I stop rowing, and slump back, holding on to the sides of the boat. My heart is racing and my body searches for oxygen with rapid short breaths.

'Keep moving, guys,' I move my legs slowly up and down without taking any strokes; I know it'll help purge the lactic acid more quickly than if I sit still. Slowly but surely my breathing returns to a more normal rate. I can still feel my heart thumping in my chest.

'That one was 1 minute 16 spot 8.' Sean tells us the 500-metre time from the bank. 'Not bad, just one left. Stick to 36 on the rate with the same push at 250 metres. Go for home from there.' Sean sounds encouraged by our speeds so far today. We're clocking marginally faster times than most of the recent Blue Boats. I doubt Cambridge can go this fast. It's also great to have Matt back in the boat. He's wearing a protective hand guard.

Our fifth 500-metre sprint of the day completed, we've only got one left. Today's session at Dorney Lake is a crucial part of our preparation. It hurts like hell as we punish our bodies with six 500-metre sprints with short rests between pieces. We're working on a new call, another BT suggestion inspired by the film *Braveheart*: the 'Hold' call. In the face of an oncoming charge William Wallace shouts to his men to hold their nerve before they attack. For us, Acer will use it to call us to steel ourselves for the final push for home. Just when we feel we can't give any more, we'll do it for each other. It also has echoes of Rudyard Kipling's *If*, which seems so appropriate.

If you can force your heart and nerve and sinew
To serve your turn long after they are gone,
And so hold on when there is nothing in you
Except the Will which says to them: 'Hold on!'

'One minute 30 of rest left, guys, let's spin the boat round,' Acer says. 'Strokeside row on, bowside back down. OK now, bow four row on.' As we row across the end of the course, I can see Isis are at the other end of the lake, readying themselves for their piece.

With the boat turned and facing the opposite direction, Acer gets us a few strokes from the finishing line. We'll be doing this last one up the course. Despite general weariness in my muscles, I notice that my breathing rate has calmed. My fitness is much improved and finally my body seems to be dealing properly with the physicality of the sport.

'Listen up, boys.' BT grabs our attention. He sits behind me in the five seat. A talisman of Oxford toughness, he usually leads the pre-race psyche-up. 'This is the last piece, we're rowing into the headwind. Let's go for this one. Let's put a time on the board that we are proud of. People think we're going to get destroyed by Cambridge. Let's fucking show 'em.'

His inspirational words sharpen us up. I need to get used to going full tilt stroke after stroke, even when I'm tired. We have to practise the hurt. When our bodies are yelling at us to stop, we must stay calm, focus and react. When I'm most tired, I have to keep my technique. This is where we forge our 'Factor X'.

James:

Monday 10 March 11:05, Putney

The front room of Winchester House on the Putney embankment is bursting with press, cameras, my Dad and oarsmen. Barry Davies steps up to the BBC Sport-emblazoned podium and calmly kicks off the proceedings. Either side of the podium sit the two crews, eyeballing each other. I haven't been able to catch Dave's eye.

'Welcome to Winchester House,' starts Davies, totally relaxed in front of the microphone. 'We are here for the traditional Boat Race challenge which dates back to 1829. The 149th race is just 27 days away. Oxford won last year, their 70th victory, closing the gap on Cambridge, who've won 77 times. After last year's epic I suppose the question is how do the two crews follow that? That's the beauty of the Boat Race. Each year has its own character and characters and takes its place in the history of individual and collective endeavour. Victory is the only reward and defeat becomes the driving force to turn the tide the following year. It is, ladies and gentlemen, a great sporting event.' Barry should know, he's been to a few. He goes on to introduce the two crews, noting I am the only survivor of last year, returning now to find my brother in the opposite crew.

'The two crews have been preparing for seven months under the leadership of the head coaches. Those two gentlemen are normally happy to remain in the background, but I believe they deserve your applause and I would now like to invite them on to the stage. Sean Bowden of Oxford and Robin Williams of Cambridge.' Light clapping breaks out and the two men take to the stage, standing uneasily either side of the trophy. They don't shake hands and there are no words of greeting. Both are of similar height and slim build, both with short dark hair, although Sean's has retreated backwards some distance.

'If you don't mind, can we start by looking back at last year,' Barry continues. 'We were all absolutely glued to what was happening on the river but it did go through my mind – what does it feel like for the coaches who sit there without any control on the proceedings? The winning coach first, Sean?'

'Just another day in the office really, piece of cake. Just sit there and it works out exactly as you planned,' Sean smiles. There are ripples of polite laughter. Smug bastard. Anger flushes through me and, I'm sure, through all the Cambridge guys in the room.

'Didn't work out exactly as you planned though, Robin,' says Barry, holding the mike up to Robin, who retains his admirably impassive expression.

'No, it was nearly as we planned. It was an emotional rollercoaster.' He mentions our issues at the start and that we were leading for 15 minutes of the race before our poor finish. The two of them subtly snipe at one another in their further comments before departing the stage to applause.

Barry then invites the presidents on to the stage. Tim and Matt face each other, looking over the trophy, Wooge almost a head taller than his opposite man. 'Tim, can I invite you to make the traditional challenge?'

'On behalf of Cambridge University Boat Club I challenge the Oxford University Boat Club to select nine good men and true to race for the Aberdeen Asset Trophy in the 159th Boat Race on 6th April from Putney to Mortlake. Do you accept my challenge?'

I hear Hugo whisper to Matze, 'I thought it was the 149th? We should be all right then, that gives us ten years to practise!'

On stage, Matt steps forward. 'On behalf of Oxford University Boat Club I accept your challenge.' The presidents shake hands in front of the trophy, Matt dropping his gaze to the photographers to his right while Tim stares at Matt. They shake hands for an awkwardly long time while photographers snap away before Barry concludes proceedings.

'Thank you all for coming. All that remains is to wish both crews an equal measure of fortune. The photo call will take place in the front garden down below.' We stand to head out but the press officer collars Dave and me and we are led to the trophy for more photographs.

'This way, chaps,' one snapper says.

'Over here, mate,' says another.

After a few more flashes, 'Could you stand behind the trophy now, guys?' More flash guns go off.

'OK, stare at each other now.' We lock glares. I almost start giggling but Dave's eyes don't flinch. There's a blankness, and something else behind them, maybe anger. He's shut me out.

'Right, now, pose right over it.' The snappers have a herd mentality; each time one tries a new angle they all have to copy, and clamber over one another to get a more centred shot.

'OK, now get in close to the trophy lid and stare at it.' Our reflections shine back, heavily distorted in the polished silver.

'Right, now lift it together.'

'OK, now snarl at one another.' What was fun is rapidly getting boring.

'Now pretend to wrestle with it.'

'Enough?' I ask Dave. 'Enough.' He agrees and we deposit the trophy back on its plinth to groans from the photographers.

Later, after group photos outside, we are interviewed by a TV crew who asks us to don Blues Brothers dark glasses and hats and stand back to back while the camera rotates around us. 'It'll look great for our link,' the journalist says.

Together we reply flatly, 'No.'

This isn't some damn light-hearted sideshow to us.

David:

Tuesday 11 March 15:58, Putney

There are lots of photos of James and me in today's papers. More interesting to me, though, is reading about the Etherington-Smiths, the first, and only other, set of brothers to row against one another in the 174-year history of the Boat Race. They raced each other on 31 March 1900. The younger Etherington-Smith, Tom, rowed for

Oxford, whilst his brother Raymond represented Cambridge. Cambridge and Raymond won the race by a record 20 lengths before he went on to win an Olympic gold medal in the eight in the 1908 Olympics in Rome.

More than a century later another set of brothers is due to race again, James and I. Instead of heavy wooden clinker-built boats with fixed seats, we're racing in lightweight carbon fibre racing shells with sliding seats which allow us to engage the powerful leg muscles. Back then, a good walk in a heavy coat, followed by steak and a glass of port, was considered to be a good training session. I doubt Sean would view it the same way now. The weights and heights of rowers have increased significantly since those days: the average weight of a Boat Race crew member between 1829 and 1836 was 11 stone 6 pounds. By 1929 the average weight had swelled to 12 stone 8 pounds and more recent crews are much larger still. The Cambridge and Oxford crews of last year were both over 14 stone on average, although I doubt our crew this year will tip the scales at much more than 13 stone. Theoretically this extra weight means extra muscle, and therefore power, to move the boat, but if not used effectively it's just dead weight. What is most surprising, though, is not the differences between 1900 and now, but the similarities. The Boat Race spirit is still one of amateur competition, sacrifice, hard work and determination to win.

The Boat Race had an interesting history long before the Etherington-Smith brothers arrived. It was inaugurated in 1829 with a challenge by Charles Wordsworth from Christ Church, Oxford, to his Harrow schoolfriend Charles Merivale at St John's College, Cambridge, to a race at Henley. It is reported that 20,000 people turned up to watch which, given there were no cars or buses back then, marks it as something of an occasion from the very beginning. Not long into the race there was a foul and the crews were ordered back to the start line to re-row. It's good to know that even then they would do anything to win. The clashing of oars, fighting for the best water, has been a feature of the race ever since.

The story has it that in those early days Oxford wore dark blue striped jerseys, whereas Cambridge wore pink, honouring their captain Snow's Lady Margaret Boat Club colours. Just before the 1836 Boat Race, someone pointed out that Cambridge had no colours on their bows, so a boy ran to a nearby shop and bought a piece of Eton blue ribbon. His choice of ribbon established the light blue of Cambridge.

Despite the great successes of the early races it was a number of years before the race became an annual feature of the British sporting calendar. In 1831 Cambridge challenged Oxford to a race, but owing to a raging cholera epidemic in London the race was cancelled. In 1836 the race moved to the Tideway in London and was held between Westminster and Putney; downriver from the current course.

The long and incident-packed history of the race gives you a sense that you are part of something special. I guess in some ways it'll mean that my name will be immortalised long after I stop rowing, even after I'm dead. I just hope that we're good enough for it to read as an Oxford victory.

James:

Wednesday 12 March 08:46, Caius College, Cambridge

Matze, Dan Barry, Breck, Ben Smith and I are tucking into breakfast with gusto. The warmth, comfort and elaborate surroundings are a pleasant antidote to the pain and sensory deprivation of the erg this morning. After extensive, selfless experimentation, the general consensus amongst the CUBC is that Caius offers the best college breakfast in Cambridge. Behind us the panelled walls of Caius dining hall glow as the morning sun radiates through the stained glass windows, illuminating the rafters of the oak hammer beam roof . The window directly above us commemorates Crick's discovery of the DNA double helix.

The ever chirpy Dan Barry is glued to *The Times* sports section, having demolished his scrambled eggs, toast, yogurt, fruit and bacon. ' "No older brother wants to lose to a younger brother and every younger brother wants to put one over an older brother," ' he reads aloud. ' "We're brothers and we both want to win but afterwards we remain brothers and friends. Blood is thicker than Thames water." Wow! Do you think you mentioned the brother thing enough, Bungle?'

'Er, I may have overplayed it a bit,' I reply. 'Let's have a butcher's.' He passes it over. The discussion turns to a dietician one of the boys met. The triallist had been feeling consistently exhausted, beyond the norm, and thought he'd look into his diet. After reviewing our man's food diary and training schedule the dietician asked whether he drank alcoholic beverages to which he admitted that he did, on occasion. The dietician was shocked and cautioned against the terrors of alcohol. Then he recommended that a better way to relax would be to use cocaine!

'Not your average dietary advice,' Matze laughs.

Looking down at *The Times* sports section there's a photo of Dave and me in 'glaring at each other' mode. I'm childishly excited to see it there. Beneath is the article. A quote from David follows the quote from me that Dan read out.

'Since I can remember I have always wanted to beat him.' I catch my breath, feeling a sudden sense of betrayal. Of course I know he wanted to win the race but I didn't think it was personal, about me rather than just Cambridge. I've got a healthy loathing for Oxford and want to win more than anything else. That means Dave has to lose. But it's an outcome, not a goal.

I reread it. 'Since I can remember I have always wanted to beat him.' Is that really how he feels? Why has he never told me this? Why tell some strange journalist he's never met before?

Right, little brother, the gloves are off.

Chapter 9
The Time Approaches

David:

Friday 21 March 05:47, Wittenham Clumps, Oxfordshire

We turn off the road down a muddy track following the 'Nature Reserve' sign. The early morning fog begins to rise as the new light of the morning tries to burn through. A few hundred metres ahead I can make out the outline of two prominent dark green hills in otherwise flat countryside. I stifle a yawn; it's even earlier than normal; dawn has just broken.

The minibus engine cuts to a halt at the foot of the hill.

'Let's go, boys,' says BT, waking Bas and Henry, who are dozing in the back. We've arrived at Wittenham Clumps, a small hilly enclave deep in the Oxfordshire countryside. I pick up my silver-painted wooden sword and shield and follow Scott out of the back of the bus. He clutches another wooden sword and a round shield. We leave the back door open. Bas pulls out an oar. A dark blue flag is tied on one end. It represents our standard. While we should have been working or seeing girlfriends we spent yesterday afternoon in Bas's garden, making wooden weapons for this morning. Today we're moving down to London, where we'll spend our last two weeks of training before the race. As a result of watching *Braveheart* and *Gladiator* a few too many times, BT decided we should survey our homeland and march on London at dawn.

Scott and I trudge up the hill together. BT overtakes us intently. His sword and outfit are by far the best. He went home especially to construct his broadsword, which is even adorned with a red rope handle. His shoulders are covered with a red tartan rug.

'It's lucky there's no one else around,' I say to Scott. As we look at one another we begin laughing at the ridiculousness of it all. Behind his

prickly, competitive persona lies an incredibly friendly and loyal character. He's become a true friend.

At the top of the hills we stop by a clump of ancient beech trees and
survey the panoramic views. To the west the cooling towers of Didcot
Power Station dominate the skyline, belching out fumes into the
unsuspecting Oxfordshire countryside. In the distance to the north-east
Little Wittenham Woods border the meandering Thames. Less than 100
kilometres away, the same water will be flowing through locks, down
the race course through Chiswick Bridge and off towards Putney.

'Boys, gather round over here,' says BT. He reaches into his pocket
and brings out a piece of paper defaced with various scribbles.

'Today we leave behind our county and march to battle. Be brave and
fight with pride. Feel the bond with those around you because when the
time comes you will believe and trust in them. Two weeks from now,
we will return victorious.'

It's a jovial, ridiculous moment and we're half laughing but at the
same time it is deeply poignant. Oxfordshire is sprawled out in front of
us. We'll return either as winners or losers.

'So let's raise our standard and march on London!' And with that BT
folds the paper and places it in his pocket, raises his wooden broadsword
and starts running down the grassy hill towards London. We follow,
shouting war cries as we go. We can't see our enemy yet but we'll meet
them on the start line in two weeks' time.

James:

Friday 21 March 19:42, Strawberry Hill, Twickenham

Across the kitchen, at the other table, I hear their laughter and then John
Adams's voice, 'And Basil was there standing on the trailer, with battle-
axe in hand when. . .'

At our table Hugo continues, 'I don't know why we don't get *Private
Eye* in the US. It's brilliant . . .' and he breaks into laughter again at the
cover of this fortnight's issue. Hugo's year in Cambridge has really
allowed him to indulge his love of British humour. I just wish that I'd
heard what Bas was doing with a battle-axe.

Outside the kitchen, in the rest of the house, the two teams dominate
different territory. Cambridge read and joke in the front room while

Oxford monopolise the TV in the living room. We're polite to one another but there is an overwhelming tension. An 'accidental' trip on the stairs or the sly addition of a laxative to a water bottle would have a big impact in a couple of weeks' time.

This weekend is critical to final race preparation for both camps. Straight afterwards, Cambridge head up to Nottingham to train on the lake there for a week before returning to Putney and the Boat Race. Tomorrow, Oxford race Leander, in effect the British national team in pink, and we race the Croatian national eight. Who's got the quality to mix with the best in the world?

The Croats were finalists at the World Championships last year, having taken bronze in Sydney. Out training on the Thames today, their boat was rock steady, as though it was on rails. Professionals. They have a kind of visceral energy about them, and their bass- and consonant-heavy Slavic discussions add to their aura. Only a few years ago there was no Croatia, just Yugoslavia. They've fought for independence and now the pride of wearing Croatian red and white drives them far beyond what the national flag might do for older, luckier countries. They've bled for the right to wear their colours.

In training they rowed down from Putney to Westminster, where none of the local clubs go because it's too rough. It didn't bother them; they just liked passing the Houses of Parliament. National symbols mean a lot to them.

They'd caused a stir on the day they arrived by drinking most of the beer stockpiled at the Crabtree Boathouse for a party happening tomorrow. 'We didn't know whether the water was safe to drink,' shrugged one of them in decent English, looking bemused. To dispel some of their magic the Goldie guys have been cracking a constant flow of jokes about the Croats' hard-line nature, like Ali's minders before a fight, cajoling the opposition, and building their fighter up. 'I heard some of them have kids just to provide an alternative to turkey at Christmas,' was about the least risqué.

For our first official races as the Blue Boat and Goldie, the coaching team handed us new racing kit. Robin said, 'Wear it with pride, like it's your battle armour. Your oar is your weapon, your blade. These are your colours. Make those that wear them in the years after you honoured to do so.'

David:

Saturday 22 March 17:07, Putney

'OK, boys,' BT starts the pre-race crew chat as we come to a halt under an arch of Wandsworth Bridge, so he can use the echo and intimacy to talk to us.

'Listen up.' He pauses for a few seconds before carrying on, 'These guys think this will be a walk in the park. They expect to crush us. Everyone's saying we haven't got a hope of beating them. They've got World and Olympic Champions. I say fuck that. We can beat Leander. We're fit and strong and fast; they won't be able to stay with us. We've put down some damn fast times over the last few weeks. We know our race plan, let's stick to it.'

'Let's not respect these guys too much,' Acer follows on. He's right. While they are the strongest club in the country at the moment, we can't afford to respect them too much. Our crew may be smaller than them physically but you can bet we want to win this race more. They are the top crew in the Leander club; for them this race means nothing. For us this is crucial preparation. It's our last full-out practice race before the big one in two weeks. Sean has run through the race plan. We're going to test out a push at 1 minute 45 when crews are fading off from the sprint start. Now the psychology and strategy talk is done and it is crunch time.

I lean forward and tap Henry on the shoulder. He silently reaches his hand back, which I touch to bond our efforts in this race.

On the other side of the bridge the pink-clad backs of the Leander crew draw up next to us. I can see Matt Pinsent's familiar hulking shape in the four seat. An Oxford Blue with three Olympic gold medals and an unbeaten run at the World Championships, phenomenal strength and aerobic power. He'll be hard to beat. I also see James Cracknell, his partner in crime, a supremely competitive oarsman in the seven seat, as well as a host of other current national team oarsmen. I doubt they feel the same nervousness about racing me, a nineteen-year-old with only a Junior World's bronze to my name.

Judging from Henry's expression he is thinking something similar.

'Don't even look at them,' I bluster, 'we can beat these guys.' I know who I'm really trying to convince.

The umpire's launch drives up behind us, along with Sean and some Leander coaches. Following them is a boat with press and some friends and family. I see Maria, wrapped up warm, standing next to my Dad, who is pointing his familiar video camera at us. I also recognise the plump, northern Leander coach, Mark Banks.

'Bow four row on through the bridge,' shouts Sean.

We head under the arches of Putney Bridge and stop near the Boat Race start.

'OK, that's fine. Both crews, hold it up.'

Our umpire for this year's Boat Race, Boris Rankov, stands up in his launch, his frizzy grey hair giving him the air of a mad professor.

'Get ready, please,' he calls.

'OK boys, let's go for this,' Acer says. 'Come forward.' I move up the slide into my start ready position, legs half flexed, back upright. I touch my index finger and thumb together. During our visualisation sessions I'd taught myself to associate this movement with thinking about all my best races. Now it instantly relaxes me and brings me confidence.

'Attention . . . GO!' Rankov screams, the oncoming headwind straining his voice.

After the first few strokes I can sense the pink backs to my right slipping back slightly. Yes, we're moving faster than them! It's a clean start, one of our best yet and we're rowing really well in time.

'Yeah, 47, that's good!' shouts Acer. The rate is very high, even by our standards but it seems to be working.

'Length. Go!' Acer calls, signifying the end of the first start phase and bringing down our furious rate of striking. A gust of wind seems to slow us slightly; Leander have stabilised their position, a third of a length down. I'm about level with Pinsent.

As we move into the next series of strokes, the moored boats along the Putney embankment seem to fly by. The rhythm feels really good, I keep trying to concentrate on a few simple clear thoughts despite the intensity of my movement and the noise of the boats and launches around me.

'Rhythm, go!' Acer calls as planned 1 minute and 15 seconds in. The rate of striking comes down slightly and we enter our race rhythm.

'Coming up to our bend, boys,' shouts Acer encouragingly, 'we've got the inside and we can break clear!'

'One minute 45, ready, go. Let's go!' he screams. We lift ourselves from this already painful rhythm into a new one, and it seems to work.

We move away to a three quarters of a boat length lead. Victory is in our sights.

'Break clear now,' yells Acer. We can beat these guys, we can actually beat them!

All of a sudden Leander veer towards us, Christian Cormack, their cox, making a last-ditch attempt to contain us. Our blades are over-lapping before I know it. My oar gets caught, entangled with Josh West's oar, and gets knocked from my grip, catching the water at an awkward angle. It digs in and shoots back towards me. The oar handle cracks into my chest, then head, and I get forced back and speared on BT's oar handle behind. After a second I recover the oar from the 'crab', but Leander have sensed a chance to attack and are moving through us. We try to pick our speed up again, but now we're half a length down and going slower than them. To get our boat back up to speed now will be near-impossible.

Any hope of getting back on level terms fades in the next minute as they break clear of our boat. I can't believe what's happened. I've destroyed our chances of winning.

David:

Saturday 22 March 17:43, Westminster School Boathouse, Putney

We lower the boat on to the slings in the dark boathouse bay. Deep in thought, I run my hand along my rigger, the dented metal backstay showing the force of impact of my stray oar. I am devastated. I am responsible for our defeat. It was all my fault. I let everyone else down and I embarrassed myself in front of my parents and Maria, who'd looked on in the following launch. My eyes well up; my pride has been punctured.

'It wasn't your fault, Dave,' says Bas, patting me on the back. He can see savage disappointment written on my face. As I lean over my rigger, my tears fall straight to the ground. If this is what it felt like to lose a fixture, losing the Boat Race would be unbearable. Scott comes over and gives me a silent hug.

Sean strides into the bay, followed by Derek, who closes the bay doors behind him, shutting out the press standing outside.

'Gather round,' says Sean. I walk up to join the others in the semicircle.

'OK, we can talk more later, but my immediate thoughts are that we had a good race. We pushed them off the start, gave them a scare. We were rowing well. Obviously we had some problems in the clash, and we lost a bit of our rhythm after that, but they were a class act. There are things we can do better but I think it's another step forward towards the race.' Sean's relatively positive summary of the fixture starts to lift my spirits.

Derek cuts in as Sean finishes. 'How do you guys think it went?'

'Yeah, we got off to a good start,' says Matt, 'and rowed well up to the Fulham bend. After the clash we lost a bit of belief and didn't row so well. We could have responded better after the crab. We can never think we've lost it, even if we're down. We have to learn from this. They taught us a lesson in clashing, but we won't make those mistakes again and we'll be better in two weeks' time because of it.'

'OK, get upstairs and get warm,' says Sean.

The rest of them clomp upstairs, their wellington boots thudding up the Westminster School Boathouse metal steps.

I stay behind. 'I'm sorry,' I say to Sean. 'I lost it for us.'

'Don't worry, Dave. Let's get your rigger checked over,' says Sean. His calm and relatively kind response surprises me. This is a side of his character I've never seen before.

Back upstairs I sit in silence for a few minutes before tearing open my pack of hot cross buns. I stuff a whole one into my mouth and stand under the showers, replaying the 'crab' incident over and over again in my mind.

James:

Saturday 22 March 18:37, Strawberry Hill, Twickenham

The front room of our family home is filled with an antique quarter-size pool table, a worn leather sofa, BBC sports correspondent Hazel Irvine, a cameraman with shoulder-mounted camera, a sound man with boom and fluffy mike, a second cameraman with hand-held camera, a lighting specialist with his lights and reflectors, David, me and Dad, videoing the scene.

'Just act natural, guys,' the first cameraman says, as I almost blind the sound guy with the wrong end of my pool cue. 'Just play a few shots and I'll check the levels,' the lighting techie requests, waving hand-held light meters. We each take a few pool shots. Not one ball goes anywhere near a pocket.

'Who normally wins these games?' Hazel asks politely. She's very disarming in a slightly mumsy way; I can see why she interviews people professionally.

'I don't know; we're both pretty bad,' says Dave, getting the awkward truth out. 'I think we'd each back ourselves.' I nod.

'The slope of the table is obviously the main limiting factor to us sinking pots; it's a nice antique feature,' I say. Hazel nods graciously. One of the cameramen raises his eyebrows incredulously.

Dave is putting on a brave face. CUBC watched the start of Oxford's fight with Leander, invisibly assessing them from the first-floor windows of our boathouse. Our spies reported what happened later down the course. I know Dave will be seething with white-hot self-loathing after letting down his boys. I'm relieved Oxford were beaten but, despite my allegiance, I feel sorry for Dave. Big Josh West, who was rowing in the Leander eight, came to the Cambridge camp afterwards to brief us on Oxford's performance and asked me to apologise to my little brother for him – it was his oar that knocked Dave's from his hand. 'I was aiming for Matt Smith's,' he explained, half-joking; he'd raced against Matt three times.

Our CUBC rowing sessions today were worryingly mixed. The first was sloppy, heavy and disappointing, which prompted a heated discussion afterwards. One of the hot topics was Matze's regular technical calls from the two seat, with some claiming there were just too many contrasting voices in the boat and we shouldn't be so negative. Thankfully, after our little shouting match, the second session – some long, low-tempo pieces with the Croatians – went really, really well. The boat had taken on a life of its own. The crew remained silent but we were able to speak volumes to each other without words and the rowing was smooth, powerful and flowing. It was hypnotic.

Afterwards Groves noted that we respond to pressure every time, which was unusually positive and absolutely right. It would make life much less stressful if we were just great every time, but it seems that's not in our nature.

The main cameraman gives a thumbs-up to Hazel, 'OK; rolling.'

'Have you raced one another before? Who normally wins?' Hazel asks, in her slightly more formal on-camera voice.

'Well, given recent results at the Great Britain trials, I would say that I do,' Dave responds quickly.

'You had the edge in the last round but this is the big one,' I counter.

'When did it to begin to dawn on you that you would be racing one another?'

'I guess around Christmas we knew there was a good chance, but it wasn't confirmed until February or so.'

At last Dave pots a ball, which is a relief for all of us.

'Peter Ebdon watch out!' Hazel deadpans.

'Is the tension level beginning to ratchet up between the two of you?'

Dave responds guardedly, 'This is my first Blue. I've done big races before but this is much more important and I'm going to be nervous.'

Later that evening Mum serves up supper to the OUBC and CUBC, who are once again staked out on separate tables in the kitchen, the Berlin Wall of the breakfast bar keeping the warring factions apart. She sees Dave is still looking crestfallen about his 'crab'.

'You did your best, Dave,' she says, smiling.

Dave shoots her back a black look which says: 'Mum, not only are you embarrassing me in front of my friends but worse, my opposition. Do not expose my weaknesses!'

James:
Sunday 23 March 11:07, Putney

We're away like a machine, pounding out strokes like a heavyweight champion at the punch bag. Each blow knocks the Croatians a foot further down, but they do not fold. We get out to a lead of half a boat length quickly, but the bearded, shaven-headed Croats are a tough lot and start holding us there, as the familiar grey of Fulham Football Club appears to our left.

'Our bend, boys, we've got half a length. Let's push out to a length! Ten strokes on the legs, now!' Jim's calls are perfectly in the rhythm of the boat, building on its natural timing. He flicks the rudder and with our extra effort we pull further ahead until their bow man is level with Jim.

Only now do the Croats wake up. Their strokeman, known to us as the Panther, and my opposite man, Igor Boraska, have rowed at two

Olympics, ten World Championships, and aren't about to be embarrassed by a bunch of students. One of them lets out a roar like a forest beast and back they come at us. This isn't over!

James:
Sunday 23 March 15:43, Putney

'OK, that's a wrap, thanks, guys,' says the producer. Wow, they actually say that. The cameraman, relieved, slings the machine from his shoulder. Dave notices a friend on the towpath and walks up the slope to meet him. The interviewer sidles up to me conspiratorially.

'So,' he starts, sotto voce, 'got any tips for a good bet?' His dark eyes gleam. 'I mean, your lot look like men, Oxford like boys,' he says with a hyena-like grin.

'Look, I'm fully confident we've got what it takes to win, but ask him,' I nod towards my brother, 'and he'll tell you the same. The odds are so bad anyway. And there's no such thing as a dead cert.'

The hyena is disappointed. He was in the press launch watching our fixture with the Croats. We'd completed two half courses with them. On the first, after our initial speed, they'd shown grit and fought back to almost level at Hammersmith Bridge, before we opened up the afterburners to return to a length ahead. On the second piece we'd gone under Barnes Bridge almost a length up, but again they managed to claw some back before the end. Afterwards we'd agreed: we need to work on our sprint, our ability to break away and deliver the killer blow. Anyway, the Croatians had looked surprised, which was gratifying.

I leave the interviewer helping with the microphones and stroll up the embankment to the road, and Dave. As I reach him a minibus horn goes; the dark blues are waving impatiently. We look at each other; the next time we'll be this close will probably be the weigh-in. Our faces are stony. I can't believe what we've become. I remember the pure joy I'd felt when as a toddler I'd first realised I had a brother. The swelling of a pure protective instinct in me. Then, for so many years we spent almost every waking hour with each other. In school, in the holidays, doing whatever hobby we were both then into, sharing a bedroom for over a decade. Now he hates being near me. Sean has turned him against me.

'Good luck,' he says.

'You too.' He lopes off to the minibus, his expression turning to a broad grin as they open the back door. They start pulling away as he dives in, to cheers and pats on the back. As the dark blue van disappears up the road, my dislike of everything they stand for bubbles upwards. At home I'd overheard them talking about some 'X Factor' they believe they have. They're welcome to their psychological crutches, I think dismissively.

David:
Sunday 23 March 17:43, Hammersmith

Matt relishes squeezing the minibus into the narrow driveway. The white Victorian town house stands proudly among its neighbours on the leafy Hammersmith road. It's our base for the final two weeks of the campaign, just as it has been for Oxford Blue Boats for the last twenty years. While Cambridge are up in Nottingham on a man-made lake we will be training on the same stretch of water that we will race on.

We will be wrapped in cotton wool for these last two weeks. There's no chance to see girls or stay up late. It's a strict diet of pasta and old race videos.

I tentatively follow Matt up the steps to the door. He has walked this path before, into the pressure cooker of the final preparations. He rings the doorbell.

Unlike Matt and the other former Blues, I know the house from my childhood. Coincidentally, the host and owner Heather Boxer is a longstanding family friend and I knew her and her children long before my Oxford involvement began. My mother and Heather became firm friends through Mum's first university boyfriend, Chris Martin. He apparently couldn't have been more different from his Coldplay namesake, with a bushy beard and a PhD in Anglo-Saxon. When Mum and Chris went their separate ways she remained friends with Heather, eventually becoming godmother to her daughter Bryony. Until recently Heather still cooked all the crew meals on the 20-year-old electric cooker that had belonged to my mum, which was rushed over to Heather's after hers had broken down at a critical catering moment.

Heather will look after us like her own. She is an unbelievable woman. She's up well before us in the mornings to prepare breakfast and retires late at night, long after our huge dinner. There's even a separate meal for Acer that looks fit for an anorexic stick insect, rowers being more accustomed to 5,000 calories a day than five.

'Welcome!' Heather, smiles engagingly. 'Matt, nice to see you again.'

'David!' she exclaims. I kiss her on both cheeks. 'How's Katie?'

'Mum's great, thanks.'

'Well, come in, make yourself at home.' She meets the whole gang and then starts allocating rooms. I'm sharing with John. I'm glad; his general calmness will put me at ease.

As she shows us upstairs we pass countless photos of previous Blue Boats that have enjoyed Heather's hospitality. I recognise many of the straining faces but I'm particularly struck by a young-looking Matthew Pinsent. His face is ruddy, as always, but his features have taken on an unusual, haunted look. I look closer and notice a swirl of water at the top of the picture, the puddle of a Cambridge oar ahead. Pinsent knows he's lost.

And he's a three-times Olympic champion. Dropping my kit on the bed, I head out for a walk along the river, wondering grimly what our photo will show.

David:

Sunday 23 March 19:03, Hammersmith

When I get back to my room, I see a letter addressed to me lying on my bed. I've been walking along the towpath just thinking about yesterday's race, unable to get it out of my mind. I tear open the letter and sit on the bed to read it. I have a few minutes before dinner.

> So, shit happens. There's nothing we can do about it – we can wish it had never occurred, we can play over and over again in our minds how we could have acted better, but when all is said and done, it is in the past and it cannot be replayed. How we react to the situation, not how we think we should have acted, is what is important. The clash on Saturday was not your fault, it was our failure as a crew to address the situation. Whatever you feel, Dave, do not question yourself as an

oarsman. Cliché as it might sound, 'that which does not kill us makes us stronger'. The situation is one that you, that we all, can learn a lot from. I have every belief that the depth of our character, of YOUR character, is so strong that we can take this blow, roll with it and adapt to be stronger. In two weeks, no one will remember our race with Leander; all they will care about is that Oxford have an awesome crew that won the race in an amazing way. That is the goal of this crew, we deserve it and we will fulfil it.

Dave, I'll be honest with you. I did not think you would be in the crew. I did not think you had what it takes. I was wrong. I tell you that now because I wish to outline to you that what you have already achieved this year has been awesome. If at the start of the year I questioned you, now I do not, not in the slightest. You have every right to hold your head with the highest dignity amongst this crew of which you are an integral part. No one could row that six seat better. There is no one I would rather swap from Isis, from Goldie or their Blue Boat to replace you. Do not let the events of Saturday blur your image of yourself because I assure you it has not changed how I or any one of the rest of us perceives you, and that is with the utmost respect and admiration. When the shit is going down on Boat Race day, when we feel so nervous beforehand, when we feel our heads will explode going under Hammersmith and when we dig deeper than ever before to draw away from Cambridge, I for one will get strength from the knowledge that I will be in the same boat as you and I know that you will be bearing that same suffering and because of that I will not want to let you down. Dave, you are one of my best friends, and someone for whom I hold much respect. I know that our friendship will endure the Boat Race and in the end, if all this year achieves is that, then it will have been worthwhile. But both you and I know we can win this race. We are the fastest Oxford crew ever and we will not be denied our rightful place as winners. If anything, do not regret Saturday, it is the type of lesson that will forge us into a crew of steel that cannot be broken.

Looking forward to the next two weeks.

Bas

James:

Sunday 23 March 21:42, Nottingham

The smell of beer, cigarettes and sweat and the sounds of S Club 7 fill the gloom of the subterranean bar. The PA cuts in as S Club 7 'reach for the stars'. 'OK, people, next to audition for *Popstars*, it's Jo!' I squeeze Sam's hand, wishing the two of us could vanish from the crowd and be alone. A greater public display of affection isn't possible, as we're surrounded on the dance floor by seven of her flatmates; a surreptitious squeeze of the hand here and a stolen kiss there will have to do. Talking over the music is also impossible.

Jo, a college friend of Sam's and mine, steps out on to the temporary stage to applause, looking not in the least nervous. She raises the microphone to her lips. Two bars into Steps' cover of 'Tragedy' there's an almighty screeching from the CD and the DJ hits the brakes.

'OK,' he says, 'change of plan. Here's Jo, she's going to sing, "It's Raining Men".' Valiantly Jo launches in, totally unrehearsed. When she finishes we applaud wildly, but sadly she doesn't get through to the next round. As we leave after a few drinks, wine for the girls and coke for me, I realise that there was a stretch of at least five minutes when I didn't think about the race once. Quite an achievement.

James:

Monday 24 March 10:42, Nottingham

The next morning Sam drives me to the National Watersports Centre where the CUBC are staying this week. It's a man-made, precisely rectangular, two-kilometre lake complete with an industrial-looking finishing tower complex. We park up behind the complex but it takes for ever for me to get out of the car. I don't want to go, leave our relaxed, intimate relationship and return to the pressure of the race. Can't I just be a normal student? Finally, when we're both very late, we say our goodbyes.

Back with the boys, the first activity is an early lunch, as I fortunately missed most of the boat rigging. In the cafeteria, which overlooks the finishing line of the lake, the English rowers reminisce about races and trials gone by. GB junior trials are held here for a week in July. Five days of three seat racing sessions a day. Five or so races a session. That's a lot of sprinting down the course, which engenders something of a Blitz spirit.

'Groves, d'you remember that time in '98 when you delayed racing because you got stuck in the ceiling void of your room?' He'd had the brilliant idea of trying to surprise a mate in the next-door room by crawling through the ceiling space and magically appearing in his bathroom.

'Remember? I've still got the burns on my ass from the hot water pipe.' A team of us had to pull him out. 'What about Ouseley and his one-lycra challenge?'

'That thing could almost stand up by itself!' One of the guys succeeded in wearing the same lycra all-in-one for every single session that week. His roommates feared the Plague might break out any moment.

After lunch, a couple of us head outside to the terrace, lean on the railings and look out over the quiet lake. The finishing line below was the scene of one of my happiest moments, when in my final year at Hampton we crossed the line first in the National Schools Championships, the fastest school eight in the country. What relief and happiness, it was a perfect moment. Winning what matters to you most, along with your best friends and your brother – what could be better? It was instant nirvana, a legal overdose of ecstasy, and the drug hasn't worn off, leaving a constant intravenous drip of pride that has reverberated through the years. Matt stroked the crew with the same dogged determination he now injected into Oxford. Dave, only sixteen, was at the other end of the boat. Throughout that year he was always quiet and overawed, intimidated and desperate to win approval. I'd tried to protect him, bring him into the group. Before racing, when he was particularly silent, I'd go and reassure him, try to take some of his load on my shoulders and not look nervous myself. 'It's OK,' I'd tell him. 'We've got this one, don't worry.' Together, his strength was mine, mine his. Then life was simple for our parents. No longer. I could see the tension building for them, particularly Mum. Her sons are being torn apart and she can only sit on the sidelines. Sport is changing them, as it had her father. Dad seems to enjoy the various press and TV interviews and the theatre of the whole thing, but Mum is intensely worried, beneath a veneer of impartiality and calm.

Dave will be more afraid than ever right now but this time I can't help him. If Matt and Dave win in a few days' time it'll tarnish my memory of everything – even our past successes together at school. It'll look as though it was the Oxford prodigies who brought us our glory back then.

James:

Wednesday 26 March 16:23, Nottingham

'OK, let's try that again,' Martin sighs, his frustrated Irish tones echoing across the water. Martin McElroy has joined us for the last two weeks as finishing coach. Along with Harry Mahon, he coached the GB eight to Olympic gold in Sydney, the first since 1912.

Martin picks up the megaphone again. 'Let the blade fill up with water. Don't tear it. Groves, leave the arms out of it, no tearing.' Somehow, as we shift up through the gears from a standstill, we're going wrong and the hull is dropping this way and that. The horror of last year's start still haunts me and the coaches are obviously equally concerned.

'Come forward,' Jim calls. 'First five again.' Solemnly we bring ourselves up to our start positions.

'Attention. Go!' Robin calls and we're away. The boat takes off fast, but unstable, like a bucking bronco. We stop after five strokes.

'Groves, you dopey arse, stop fucking tearing it!' Martin angrily belts out at top volume. As the echoes die away Robin pipes up, 'Again. Do it again.'

The next start, the boat fires off, straight and level as an arrow. Groves doesn't tear the first stroke and none of the rest of us incur Martin's wrath. After several more good starts 'for the bank', we 'battle paddle' back.

Martin picks up the megaphone again, 'Bow four, move through the feet at the front end.' He's working on the change of direction off the front of the stroke. It's got to be perfect or the stern of the boat will drop and dig into the water. A few more strokes. 'Grip the foot stretcher at the front end with your toes, like you're trying to pick up a tennis ball with your feet.' Instantly the boat lifts out of the water and it feels as though 40 kilos have been taken off my shoulders and the rest of stern four's.

In our debriefing later, under the gathering darkness, the precious boat stowed for the night, Groves is in one of his deep, dark moods. Silent, with arms crossed and thick, dark eyebrows furrowed. He doesn't offer a word and walks off by himself when the meeting is concluded.

Martin grins at me as we watch him go. 'You were pretty hard on him,' I comment.

'He needed telling. It's hard to get inside that thick skull. He won't tear it now,' he says robustly, clearly glad to have had such an obvious effect.

Later on the mood is lifted by the Goldie guys. It's Ellie's twenty-first birthday and they're playing a new version of blind date to celebrate. JA, Andrew Shannon, Ewan Robson and Dan Barry are all dressed up as girls, Dan having earlier managed to persuade the cleaner to lend him a couple of pairs of tights. In an odd role reversal, Ellie gets to ask three questions before picking her ideal woman.

Andy Smith revises in his room alone. He and Breck are ploughing a lonely furrow in their spare pair, cruising up and down the lake without any coaching, with only their thoughts and each other for company.

David:
Wednesday 26 March 19:30, Hammersmith

The rest of the crew are lounging in Heather's semi-basement dining area, our crew room, looking forward to the fourth meal of the day. I'm making myself a cup of tea in the kitchen with Derek, our assistant coach. Having been cooped up together every day for months, virtually every topic of conversation has been explored and exhausted. For the last week our crew has been debating the relative popularity of horse riding and rowing.

'Derek, do you think there are more competing rowers or competing horse riders in the UK?' I ask casually.

'I think there are more horse riders, actually,' our assistant coach replies firmly, in his light Scottish accent, unsurprised by the odd question. I should have expected that. Derek, a horseman first and foremost, once claimed that dressage competitions are more tiring than 2,000-metre ergometer tests. I have never seen one of those riders in jodhpurs roll off their horse in agony after trotting round the course. It caused huge debate.

It reminds me of a story told by Mick McKay, one of our guest coaches. In the run-up to his second Olympic gold in 1996, a serious disagreement almost tore his Australian four apart – all about whether fish feel the cold. After the hour-long argument escalated into a heated shouting match, the crew simply refused to talk to one another. After several days of sulking, the coach put an end to the fish argument with some hasty research, and they got on with the business of winning gold.

Returning to the living room to join the other guys, I squeeze on to the sofa between Bas, Matt and a number of Heather's cats as Acer puts on *When We Were Kings*, the documentary about the 'The Rumble in the Jungle', Mohammed Ali's famous fight against George Foreman.

When the fighters stand together for the press I'm struck by the size difference. Ali's stature is a joke compared to Foreman's. The parallel between my crew and Cambridge's is immediate.

The footage cuts to Foreman demolishing a heavy punch bag. Watching his power, I think it is no wonder the pundits thought Ali would be killed in Zaire.

In the fight Ali takes huge amounts of punishment on the ropes. He's not dancing round the bigger man as everyone expected. I watch the punches rain down, expecting each one to be the end of Ali. Gradually, though, Foreman's punches start to weaken as he tires. Ali re-awakens. Soon the tables turn and Ali finally knocks out Foreman.

'Unbelievable!' I say out loud as they replay Ali's knockout blow.

'I knew you'd like it,' says Matt, who'd insisted on it in the video store. 'That's what we're going to do, guys. Let the big Cambridge guys tire themselves out. Then we break them.'

James:
Thursday 27 March 11:30, Nottingham

The impending race is weighing heavily on us all. We only have ten days left. Wooge is taking it across his shoulders and is quiet in the boat. Occasionally, when he leans away, I can share a smile or cheering comment with Jim, but Tim is a 'black hole of negativity, sucking away any positive thought' as Wayne puts it. When we're turning the boat, I'll turn to young TJ if I've got something to say. Off the water Tim's more relaxed.

What adds to it is the confined space. We've agreed not to bring any personal vehicles so we're together all the time, no escape. The lake, the centre, the minibus. The coaches have sensed this, and this morning we've moved to the River Trent. They're setting us free of the right-angled confines of the buoyed lake.

On the landing stage, about to push off, Martin tells us, 'When you are back here in an hour and a half I don't want you to regret anything.' It's a rare, glorious, sunshine-filled day.

We row off and run through our standard race warm-up, some fast-moving speed work after some low-tempo power strokes. Then we build into a solid paddle working on our targeted technical focuses, the coaches occasionally glimpsed between banks of trees on the towpath, cycling alongside and not saying much.

We pass Nottingham Forest Football Ground and continue, under the city bridges until we are out with only fields to either side. Despite the freedom of rowing on curves and bends in the river and the rare sunshine, frustration builds in me. The boat feels heavier and heavier, so I attack each stroke more and more, causing old technical faults to appear, prompting comments from Robin and Martin. Whenever we pause, Tim mutters darkly under his breath and stares moodily away from the boat. He won't repeat his comments when I ask him to. He only shouts to the coaches that the boat is still sitting on strokeside, making it uncomfortable for him. I'm at boiling point as we spin to row back with the stream. I turn to the crew, 'We all need to take more personal responsibility for the speed,' I say, exasperated.

The row back feels no better to me, so by the time we carry the boat back from the Trent to the Watersports Centre, I'm fuming.

I walk back with Robin, with Martin a few steps behind, on the phone.

'Can you have a word with Tim?' I ask him. 'It feels like he'd rather be rowing by himself out there.'

'Yes, OK, I will,' he says gravely. Just telling Robin how I feel helps most of the steam built up in me evaporate.

'Did you see their fixture in Putney?' I continue, referring to Oxford's race against Leander.

'Yes.'

'They're good, aren't they? They seem able to cruise at 38 strokes a minute.'

I'd watched Dad's video of Dave's race at home. Before the clash they'd been roaring along, looking smooth, at an incredibly high tempo with no signs of fatigue. Equally, earlier that afternoon, Dad had found Dave watching his video of my race against Croatia. Apparently Dave was 'somewhat subdued' afterwards.

'They're good but not superhuman, James. Who knows, you might just cruise away from them after the first mile.'

God, that would be so wonderful.

James:
Thursday 27 March 15:45, Nottingham

'Up two, now!' Jim calls defiantly as we pass the marker buoy and seamlessly shift up a gear, and start moving further away from Goldie, who are alongside, battling to keep in the game. After a further 250 metres we reach another marker buoy. 'Push out, back on the rhythm. Good, 36.' Another 20 strokes later and we're over the finish line, panting.

'Turn the boat, one minute.' Robin demands. Still breathing hard, we start bringing the hull around for another pass. In our work-out this afternoon we're practising the knockout blow. Lifting from cruising speed either to break Oxford entirely or to respond to their having thrown down the gauntlet.

It's glorious to be able to lose yourself in the work and the pain, able to do something about all the built-up worry and nerves. Just pull harder. The coaches on the bank are recording our times but we agreed before we set out that Robin wouldn't shout them out to us as it would put too much of a focus on outcomes when we need to focus on the processes required to get that high speed.

Wooge can't restrain himself, though, and calls to Robin to disclose the times. There's some unhappy shouting from further up the boat and Wooge swivels round, 'Hey, I just want the fucking times.'

Matze shouts back, 'Why don't you row a single, then?' which silences everyone. Tim bites his tongue and turns quietly back to Jim.

'Right, more pieces!' Robin demands. We sprint, stop, turn the boat. Sprint, stop, turn. Sprint, stop, turn. If Tim is angry it doesn't affect his rowing.

As we pull into the landing pontoon after the last piece, there's more tetchiness. 'We need to do a proper warm-down; the lactate won't have cleared from our legs for the next session. It's not professional,' Matze insists.

'Do it on the fucking ergo,' Wayne offers Matze aggressively from the bow seat. Emotions must be running high for calm, responsible Wayne to be short with his close friend.

After a slightly morose crew chat in the fading evening light, we all spontaneously go for a long warm-down run around the top of the lake, still in our wellies. Our feelings settle as the sun sets.

Matze chips in, 'Guys, I'm sorry about earlier,' looking particularly to Wooge and Wayne. Matze is just so passionate about this race and about his friends. 'This is the last two weeks we'll be together as the 2003 crew. Let's really make the most of it.'

On the return leg of the jog Groves leads us in marching songs.

'I wish all the women,
were waves on the ocean.
And I were a pleasure boat,
riding them all day long!'

There's a greater unity than ever before. Over dinner, Robin reveals the times. They're fast; the fastest would challenge any international eight.

James:

Saturday 29 March 20:15, Strawberry Hill, Twickenham

I get home to find David's irritating dark blue kit bag in the hall and David in the kitchen. It's his last day off too. Poor Mum is struggling under a mountainous pile of washing: horrific-smelling lycras, sweat-drenched T-shirts, sodden socks, waterproofs and hats. Typical of Dave. I doubt he even knows how the washing machine works. Dad sits recovering after a six-hour driving marathon, picking up Dave's stuff from Oxford, then me from King's Cross. Neither of them has uttered a word of complaint. Not that they would normally, but I think they are worried about the stress we're under and want to make life as easy for us as possible. Tonight, for one night, we can almost be a normal family.

I've been joking with the parents about our 15 minutes of fame. Dad's been inventing tag-lines for a possible future advert: 'The mother of the Livingston brothers recommends Body Wipes, by Lenor,' he quipped after passing a little too close to Dave, who hasn't had the chance to shower since training yesterday. Dave sits reading some biology notes on the breakfast bar.

'So do you think you're the fastest Oxford crew ever?' I ask Dave, stirring things up. I try to keep the disdain from my voice.

'Maybe,' he replies coolly, barely raising his head from his notes.

Is he being serious? Oxford have had some really fast crews. Is he bluffing? I can't read his cold face. It's frustrating.

I've heard from the parents that Dave is particularly proud of one of their timed 500-metre pieces.

'Dad said you did a quick 500.' He shrugs non-commitally.

'So what did you clock? 1.16?' I hazard, watching his reaction. One minute 16 seconds is a fast time, one that I'd hoped they couldn't have clocked. He shakes his head.

'1.15?' Again a shake.

'1.14?' I offer, feeling a knot of tension in the pit of my stomach.

He looks up. 'Do you really think I'd tell you?'

Damn, he's bluffing. What an idiot. I'm just so desperate to know what we'll be facing.

Later that night, I lie awake in my boyhood bed thinking about sitting on the start of the race, trying to picture it in my head. The crowds, the screaming. Helicopters buzzing. Dave and the other dark blues, sitting there next to us, defiant. A Sean Bowden quote about me drifts into my consciousness, 'This is his last year to win and his little brother is in the way. Who's under pressure?'

David:

Saturday 29 March 23:58, Strawberry Hill, Twickenham

I toss and turn, my fitful sleep interrupted by nightmares of the impending race. I see myself losing to Cambridge. The desolation on the faces of my crewmates. Worse, it's my fault. I caught another crab. In front of millions of people. A filthy unworthiness washes over me. Then I'm awake and sweating.

James is lying just next door. Is he as fearful as me?

Earlier he seemed composed and almost friendly. It put me off guard, but there is still a wall between us, maybe not from his side but certainly from mine. If he wins I fear my envy may consume our relationship entirely. I've always had to live in his impossible shadow. This is my chance to escape it for good.

I close my eyes again, take some deep breaths and try to calm myself. Many listless minutes later I finally fall back to sleep.

James:
Sunday 30 March 10:15, The Bank of England Club, London

I grab breakfast and then Dad gives me a lift through Richmond Park to the Bank of England Club in Roehampton, our base for race week, five minutes from Putney. My legs feel more cramped than normal in the car. After our first day off in a month yesterday they are begging to do something; they won't be still. At the lodge, a large white building in the gardens of the club, there is an electric sense of excitement in the air radiating from everyone as we trickle in with bulging kit bags and the odd pillow for some over-sensitive souls. Most of us haven't seen each other for a day but it feels like weeks, which shows the intensity of the six months we've spent together. I'm overjoyed to see the lot of them.

David:
Sunday 30 March 10:44, Hammersmith

The hub caps make a horrible grinding sound as they scrape against the curb. Maria pulls the car forward, trying to straighten it up, but only grates the wheels still further. Across the road is Heather's house.

'That'll do,' she says. The engine off, silence embraces us. Neither of us wants to talk about the inevitable. 'Will I get to see you again before the race?'

'I'm not sure. I'll try and make it happen.'

She sighs; she's heard it so many times before. I'll try my best but the next week will be so intense.

Suddenly I remember I have something for her. 'Wait, hold on a second.' I hop out of the car and rush round to the boot. Scrambling in my bag, I find the item. Climbing back into the front passenger seat, I hide it behind my back.

'This . . . is for you. Ta da!' I whip out the dark blue T-shirt with an 'OUBC girlfriend' insignia on the front. 'Funny, don't you think?' I chuckle nervously. She breaks into a smile.

She turns it over to see the bold white writing on the back: LUCKY GIRL.

'Lucky girl?!' she says incredulously. 'Yeah, right.'

James:

Sunday 30 March 19:15, The Bank of England Club, London

'I'll read out the best times of Cambridge Blue Boats for the last half decade and you can take your own view on your speed.' We've settled in and unpacked in our rooms assigned by crew order. Now we are gathered in the main living area for Robin's review of the year.

As he reads off the best times for Cambridge crews over 500 metres, 1,000 metres and 2,000 metres, we come out equal fastest with the 1998 crew, the current Boat Race Course record holders. They were bigger than us, the heaviest on record until the crop of massive guys in 1999. We are much faster than the 1997 crew I idolised as a school kid. What a confidence booster.

'You can't argue with times; there is nothing relative about them. They're fast,' says Tim Wooge. 'Now what we need to do this week is tweak the things we can change in a week.'

A week, not long.

'I'm going to try to be more positive this week. When I'm unhappy it's not that we're shit, just that we're not as good as we could be,' Tim says.

'Now I'd like us to each talk a little about our individual strengths,' Robin suggests.

KC kicks off in his Aussie lilt. 'Well, I'll be pulling hard at the start and when it comes to the end I'll still be there, pulling just as hard. My fitness has always been my strength.' He's not wrong. The best runner of any of us, a tough cyclist and most importantly a great oarsman with not a pound of excess weight. He's come into the sport late but is already making his name.

Next is Hugo, who makes the point that he is very experienced, given his years of racing at school and, more importantly, Harvard. At almost 100 kilos he is one of the bigger men of the crew and has the power to go with his bulk. A good man for the three seat.

Jim is next. 'Well, I guess I bring an intensity to the crews I'm coxing. I'm aggressive, and like the other guys,' he nods at Wayne and Hugo, 'experienced. I've done a lot of side by side eights racing. I never give an inch of water away.' He's confident as well, vitally important. Who's going to have confidence in his steering and directions if he doesn't? His calls in the warm-up for a race set pulses racing right away. He understands the guys in his boat perfectly, and can sometimes put across the coaches' thoughts better than they can themselves. A consummate professional.

The next man in the circle is Wayne. 'I've won plenty in the bow seat of eights,' he says modestly. He had an unblemished record at Harvard, always at bow, a difficult seat to master as the bows of a racing eight leap out of the water during the drive, which demands extreme technical skill from the guy in the sharp end. It's a crucial part of the jigsaw, not only receiving the rhythm from the stern but reflecting it back. 'And of course,' Wayne concludes, sweeping his palm over his bald head, 'I'm aerodynamic.' He grins.

Then it's my turn. 'Well, I think my greatest strength is that I want to win this race more than anyone else. I've grown up with the event. I know that river blindfold. For the last four years I've put everything into winning this. We should have won last year and I put life on hold to come back for this, my last chance. No matter what happens I'll never give up – the last time I was in the seven seat on Boat Race day, in Goldie in 2001, we ended up winning by six lengths. And of course pride won't let me lose to my little brother.' There are knowing smiles.

Groves, TJ, Matze say their bit and then Wooge is last to speak. Like Wayne specialising at bow, Wooge has won a huge number of races at his end of the boat, in the stroke seat, setting the length and rhythm and perhaps most importantly choosing when to hit the gas and break the opposition in half. While his high standards can come across as criticism, there is no disputing that he has a fantastic record. He stroked North-eastern University to some of their greatest victories of recent years, winning the Eastern Sprints in the USA, crowning them the fastest eight in the country. When, later, they were disqualified on a technicality – one of their crew had missed one too many classes and hence didn't qualify as a Northeastern student – Tim dutifully sent his gold medal to the stroke of the silver medal boat. He got it back in the post a few days later with a message that simply said, 'Keep it, you earned it.'

More importantly though, Oxford are scared of him. He's our talisman and our figurehead. I'm very glad he's here.

David:

Tuesday 1 April 12:59, Winchester House, Putney embankment, The Weigh-In

The Oxford crew lines up outside the Winchester House function room, each of us adjacent to our opposite man from the light blue camp.

'Just hold on here for a few minutes, guys,' says one of the organisers. 'I'll call you through when they're ready for you.' Next door I can faintly hear Barry Davies's familiar voice introducing the race to the national and international press and TV crews.

There's no hiding our physiques from the opposition – or theirs from us – as we're all wearing racing suits, all-in-one lycras. It's easy to see that they dwarf us in size, age and experience. I knew it was the case, but now it is starkly obvious. I'm taller and heavier than my opposite number Tom James, who I'd raced with at Junior Worlds, but I'm the exception. We've decided not to try to weigh in 'heavy', an old Boat Race trick to try to physically intimidate the opposition. In the past some have taken this to extremes: one Cambridge oarsman drank so much water to weigh in 'heavy' that it made him sick and he couldn't train that day. It didn't do him any good that year or any other as he ended up losing all his Boat Races. Instead we're hoping to weigh in light and for Cambridge to underestimate us before we've even taken a stroke.

In the waiting area Wooge turns round to his guys nearest to him. 'Smell ze fear,' he says under his breath in his thick German accent.

'Fuck you,' I mutter under mine. How dare he patronise us? His arrogant comment belittles our belief in what we've been building.

Maybe man on man they have the edge but as a unit we're unbreakable. The Tabs smile and laugh, seemingly relaxed and confident. By contrast we're silent, nervous, realising that to win this race we'll have the fight of our lives. He's right, we're scared, but at the same time, I know we can beat these guys. James stands just in front of me to my left. I glance over and see the back of his head; he stands at ease.

'It's my pleasure to present the Oxford and Cambridge Boat Race crews for the 149th Boat Race,' Barry announces. The organiser beckons us in and we file into the room.

The number of reporters, PR people, cameramen and others takes me aback; the big room is packed. I spot Dad, behind the red light of his video camera, and also Martin Cross, my old Hampton School teacher. We take our seats in front of our Isis counterparts, on the opposite side of the stage to our light blue foe.

Barry begins the weigh-in process by announcing us one by one from bow. With each subsequent pair of oarsmen the disparity in weight between the two crews becomes more and more cruelly underlined.

'And at six for Cambridge, Tom James, and for Oxford, David Livingston.' I shuffle along the line and up the stairs on to the stage and take my place on the scales, my hands clasped behind my back. I look ahead over the photographers but don't focus on anything in particular.

'Tom James is 81 kilos, that's 13 stone 4 pounds. David Livingston for Oxford, weights 89 kilos, that's 13 stone 12 pounds,' says the weigh-in official. A few camera flashes go off. I leave the scales and walk down the steps to take my seat again.

'At seven, for Cambridge we have James Livingston, and for Oxford, Henry Morris.' As they stand next to each other, Henry suddenly looks diminutive compared to James. I feel no affection for James; his light blue attire only serves to stir hate. 'James Livingston weights in at 94 kilos, Henry Morris at 81 kilos.' Henry returns to his seat next to me.

'Next we have the presidents and strokemen, Tim Wooge for Cambridge and Matt Smith for Oxford.' As they take to the scales and their weights are read out there is a noticeable intake of breath from the crowd, and the photographers in the front row burst into action. The weight difference between the crews is epitomised by the two leaders. Smithy looks like a kid next to old man Wooge. 'Tim is the tallest and heaviest oarsman in the race this year,' Barry expounds. 'Tim

Wooge weighs in at 100 kilos, Matt Smith at 80 kilos. Thank you, gentlemen. We'll just wait for the crew averages to be calculated.'

'The Cambridge boat have an average weight of 91 kilos or 14 stone 5 pounds per man. Oxford have an average of 84 kilos or 13 stone 3 pounds per man. The difference between the crews is over a stone a man. If Oxford were to be victorious they would have overturned the greatest weight disadvantage in the history of the race.'

After the weigh-in I change back into my chinos and dark blue jumper still angry about Wooge's comment and relishing the enormity of the challenge before us. Walking back into the main hall, I'm grabbed by Caroline Searle, our press officer, for more interviews and photos. Over the past few weeks we've spoken to Sky TV, BBC Sport, BBC News, ITV, had interviews with *Times* and *Telegraph* feature writers like Andrew Longmore and John Goodbody. We even had a photo shoot for *Country Life* magazine. Having been promised the front cover, James and I were relegated to an inside page, in the section normally reserved for debutantes and eligible bachelorettes who are daughters of Lord Lieutenants or Admirals of the Fleet. I'm extremely glad we didn't make the front page; the photo makes me look like I'm pregnant with twins, as I'm leaning back on an unseen railing, while James's face is half in heavy shadow and half in sunshine, making him look creepily like Hannibal Lecter. The most extreme request was to go on the reality TV show *The Salon* with promises of massages from Swedish twins. Appealing as that sounded, I couldn't take the time off training to do it. James was quite up for it and was disappointed by my response. The National Lottery even asked us to 'press the button' on Saturday but it's the night before the race so there isn't a chance we'll be doing that.

David:

Tuesday 1 April 19:45, Hammersmith

'This question will decide who's going to win the Boat Race this year,' says the Five Live presenter who is giving James and me a live radio interview over our mobile phones, each of us installed in our crew digs. 'Which team won the FA cup this year?' Silence. James and I are both stumped. The seconds tick by.

'Errr, was it Chelsea?' James answers hesitantly.

'No, that's wrong,' the presenter replies, overjoyed at the break in the silence. 'David, have you got an answer?'

'Arsenal?' I guess, sounding equally unsure. I haven't paid attention to the outside world in what seems like months.

'That's right, David! Well done! It looks like an Oxford victory! We look forward to seeing you racing each other this Sunday in the 149th University Boat Race. Coverage will begin from 12 p.m. here on 5 Live. Do you have any final words for each other before the race?'

'Have a good one, bro,' James replies.

'May the best man win,' I reply.

'Great guys,' the commentator wraps up. 'Thanks a lot for being with us tonight.'

'Thanks,' we reply in unison, our voices sounding very similar. That wasn't the most compelling interview in sports history.

I hang up my phone and go downstairs to the play room where the rest of the guys are watching a film. Maybe it was a good omen that I guessed Arsenal and got it right? Last year in the pre-Boat Race media hype *The Big Breakfast* put on a 'Goat Race' a couple of days before the event, with Oxford and Cambridge goats racing around a mock-up Thames. The goats were cheered on by some of the crew's girlfriends, including an embarrassed-looking Sam. The Cambridge goat faltered on the final bend, allowing the lagging Oxford goat through to victory. It was an eerily perfect prediction of the outcome of the actual race.

That Radio Five Live interview will be the last time I speak to James until the race is over. Now he's just one of them, the enemy. That's how it is; my loyalties are focussed elsewhere for now, and maybe for ever.

James:

Wednesday 2 April 19:44, The Bank of England Club, London

I don the Blues blazer reverently and head out to knock on the doors of the adjacent rooms. TJ is critically examining the cut of his new blazer in front of the mirror. We were measured up two weeks ago and tonight is the first night we are allowed to wear them: dinner with the 1993, 1983, 1973 and 1963 crews.

'Looks good on you,' I comment.

The youngster grins. 'Thanks.' A Blue in his first year. We gather with the others in the hall. We nod our recognition at the sight of each other in the sacred blazer. Tim leads us into the main room, which has been set out with many tables for the dinner and is filled with suited men of various ages who stop their bright-eyed reminiscing and applaud us respectfully as we file in. We disperse amongst them and start listening to tall tales of races gone by. Goldie have arrived from their lodgings too, in their gold, blue and British racing green striped blazers. It's great to be together as a team again.

Soon I find myself in a cluster with Hugo and some of the oldest Blues there. One, leaning on a stick, is talking about the 1973 race energetically. 'We were ten lengths up at Hammersmith!'

'What happened next?' someone asks.

'Well, Bill, our stroke, made the sensible decision that we should save ourselves for the dinner! What a night we had.' I wished we could have that luxury. It'll never happen.

We take to the dinner tables, the current squad spread out in ones and twos amongst the old boys. It's noticeable that the crews that won their races generally have full turn-outs, some of them having flown over from the USA or the Far East. The losing crews on the other hand tend to have just a handful in attendance. When we're seated, the bowman of Goldie, JA, stands and introduces the speaker, an admiral. A surprisingly short 60-something man, with black hair swept neatly back, rises to his full height. Some of the others of his generation shout, 'Stand up, stand up!' one of them laughing himself to a coughing fit.

'Thank you, thank you.' He thanks the 2003 squad for our invitation and laments that several of his crew cannot be here, noting they will be looking down on us from above on the day.

'I coxed the Cambridge Blue Boat in 1962 and 1963. My God I was petrified on both occasions! After Cambridge I went into the navy and gradually rose up the ranks. I was captain of one of our first nuclear submarines, a slightly bigger boat than I'd got used to at Ely. On exercise one year, about 2,000 miles north of here, under the pack ice in the Arctic Circle, we hit a submerged iceberg. All hell broke loose. We began taking on water but we couldn't surface because of the thick ice above us. In the midst of that, though, I quite clearly remember thinking to myself. "This still isn't as scary as sitting on the start of the Boat Race".'

Everyone laughs. As it quietens I swallow audibly, attempting to moisten my dry mouth. I'm grateful for the collective admission of fear.

The admiral concludes, 'In three days' time, gentlemen, when you face Oxford on that start line, you are not alone. We are all there with you. Good luck.'

Part IV

'We few, we happy few, we band of brothers;
For he to-day that sheds his blood with me
Shall be my brother; be he ne'er so vile.'

Shakespeare's *Henry V* (1598) act 4, sc. 3

Chapter 10
Triumph and Disaster

David:

Wednesday 2 April 19:25, Putney

The model ushers us into the sleek, contemporary lift. In her heels she is taller than quite a few of the guys. At least I salvage our team pride. As we rise silently through the floors, the mirrors in the lift remind me that it's our first outing in Blue Boat blazers; they are very smart but also annoyingly subtle. There is no crest on the jacket. It could be any dark blue wool blazer. Unlike the colourful blazers worn at Henley Regatta, which shout the wearer's allegiance, the only way you really could tell it belonged to an Oxford rowing Blue are the bronze buttons, which have the emblem of a Roman galley circled by the words 'Oxford University Boat Club'.

This evening we've escaped Heather's house and the constant presence of the coaches to attend the opening of a new luxury riverside development. A property developer who saw us on the river bank this morning said the theme for the showcase of their penthouse flat was Blue and he'd love us to show up; no pressure, just a few free drinks. He'd pointed to the newly built block of flats just up the road, on the other side of Putney Bridge.

The lift is very cramped. Please, no one fart, I think. A terrible side-effect of our huge diets.

'How much is it on the market for?' Macca asks, breaking the silence.

The blonde model turns and gives him a look of distaste. 'It's already sold actually. It went for three.' She turns round again to face the lift exit.

'Very reasonable,' Macca retorts quietly. John and I exchange looks, dying to laugh. I assume she means three million.

The doors slide back and we exit into the foyer. Another hostess holds trays of drinks at the flat entrance.

'Champagne?' she asks.

'Orange juice, thanks.' I reach over the back of the tray and take a solitary orange juice. The others swarm around the other tray, which offers more non-alcoholic offerings. The party is already rocking by the looks of things; there must be about fifty people here. Most are slick, in their thirties, and look like they might actually be able to afford the flat. Quite a few give us strange looks; I guess they must wonder why nine guys have wandered in, dressed in identical blue blazers. They probably think we're the band or a barber's shop octet.

I wander over to the massive, frameless, glass windows. Even in the darkness, the view is impressive from the seventeenth floor. To the east, I can make out the MI6 building at Vauxhall. To the west, Putney, Fulham and Hammersmith Bridge – the Boat Race course. The river snakes through the lights of London.

As I survey the view I think of a completely different world. Red Deer, Canada, a small, rural farming town. On the drive over Scott had told me that his uncle had been bragging to his fellow hog-farming friends about his nephew making this year's Oxford Boat Race crew. One of the other farmers exclaimed that he had two in the race – my great-uncle Roy. Scott and I had laughed together. Small world, he'd rightly pointed out. I break into a chuckle whilst thinking about our crew's new nickname for Scott: Scotty-too-hotty, a joke mainly about his temper which we passed off as a comment on his good looks.

The main penthouse living room is amazing. Imagine owning this place. A gaggle of models – I'm not sure what the collective noun is – stands together in the other corner of the room. How many models did they hire? One of them catches my eye. Oh no, she's coming over. Maybe what I've been told by the old Blues is true. Maybe this jacket does emit some sort of electro-magnetic pull to the opposite sex. As she gets closer I realise she's actually quite average-looking in every department except her breasts, which are enormous, like two inflated balloons. God, don't let her catch me looking. Unlike Acer, I'm not a breasts man, I find them daunting.

'Hey, how are you doing?' Her Australian accent is easy to place. I wonder if they're real.

'Fine, thanks. I'm with the Oxford rowers, the other guys in the same blue blazers. We were invited this morning.'

'Oh great. Can I ask you a question?'

'Sure,' I reply, waiting for her to ask my height.

'I hope you won't think I'm stupid, but what is the river outside called? I've only been in London for five months.'

'The Thames.'

'Uh huh,' she nods.

At least for some people there is another life apart from that damn river.

James:

Friday 4 April 14:20, Putney

Friday. We have only one outing, with the rest of the day free to ensure total freshness for the race in two days' time. The aim of the session is to put the finishing touches to our start. This morning's outing is one of the few remaining chances we have to practise from the stakeboats with the umpire in race positions. It must not be wasted.

We boat up, and begin running through the race day warm-up exercises to get us physically and mentally ready. It is going well. We've performed this routine of warm-up bursts and starts hundreds of times before and now it is getting close to perfection. The boat sings through the water, fast and effortless.

We turn the boat around near the start line to complete the final piece of our warm-up – the 'jet speed' burst, a maximum bore sprint of 15 strokes. We're right in front of the boathouses. I see the Oxford minibus has arrived. No doubt they'll be watching.

'Get a load of this!' I think to myself.

David:

Friday 4 April 14:30, Westminster School Boathouse, Putney

Bas, Scott and I stand on the balcony of Westminster School Boathouse, the Oxford training base during Boat Race preparation. Notionally we're assessing the river conditions before our outing but really we're watching Cambridge.

Their last burst before they started turning round looked good. Maybe, just maybe, they deserve their mantle of pre-race favourites, and not just because of their massive stone-per-man weight advantage. As if sensing what I'm thinking, Scott mutters, 'Nothing special,' and stomps off down the metal stairs in his wellies. His confidence in our ability is seemingly unshakeable. With a last look at Cambridge, who have just finished turning their boat around, Bas and I follow Scott downstairs. We have 18 minutes until we hit the water. We're running to a strict schedule, as we will on the day.

James:
Friday 4 April 14:35, Putney

'Yeah, boys, 41. That's good,' Jim shouts. The boat has transformed, it's sprouted wings, we're flying free of earthly hindrance, the water disappearing away beneath us. We've left Robin's coaching launch far behind. I'm grinning through gritted teeth.

There's even some cheering from the bank.

Then Jim screams, 'EASY THERE! HOLD IT UP!!'

The naked fear in the rushed words is petrifying. A fraction of a second later, before we can even slam the blades in the water to slow the boat, there is a massive impact and a deafening *crunch* of smashed carbon fibre and metal against God knows what. The boat judders to a grinding halt.

David:
Friday 4 April 14:35, Westminster School Boathouse, Putney

I'm tightening my foot stretcher with a spanner when urgent screams outside the boathouse make me look up. Through the wide open boathouse door, I can see Cambridge rowing full pelt, straight towards a large tugboat which is powering down on top of them.

How can the two boats not see each other?

Someone could be killed. My God – James.

James:

Friday 4 April 14:35, Putney

A dark wall fills the left side of my vision, not even a couple of feet away, and I duck right instinctively.

The bows of the huge black launch smash into my oar, which knocks me backwards. Hot with adrenalin, I wrestle the oar handle back from parallel with our boat, pushing it forward over me, and stare incredulously at what is now the stern of the passing craft, noticing the shocked expressions of the men standing on the rear deck.

Heart pumping hard, I turn to see the worst. Wayne and Hugo's oars are splintered and broken in two. Groves's oar has a huge splintered crack halfway down the shaft. Everyone's still there, though. There's shouting from somewhere.

'Get your feet out. We're going down!!' Kris bawls from the bows, with genuine alarm in his voice. I turn back to get my feet out of the shoes that are bolted into the footrest. Tim's head is in his hands; I can hear obscenities emanating from him in both English and German. Jim is absolutely silent and clearly in shock.

Robin's coaching launch pulls up alongside and Martin shouts, 'Is anybody hurt?' in desperate Irish tones. I don't immediately hear a reply and the panic coursing through my veins drops a little. There doesn't seem to be any water pouring in either. The boat remains afloat.

We've just had a virtual head-on collision with a 15-tonne tugboat and escaped without injury. Jim, regaining some composure, calls Groves and me to take a few strokes as the boat has drifted square across the river. Robin drives past, up to the bows. There's a nasty crack behind me as Groves's broken oar snaps in two. A large chunk of it drifts off upriver to Fulham. I hold on to my oar all the tighter – now that the rest of bowside are oarless passengers, it's all that is stopping us swimming in the filthy Thames. I turn and see Wayne climbing, with great difficulty, into Robin's launch. Robin guns the engine and they pull into the stream and make for the bank. Wayne is holding his arm like a bird holds a broken wing. At that moment the potential disaster of an injury doesn't hit me – as the only remaining bowside oar, I'm more immediately concerned about getting us into the bank, before the Thames carries us off downriver.

The press launch alongside is a frenzy of hacks jostling for the best view, whirring motor drives, and waving lenses as we weave gingerly between the moored boats into the bank, with the help of the other coaching launch at our bows. As we come into the bank some of us start to joke shakily about how it had been a damn good last burst. Jim is still white and when he gives his calls his voice is dead and soulless.

As we carry the boat in, Martin grabs the shattered oars and rushes them to the back of the boathouse. We put the boat down on to trestles and hurry to the bows to examine the damage. It's bad. The shoulder of the boat near the bows has crumpled. Delicate carbon fibre racing boats, painstakingly finessed to microns of accuracy to be ultra-thin walled and light, don't take well to any impact, let alone what we've just put our boat through.

Alan, our coxing coach for Boat Race week, says determinedly, 'We've had worse. In '86 six foot of our bow was entirely ripped off and that was 15 minutes before the race.' He is referring to the notorious year when Cambridge slammed into a barge during their warm-up, crippling their boat so badly the bow pointed jauntily skyward. They promptly sank. The race was delayed to the following day, giving Cambridge time to borrow a boat. Alan was chief coach at the time. 'We got through that. I'll be damned if we don't get through this.' It is good hearing his reassuring words.

The press pack have now disembarked from the press launch and are rushing up the bank. Others are hurrying along the Putney embankment towards us. They've smelled fresh ink. We slam down the shutters of the boat bay to prevent them snooping round the damaged boat and head upstairs to the changing rooms. Wayne is already upstairs, sitting with his left forearm upright and wrapped in ice, being looked over by a doctor. Caroline Searle comes in and says she's put guards on the door to stop the press getting up here.

I hand round newspapers which I find on a side table in an attempt to distract everyone. The sooner we get ourselves back to a normal, calm state, the better. After a few minutes, Robin decides we should head home for the day and try to relax.

'We won't be doing any more rowing today with five oars, boys,' he reasons. Robin drives Wayne off to a local hospital with the doctor; the rest of us change and go straight down to the bus without speaking to the milling, and now very agitated, press. Wooge drives us home.

David:

Friday 4 April 14:58, Putney

I wade into the familiar murky Thames water and lower my blade into its gate. We are already several minutes behind schedule, so I hurriedly slip off my size 13 wellies and do my best to cram them under my seat. This is one of our final rows but Cambridge's terrible crash has unnerved me. Incredibly, it looked as though they got away with an almost head-on collision with only a few broken oars. I watched James carry their boat up the bank with the rest of the crew. They all looked fine and they'll be able to replace their broken equipment, but one thing's for sure: we've all been reminded of the utter faith we place in our cox, Acer.

The warm-up begins and I zone in on the job in hand. I have only four outings left to make last-minute improvements that will increase our speed. It seems like I've been working on the same technical points all season.

As we manoeuvre on to the fixed stakeboat for our first 15-stroke practice start, I can't fail to be aware of the umpire's launch lurking behind us.

Sitting inside it is Boris Rankov, the most successful Boat Race oarsman ever, and the umpire for the race. I'd heard that in the early months of 1983, during the run-up to his final Boat Race, he received death threats from a Cambridge supporter who wrote that should Boris compete, he would be shot from Hammersmith Bridge. Apparently unfazed, Boris rowed his sixth race and won by a handy margin.

'Fifteen-stroke start, boys,' repeats Acer. Boris stands up to give us a practice start sequence.

'Oxford, get ready, please,' announces the umpire. This is the command we have been waiting for.

We sit forward. I take a deep breath.

'Attention . . . Go!' We square our blades into the water, taking the weight of the heavy stationary boat, and it begins to move.

Acer screams rhythmically with each stroke, 'Drraawww, Draw, build . . . NOW!' These code words initiate changes in our rowing in an automatic, almost robotic way. By the fifth stroke the boat has sped up and is moving well but over the next ten our progress becomes erratic and the boat unstable, making it difficult to row effectively.

'Wind down, wind down,' shouts Acer on the fifteenth stroke.

We start to turn the boat. From the stroke seat, Matt swivels to address the crew.

'Guys, we let the conditions get of the better of us. Let's sharpen up the next one.' His analysis is spot on: the performance had been poor by our high standards and the conditions were not that bad. The crew is subdued as we begin to row back for our second start.

We are passing under the archways of Putney Bridge when Bas suddenly shouts, 'Fucking hell!'

Just Bas being his usual over-emotional self. He's always either exuberantly happy or inconsolably miserable.

'Someone tell Bas to shut the hell up,' comes Matt's retort, which carries over Acer's microphone.

I'm with Matt; nothing is more annoying in a boat than having someone making negative, unconstructive comments. Then I faintly hear Bas grunt, 'A bloody water balloon hit me from the bridge!'

The rest of us start laughing. Bas is not amused.

James:
Friday 4 April 17:05, The Bank of England Club, London

Back at the Bank of England Club, Hugo, Tom, Matthias, KC and I play snooker, very badly. Wooge joins us after a few games. No one wants to be alone with their thoughts, apart from Groves, that is. When we'd last checked on him and asked whether he fancied joining the game, he was lying on his bed and listening to Counting Crows' melancholy master-piece 'Colourblind', over and over. Set on repeat, the soft piano melody drifted around the room, rising and falling, while Groves stared at the ceiling, unseeing.

Jim is in meetings with the harbour master and the river authorities. Someone could be in deep trouble.

Everyone is still in a state of shock. As we loiter, too churned up to do anything, playing half-hearted games of snooker, our phones buzz with messages from shocked friends and relatives who have just seen news of the crash on TV. 'Are you all OK?' they enquire. We don't know. The waiting for the hospital verdict on Wayne's injury is terrible. Thoughts are no longer on the race; there's now something even more pressing that holds our attention. He'll be fine, we tell each other, some ice on it and he'll be great. He just has to be able to row. It's unthinkable that he can't.

I chat to my father on my phone outside the snooker room. Dan Smith, Matt and Ben's father, had rung him at his office to let him know the news he'd heard from Matt. Oxford, after all, had had a ringside seat to our high-velocity crash, as had the press.

Dad says he is glad no one has been killed but he can't hide the concern and shock in his voice when I tell him that Wayne has been rushed to hospital. Dad knows Wayne well as he's often stayed with us in London throughout the year. 'It's probably just a precaution,' he says, trying to reassure me. I hope he is right.

Finally Jim knocks at the snooker room door. We are relieved to see him; he must be bringing news of Wayne. The waiting will soon be over. He tells us Robin has called a meeting but he doesn't say anything beyond that. On the short walk across the gardens back to the lodge he tells us how he'd had to go over his account of the crash again and again to the authorities. Someone was really going to be for the high jump, and we were all confident it wouldn't be Jim.

We follow him back to the lodge and in through the kitchen. As we walk briskly through into the main room, our impatience hurrying us on, I notice a brown A3 folder, partially open on the breakfast table. Inside is the unmistakeable, shiny dark film of an X-ray. Slowly it registers. There is a red arrow on it.

In the main room stand Donald Legget, the Goldie coach, Robin, Rob Baker, our boatman – and Wayne. We draw up chairs in a circle. No one says anything. Wayne is expressionless and doesn't meet any of our questioning eyes. The atmosphere is thick with tension. It is suffocating us all. Then Robin speaks.

'We've just got back from the hospital. Wayne has a hairline fracture to his wrist.' There is a collective intake of breath and all our eyes turn to Wayne, who stands staring at the floor. 'He won't be racing with us on Sunday.' My chest tightens as the news hits home, and I pull at the collar of my shirt for breath. All our hearts break for Wayne right then. 'Ben Smith will be taking his place.' Another intake of breath. After a few moments Robin concludes. 'I know it's tragic and awful, but we don't have time to feel sorry for Wayne. We just have to come together and win this race.'

There is a silence as everyone gathers their thoughts. Many of us stare wide-eyed at the floor. As the only veteran of last year's crew, I'm conscious of the need to keep everyone fighting, everyone's heads up. I don't want anyone giving up before the race has even started. I feel I have to say something.

'Firstly, I feel awfully sorry for you, mate.' Wayne doesn't look up. 'Secondly, I have total confidence in Ben. I've known him for years. He's technically excellent and a real performer. If anyone can step up to the plate it's him. In his last year at school he spent the winter playing football but he couldn't keep away from rowing and jumped in a boat as soon as the summer season started, rowing in the Hampton second eight with his friends. At the end of that season he went to GB junior trials for a laugh, ending up in the British eight at the World Championships which won a bronze medal. He is perfect for this. Let's go do it for Wayne and the rest of us, and win this race.'

Jim starts, his voice strained as he fights the lump in his throat. There are tears in his eyes. 'Wayne, I'm really, really sorry. I'm just glad you're alive. When I saw that ship come out at us I thought somebody was going to die.' I can see from the state of him that he really did. 'I'm just glad you're still here,' he says to Wayne and they embrace with emotion. They are still great friends.

'You've got ten men now,' says Rob. 'Wayne will be with you all the way and do everything he can do with you.'

Finally Wayne speaks, breaking his conspicuous silence. He is heroic. 'You guys go and win this. I don't want or need you guys crying on my shoulder. I don't think it's sunk in yet.'

I remember how it hit me when I walked into the doctor's surgery in Hamilton, New Zealand, all those months ago, on my first day in the country for a three-week rowing tour, to see them studying an X-ray of my shoulder. The collar bone was so obviously broken it almost felt like I'd been struck again. I had been totally gutted to miss that race, and that had been a regatta that meant almost nothing to me. Wayne came to Cambridge to race the Boat Race. What he must be feeling now, after enduring all the months of 6 a.m. starts, freezing weekends on the Fens, sacrifice and selection, is beyond comprehension. Only yesterday his family flew in from Canada to support him. I suppose at least they are nearby to comfort him.

Donald adds forcefully, 'Do not worry about Goldie.' It hasn't really hit me, but taking their strokeman, the key man in the stern of the boat who sets the rhythm, so shortly before the race is a massive blow. They are sacrificing one of their best and most vital crew members for us to go on. It can't all be in vain, surely. 'They are the reserve crew. That is their function. In 1962 the Cambridge president resigned from the Blue Boat the week before the race. A sub was brought in from Goldie. They won handily.' He reels off a handful of other cases of last-minute substitutions that went on to be winners. Don's a walking dictionary of Boat Race trivia.

I imagine how Matt will feel about suddenly seeing his little brother in the Cambridge eight the day prior to the Boat Race. If anyone knows, I do.

'Ben should room with David or Tom; he knows them best,' Rob points out, mistakenly swapping my brother's name for mine.

'Er . . . James,' I correct him. Everyone laughs out loud, breaking the tension.

'Oh God,' winces Wooge. 'This brothers thing is going to be unbearable.' There are now to be four brothers, all from Hampton School, competing in the race. Wait 100 years for the next set of brothers to follow the Etherington-Smiths and all of a sudden two pairs come along at once! It's a real first, no longer a first time in 100 years. If the race runs another 100 years it might never happen again. The manner Ben has come into the boat is a hack's delight, if not ours.

Robin, Rob and Don leave to pick up Ben from the Goldie house. The sooner he is with us, the sooner he'll become a part of the eight.

After they leave all is quiet. Gradually we begin to move around, watch TV and try to do normal things. All of us go up to Wayne individually and say a few words of consolation, as you would to the principal mourner at a funeral. It must be torture for him. Matze looks really heartbroken as he tries to console one of the best friends he has made this year. The German and the Canadian recognised similar strengths in each other and have become close friends. They make each other laugh. They are similar guys, but from very different backgrounds. I recall that Matze lost his grandfather earlier in the week; it has been a terrible few days for him. I just pray things won't get any worse.

David:

Friday 4 April 20:27, Hammersmith

After dinner most of us return to our crew room, our minds plagued by discussion of the crew charter – how we want to be remembered. In the end it always comes back to our tenacity and aggression as out-and-out racers. We'd pledged never to give in. To us it doesn't matter that no other crew in the race's history has ever overturned such a big weight disadvantage. Cambridge are there to be beaten.

Two such embodiments of this spirit are Bas and Scott, who finish an aggressive game of chess and then start on another one while I watch TV with Henry and Macca. I am growing more and more impatient. Maria should be arriving soon. I keep looking out through the bay windows, hoping to catch sight of her unmistakable, luminous yellow Volkswagen Polo.

I check my watch. She is already half an hour late, probably due to my poor directions. I can't wait to see her; I have missed her so much while off limits on training camp and my emotions are running high with the race so near. I have spoken to her most nights but it's just not the same as seeing her in person. I'm looking forward to spending time with her after the race, particularly the skiing trip to Meribel we've booked a couple of days after the big day.

Finally the doorbell rings. Charged with excitement, I jump off the sofa and stride into the corridor to answer the door. I can make out a blonde girl through the frosted sidelight of the large oak front door. It must be her!

'Hey!' she screams as I open the door.

I grab her in my arms and kiss her, lifting her off the floor. Then I pull back and look at her. She is stunningly beautiful and her beaming smile makes me immediately happy and carefree.

'How are you doing?' I ask her through my smile, elated by her presence.

'I'm really well. How are you?'

'Come upstairs,' I say, avoiding her question. I take her by the hand and lead her along the corridor to the sound of sniggering from Heather's TV room. They probably think I am about to break the pre-race sex ban but I just want us to be alone together. I lead her upstairs past all the old Boat Race photos and into my room, closing the door behind us. I embrace her again and kiss her for a few more seconds. 'So what have you been up to?' I ask her, collapsing on to my bed.

'Busy in Bristol as always. Maddie came up the other night and pulled a guy. You know the kind.'

'Oh no,' I chuckle knowingly. Maddie is notoriously indiscriminate.

'By the way, I have fixed myself up for Sunday. I'll meet up with Henry's girlfriend Kathryn to watch the race from Hammersmith.'

I look into her deep brown eyes and take her hands in mine. Although I'm so thrilled to see her, I can't stop thinking about the race.

'Maria, this race is going to be really tough. It is going to hurt like hell. Cambridge will not give up but I know if we row our best we can win it,' I say, aware I have completely changed the tone of the conversation. My feelings are laid bare. She squeezes my hand.

'You're such a great rower, Dave. So dedicated.' She knows only too well the sacrifices I've made for this.

She continues, 'I'm so confident in you but I'll be proud whatever happens. And just think, when it's all over we can go out and have fun.'

'I can't wait,' I say. But thinking beyond the race is unimaginable.

'I wanted to give you this,' she says, reaching into her bag. She brings out a decorated plate. 'I just wanted to wish you good luck,' she says, on the verge of tears. As I take the plate I feel the surprising weight of the large white and blue square china. I turn it over to reveal dark blue bold letters at the top of the plate saying, 'GOOD LUCK'. Underneath, two rowing crews are battling away, the dark blues leading the light blues.

'This is amazing, thank you so much,' I say, hugging her briefly, overwhelmed by the special effort she has put in to the gift. 'How did you make this?' I notice how unusual it feels to be smiling.

'I painted it in Bristol; there is one of those places where you can make your own pottery.'

'I didn't know you were such an artist.'

I lean closer to her to whisper, 'I love you.' She breaks into a smile.

'I love you too, Dave.' We fall onto the bed and I kiss her again. I can't wait till after Sunday.

James:

Of all the people you could choose to take on a Herculean task at the very last minute under enormous pressure, Ben Smith is surely the most laid back. After a few quiet hours, he arrives at the club house smiling the happy-go-lucky grin of one who knows that he can only do his best, and no one could ask for more. The atmosphere lifts wherever he goes.

At dinner we laugh and joke as best we can. Ben suggests this could be the subject of a great film; potentially better than *True Blue*, the movie about the Boat Race of 1987 and the famous Oxford mutiny. My brother can quote from it verbatim.

'Who'd play us, then?' I ask; a spot of entertainment is needed to raise everyone's spirits.

'Vin Diesel for Wayne, I think,' says Matze, grinning at his friend. This elicits a smirk from the otherwise downcast figure supping his soup with his good hand.

'Or the bald dude from *The Dirty Dozen*,' somebody else chips in.

'I think Groves could be that guy out of *Gladiator*,' I suggest, watching his face for a response. Just a hint of a smile plays across his saturnine features and his right eyebrow, the one with the ring through it, rises just slightly. If he wears it on race day it will be a Boat Race first, apparently. I wonder what the old Eton boys will make of that and the grade-two hair cut. 'And of course Young'un here could be Macaulay Culkin,' I say, gesturing to TJ, sitting next to me. Everyone laughs.

'No, no. He is too old now,' says Wooge in his guttural voice. 'The kid out of *The Sixth Sense* would be perfect.' More laughs, not least from TJ himself.

KC suggests that the hulkingly large Wooge should be played, not by an actor, but by Darth Vader from *Star Wars*. Images of Darth sitting on the start in his big black helmet keep us entertained through the main course of pasta and vegetables.

By dessert, we've decided that Paul Hogan as Crocodile Dundee would have to be KC, Groves having bagged the other well-known Aussie. Robin could be played perfectly by Kevin Spacey, we all agree, with his slight frame and scheming eyes.

Of course Spielberg would direct. 'But who'd play me?' I put to the table. 'I think Tom Cruise, stretched a bit, could do a decent job, or maybe Mel Gibson.'

'No way,' TJ says instantly. 'Hugh Laurie in Lieutenant George mode,' he grins at me. 'And he's an old Cambridge Blue.' There is a chorus of agreement. At least I'm a *Blackadder* fan.

Robin has quietly asked me to look after Ben. As he moves his stuff into room no. 7 to share with me, he is bubbling with nervous excitement. 'I was born for this moment,' he says, without a hint of complacency. It's a statement – no reply or further discussion required. There is no doubt in my mind, as I fall asleep, that if there is anyone who can handle the drama of having this thrust upon them, cope with the intense media attention and perform to their best in front of millions, it's Ben.

David:
Saturday 5 April 09:01, Westminster School Boathouse, Putney

The day before the race of our lives dawned three hours ago, without a cloud in the sky, and we are now beginning our final preparations in earnest. We stand in a semicircle to listen to Sean.

'OK, guys. Today we're going to row up to Hammersmith Bridge. Normal warm-up. On the way back we'll do three sets of thirty power strokes in fours. Then some all eight. From here on out we are building the intensity until the race. OK, let's go.'

Walking down the shingle to the water I'm very aware this is one of our last outings; better make it good.

Everyone must be thinking along similar lines, as the row starts well. We soon pass Hammersmith Bridge and decide to carry on up to Chiswick Eyot, a couple of kilometres further than expected. The boat is really flying, surging along between strokes. It feels great. This is what the sport is all about.

On the way back, the stern four cease rowing and the bow four begin their power strokes. With stern four sitting as deadweight, and balancing the boat, bow four can get a higher resistance on the end of the blade and develop maximum power. Technique goes out the window to an extent, as they pull with eye-popping effort.

I sit there, a passenger, as the boat powers along, joining the others in shouting encouragement.

'Yeah, John! Yeah, Bas! Let's see it!'

I can see them respond, making even bigger puddles of churned water after each stroke. Then it's my turn to unleash some of the bottled-up tension and frustration that has developed over the last two weeks. When we row all eight it's a bit rough, but fast. As we come to the end of the outing, I'm pleased with the morning's work and can't wait to race. We can win this.

Back at Heather's, Sean calls yet another meeting.

'I'll get straight to the point, guys. Wayne Pommen will not be taking part in this year's race. He fractured his wrist in yesterday's accident.'

I catch Henry's eye, both of us frowning, our faces screwed up in disbelief.

'Ben Smith will move up from Goldie to take his place at bow.' Eyes go even wider at this surprise.

I'm instantly hit by a bag of mixed emotions. I feel desperately sad for Wayne, whom I've met during his visits to our family home with my brother. Despite our different allegiances he seems like a good guy. He has trained too long not to take his place in the race.

However, I'm very happy for Ben, one of my best friends from school days. Then I remember his skill with an oar. I cut into the excited discussion.

'Let's not underestimate them. I rowed with Ben at school and he is a talented guy.'

Matt, Ben's brother, is silent. He looks torn. When Bas presses him on how he feels about racing his brother, he says simply, 'I've still got a job to do.'

The press have asked me over and over, 'How will you feel racing your brother?' and every time I've fobbed them off with an appropriate soundbite – it being a 'great honour' or my being 'really excited'. The truth is that I still haven't come to terms with racing against James. I don't know what I feel; the washing machine of emotions is too full and mixed for me to understand.

It is far easier to compete against a crew that you can make an object of hatred. Last year, with no family connections in the boat, it was easy to take the relatively benign features of the Goldie oarsmen and transform them into enemies we would love to vanquish.

This year it is much less simple. However, I have committed to achieving my dream and James and Ben can't stand in my way. I will deal with the consequences afterwards. Like Matt, I too have a job to do.

James:
Saturday 5 April 12:07, King's College School Boathouse, Putney

Down in Putney, Rob, the CUBC boatman, is helping Ben adjust the bow seat to his requirements, moving the foot plate further away from the seat to make room for Ben's longer legs. The height of the gate, the black plastic collar which holds the oar, is raised as well, to give him enough room round the finish of the stroke. That done, the eight rowers of the new Blue Boat jog a little way along the towpath to warm up, looking ridiculous running in wellies, but feeling a strong sense of togetherness. The cruelty of recent events has brought us even closer. Ben wears a Blue Boat all-in-one I've lent him. Everyone, not least Ben himself, is wondering, hoping and praying that he'll just slot into Wayne's empty seat and that we won't be any slower.

Out on the water, after letting Ben settle in for a few kilometres, we start going through our routine of race pace bursts and starts. During one burst Jim calls for the 'silent push', during which the boat lifts right out of the water and takes off, without apparent effort. As we wind down after the burst, Ben calls down, frustrated, 'OK, guys, you've got to fill me in on a few things.'

He is right, of course, and he continues to shout down to Jim, as we stop.

'I mean, in the race you can't just go, "Silent push, GO!" and then whisper, "OK, Ben, a silent push is . . ."' Matze and Hugo, the nearest to him, turn and explain as best they can our special calls and moves to him. It is fortunate that he's been around us enough to know our culture, the way we do things, and only the nitty-gritty of calls need explaining. The rest of the bursts are excellent despite the press launch sitting closer on our stern than ever. Between them Wayne offers some useful comments from the coaching launch.

I feel a sense of relief when we get off the water. One disaster has happened and there is nothing that can be done about it now. Another seems to have been averted. We all knew that if the crew hadn't worked with the substitution, well, that would have been it. Game over, good night. Try to put up a fight in the race and commiserate at the dinner later on.

After the session, I walk back up the stairs of the boathouse and turn to look at the quiet Thames. It is difficult to imagine the river banks, empty now bar the odd jogger or mother pushing a pushchair – packed with hundreds of thousands of people tomorrow. The flotilla of launches that will roar off behind us is equally hard to visualise now, as the empty Thames meanders slowly past on its journey to the sea.

I turn back and head through the doors into the boathouse and spot Breck avidly reading a newspaper. When he looks up at me he avoids my gaze and his eyes flick back to the paper.

'What'ya reading there, Breck?' I ask, walking round and squinting over his shoulder. My photograph stares back at me from the *Telegraph* sports section.

'You probably don't want to read this, Bungle,' Breck says as he watches my facial expression. It is a great photo, I have to give them that. One from last year's race, after the finish. Seb Mayer is lying back prostrate across my legs, with his arms over his head. I'm sitting hunched, my right hand on the gunwale of the boat and the other gripping my oar. My eyes are staring up towards the sky. I'm trying to ignore the crowds on Chiswick Bridge, the nine dark Blues whooping with delight in their nearby boat and the semi-conscious German lying across my legs, mumbling 'Scheisse, Scheisse' over and over. I'm looking for escape but there is none.

I take the paper from Breck, who hands it over without further comment. Alongside the photo is an article, written by Tim Foster, part of the Sydney gold medal four, commenting on Ben's last-minute substitution. Part of it says, 'If the greatest ever oarsman subbed into the Cambridge boat now it would only go slower for it, being such a finely tuned machine, with so little time to readjust.' The awful thing is I know he is right. I knew it before I read the article.

But I also know we that we are still damn quick and that Ben has a sort of magic about him, making things work when they shouldn't, most of all rowing boats. We might have slowed down fractionally but we are still faster than Oxford. I just know it.

Chapter 11
The Race

David:

Sunday 6 April 03:48, Hammersmith

My watch glints green in the darkness. 3.48 a.m. I'm awake, listening to the sound of John's heavy breathing, metronome perfect. How can he sleep so deeply? Is he not nervous? Closing my eyes, I try to still my mind but racing scenarios flash through it, one after another. Every race in the 148 preceding years has played out differently, with sinkings, collisions, crushing defeats and agonisingly tight victories – what will ours hold? Will we lead off the start? What if the two boats collide? What if I sleep through the practice row?

Last night, when Matt had issued the summons, 'Let's go, boys, a tradition needs to be fulfilled,' we strode unquestioningly out of Heather's into the dark night. Ahead of us Hammersmith Bridge loomed, illuminated. Halfway across the bridge, I turned to look down at the murky water. I had never felt emotionally close to a river. Would she look after us? Give us her fastest currents?

'OK, boys, the time has come,' Matt called from the other side of the bridge. 'This is our lucky tradition from last year, it HAS to be done.' With that said he unzipped his flies and began to urinate off the bridge into the sacred river below. Rather self-consciously, we all joined in, fully hydrated from drinking pint after pint of water. It was like a sacrifice to the river gods, though perhaps not one they'll hugely appreciate.

John and I walked back together. We were in last year's winning Isis crew and this year we've pushed each other along in training. John's father, Peter, has very thoughtfully sent me several letters of encouragement throughout the year.

'Isn't it strange, John,' I'd said, 'Twenty-four hours from now, we will either have won or lost the Boat Race. I can't believe it's almost over.'

John turned to me. 'It has been an incredible journey. The outcome is in God's hands. All we can do is our best.'

John is a very committed Christian, and places considerable faith in God. I also feel there is an element of destiny in tomorrow's race.

It's certainly helping John sleep.

David:

Sunday 6 April 06:29, Hammersmith

6.29 a.m. The day has finally come, 6 April. I've never felt so alive at this time of the morning, instantly electrified with excitement and ultra-conscious of every muscle and taut sinew in my body.

Downstairs I can hear Heather and her team of helpers preparing our first breakfast. The routine we have practised over the previous two weeks begins afresh.

I bump into Bas at the bottom of the stairs.

'Morning, Bas.'

'Hi, Dave, how are you this morning?' He hails me cheerily, his speech a little faster than normal.

'Feeling well, if a bit nervous,' I admit. He nods in agreement with a pained smile. In the kitchen we join our drawn-looking president, Matt, who is obviously trying to set an example by his punctuality.

I fill up a sizeable bowl of Shreddies and a glass of apple juice, as the guys filter in to join us. The stark contrast between our usual noisy banter and the suffocating quiet now filling the room is all too clear. Everyone is internalising their various conflicting thoughts and emotions concerning the day ahead.

We are all proudly wearing the OUBC Race Day kit. Today we earn the highest sporting honour of our university, the Oxford Blue. Only a select number of sports are eligible and a Blue can be awarded only in competition against Cambridge. It doesn't matter if you are the first team in every other competition that year, it is the Oxford–Cambridge match that counts. To be awarded the rowing Blue you must pass the Fulham Wall, about two minutes down the course. The cruelty of sinking would be doubled if it happened before that point. Thankfully sinking conditions were not forecast, and bar disaster, we will become Blues and a lifelong part of university sporting history and tradition. Even if we lose.

7:15 a.m. According to our schedule it's time to go for our warm-up outing. When we arrive, I notice that, despite the TV cameras, barriers, flags and banners that have been erected, there is almost no one here. It feels a bit like any other day down at the river bank at Putney.

We row off to do our regular warm-up, but it doesn't feel normal. The usually neat and coordinated movement of the oars is shaky this morning, which only serves to make everyone even more jittery.

After we finish our first practice start Sean pulls up next to us in the launch. He's been quiet all outing, knowing today is up to us. 'Guys, how was it?' he enquires.

'Yeah, OK,' says Henry.

'OK is for practice. Today we race. Let's go for it! Lose your inhibitions.'

I sit forward for the second practice start and just know it is going to be fantastic. We fly off the start with the rate at 49 strokes a minute. It's beautiful. When we stop at the end of the Putney embankment, I see some of the Cambridge rowers have been watching from their boat-house balcony. 'Watch and learn, boys. This is what is coming today!' I say under my breath.

James:

Sunday 6 April 11:05, King's College School Boathouse, Putney

After the final warm-up outing I bump into the Goldie cox, Ellie, sitting on the steps up to the boat house, still in her coxing gear of lifejacket, cap and waterproofs. She looks sad and withdrawn; we have stolen Ben from her Goldie crew at the last minute. The coaches have brought in Andy Smith from the spare pair and reshuffled Goldie, with the determined American Nate now at stroke. Ellie's body language is defiant; she won't give an inch to Isis.

'How do you feel, in your heart of hearts?' she asks me, her eyes betraying her own emotions. I return her gaze and think for the briefest of seconds, to make sure I really believe what I am about to say.

'I still believe we can win.'

She smiles, clearly glad that the sacrifice of her vital strokeman is not going to be in vain.

Andy Smith bounds up the stairs past us, wearing his new Goldie kit, giving us a cheery 'hi'. After all that slog in the spare pair he's now at least getting a row on the big day.

Heading back to the minibus, I stop to look at the river. It's no different from any other day. A jogger passes, then a couple with their dog. I notice a couple of men putting railings out but I wonder whether they'll be needed. There's no one here. Maybe no one will turn up? We can just race our hearts out privately.

James:

Sunday 6 April 12:35, The Bank of England Club, London

'James!' Sam sounds surprised.

'Hey.' I say. I'm sitting on my bed, staring at the trees out of the window, assessing the breeze.

'Is everything OK? I didn't expect you to call today.'

'I just wanted to hear your voice,' I reply. In the background I can hear the babble of conversation. 'Who are you with?'

'I'm at KCS.' Our boathouse, which is putting on a reception for our friends and family. 'Your mum and dad are here. And your headmaster. Your uncle and aunt are talking to my parents.'

'Is Mum OK?'

'She's a bit quiet.'

There's a knock at my door and TJ pops his head round. 'Lunch is up,' he says.

'Got to go, babe, I love you.'

'So much luck! You'll be fantastic.'

'Thanks. I love you.' And I ring off.

James:

Sunday 6 April 13:40, The Bank of England Club, London

We assemble outside our lodgings for the last time, next to the coach that will take us down for the race, decked out in identical blue jackets and carrying our bags, which we have all fastidiously packed, repacked and packed again.

'Good thing you're the same size as Wayne, hey?' I nod to Ben quietly as we board, his top fitting him perfectly. He smiles back, looking humble but nervous and obviously thanking his lucky stars for this chance.

Disappointingly, the police escort is late, and Robin makes the decision to start our final journey from the Bank of England Club to Putney without it. The atmosphere is tense and on the bus each of us is lost in thought. Someone hands a tape to the driver. The *Gladiator* soundtrack rises out of the speakers.

Russell Crowe calls out, 'Brothers! Three weeks from now, I will be harvesting my crops. Imagine where you will be and it will be so. Hold the line! Stay with me! If you find yourself alone, riding in green fields with the sun on your face, do not be troubled for you are in Elysium and you're already dead!' His cavalrymen laugh with him. Wooge, TJ, Matze and the others – these are the men I'm going into battle with. They are my brothers now. I feel I would die for each of them.

'Brothers,' Russell Crowe calls again, 'What we do in life . . . Echoes in eternity.'

The result of this race will be gilded on to the ceiling of the Captains' Room. Long after I'm dead Cambridge students will look up, read our names and the word above them. Won or Lost.

I vow to myself: this is only fifteen minutes of my life. I will give it everything. I will offer myself up and go through the white hot pain. It won't kill me, but even if it does, better that than fail my brothers.

When we arrive at Putney, the coach is stopped by the police as we turn on to the river bank; apparently they've got to keep it clear for the Boat Race crews. Martin puts his head out the door and gives the officer an ear-bashing. By some bizarre quirk of fate they recognise each other. It seems they attended the same tiny primary school in Ireland. We're waved through to strains of, 'What are the chances of that . . . small world!'

The packed crowds on the embankment stare at our coach and wave, cheer or boo. I wave back solemnly, slightly shocked that people have turned up. As we get off the coach at our boathouse, a huge cheer goes up and we climb the stairs to rapturous applause.

We walk through the function room to our changing room to heartfelt applause from our family and friends. On the way through Dad pats me on the shoulder. His tie is half light blue, half dark blue, I notice. Mum wishes me luck, looking ashen. Sam mouths, 'I love you.' On the way through, my gaze meets that of my old Hampton School headmaster. He gives a simple thumbs-up.

David:

Sunday 6 April 14:01, Hammersmith

I close the door behind me as we leave Heather's house. We will return either as winners to champagne or as decimated losers; either way we'll soon be commemorated on her walls.

I climb into a free seat in the minibus. Sean's driving today. BT in the front seat pushes in the tape he's prepared specially – songs interspersed with Boat Race commentary and quotes. It's the start of our psyche-up.

The pounding beat of Eminem's 'Lose Yourself' begins and my emotions surge. This is my one shot, my one opportunity. Can I capture it? I think back through our season: my experiences at the Fours Head, Trial Eights and against Leander. Our run down from Wittenham Clumps. It has all led to this.

Crossing Barnes Common I look out of the window. A couple walk arm in arm with some shopping bags; for them it is a normal day. For me, three-thirty is the end of my life.

Now Moby's 'My Weakness' echoes around the bus. Then it cuts to old Oxford president Dan Snow.

'This race means everything. I know that if we lose this race, it will all have been for nothing.'

Moby's sombre tones resume. There is no chatter in the bus. Today each of us struggles with the myriad internal thoughts, doubts and hopes.

We turn on to the Putney embankment. People everywhere.

This is it, 600 strokes of back-breaking effort, for the whole year, for the other eight guys who have come on this incredible journey. It is coming to the end; the one and only definition of the entire year, more in fact, of my life to date. Finally I am ready. I reach up and wipe away the tears with my sleeve.

David:

Sunday 6 April 15:45, Westminster School Boathouse, Putney

John stands, a solitary figure looking out of the window of the boathouse changing rooms. He seems eerily relaxed. The rest of us are stretching or just sitting on blue mats placed on the floor. Bas is in one of his usual improbable stretching positions, making the rest of us feel inadequate. The ever-intense Scott, who never believed in stretching anyway, listens to his iPod, nodding along to the rhythm of the music. You could hear a pin drop.

Sean breaks the silence as he enters the room. His sharp features are accentuated by his race-day frown.

'Guys, let's run through the race plans for both stations one more time before the coin toss.' Headphones come out and everyone tunes in to him. 'You can think of the race as a series of rounds, roughly six equal ones. First of all, secure yourself against defeat,' he pauses. 'Get out of the start clean and fast. Our first big effort is around two minutes in, as you come to the first bend and Cambridge begin to settle their pace down. Keep moving there at 37 strokes a minute; that's our race rate. That marks the end of the first round.' Such intensity has never before been attempted over the entire course. Only a few years ago it would have been thought impossible.

Acer chips in, 'The phrase I'll use to trigger our push at two minutes will be "smell the fear", boys.' It's a reference to the comment made by Tim Wooge, the Cambridge president, at the weigh-in on Wednesday.

Sean continues, 'To win the race, you have to either win more rounds than them, or deliver a knockout blow. Don't be fooled. It will be a close race but I believe you will win. You have done the training; you can go the whole way.' He then reminds us what each bend is worth on each station – where we have to attack and where we have to defend. I visualise each sweep of the river.

'I've just got one thing to add, says Acer. 'The most important call will be the "1963" call.'

'1963' refers to the year a crew as light as us last won the Boat Race. Appropriately it was an Oxford crew. He continues, 'If I call it, we will be in a situation where the race will be lost in the next 30 seconds if we don't make something happen. It's pretty drastic. We'll need to respond with a huge push to save the race. When we put our heads up after the move I may have the dubious privilege of having to call it again. As you know though, unless we stop Cambridge breaking clear at that point the race is effectively over.'

The thought of being in a losing position petrifies me and ties my gut in knots. I desperately hope I will never hear the '1963' call. If I do, I'll throw in everything. And if that can't get us back on terms we'll be dead in the water.

James:
Sunday 6 April 15:47, King's College School Boathouse, Putney

Robin brings us together in a huddle before we step outside. 'Guys, remember we're all nervous today. Those nerves will help you deliver your best. Use them in a positive way. Imagine the crowd are here for your birthday, or that you're a rock star about to go on stage. Good nerves.'

With that we walk out of the doors of King's College School Boathouse on to the Cambridge light blue carpet to the sound of cheers. We are led through the packed crowd by girls dressed in the sponsor's corporate colours. We make our way to the wooden podium for the traditional coin toss for stations; hundreds of familiar faces line our route. It's like everyone I've ever met is here – rowers, Cambridge students, school friends and their parents. Everyone is wearing or waving their colours of allegiance, in the form of scarves, caps, rosettes, badges or placards. The general buzz, enthusiasm and yelling from the crowd make our already nervous hearts soar. I greedily drink in the scene.

'Go, Cambridge!'

'Kill 'em, Cambridge!'

Even the occasional, 'Go, James!'

By the time we reach the podium, we have left pure light blue territory behind.

David:
Sunday 6 April 15:48, Putney embankment

In one line from stroke to bow we walk out into the crowds and a massive cheer goes up. The nerves which I'd begun to get under control resurface quickly. I know why all these people are here. They are here to see one crew, their crew, win, and the other publicly humiliated. Out of the corner of my eye I spot Maria, but I don't stop to speak.

Cambridge are already lined up on the podium as we climb on to it. It is the first time I have been up close to them since the weigh-in. James stands among them as well as my old friend Ben Smith, now taking Wayne's place. Their expressions are, to a man, relaxed; some are even smiling. Our boys look grim-faced, etched with fear and aggression. I try not to look at James; we are not brothers today. We are enemies.

James:
Sunday 6 April 15:48, Putney embankment

Dave looks pinched and pale, and doesn't meet my eye. For a second I feel as if I want to go up and hug my little brother and tell him it will all be OK, but I dispel the urge as quickly as it arises. As I look along their line I see that all their faces are tense tight as a drum.

I look over my shoulder and up the river. A blustery north wind blows into my face, from Hammersmith towards us and Putney Bridge. That will mean a solid headwind for the first half of the course, with rough water whipped up by the wind blowing against the incoming flow of the tide. Ideal for our weight advantage. Oxford will be blown away by the conditions. We will roll over them like a tank.

A boom-mounted camera swings past and brings me back from my thoughts. The presidents now stand together in the middle of the podium with their backs to the crews, Matt once again dwarfed by the colossal Wooge. The BBC anchorman, Steve Rider, manoeuvres them into a more eye-catching shot, and in the move, Matt is positioned much nearer to us than to his own troops. Groves, to my right, on the other side of young Tom, mutters maliciously, a slight smile on his face, 'Wouldn't want to be a-stone-a-man down and race into *this* headwind.'

I can't help myself and my controlled, impassive stare breaks into a smile. The comment was loud enough for Matt to hear, he is no further away than I am; but if he did his solid, high-shouldered posture gives no indication. But then he couldn't stiffen any further without the insertion of an external object.

Steve Rider produces the 1829 gold sovereign, which only narrowly survived last year's event. It rolled off the stage following the toss, and would have certainly continued down the concrete embankment and into the flowing Thames had it not been for some speedy footwork by Rider. The big gold coin, with 170 years of Boat Race history attached, is handed to Matt, who flips it into the air, stony-faced. No signs of the easy-going and awful bass guitar player of our teenage band days.

Wooge calls, 'Tails,' as it flashes into the air.

It clatters to the ground, gold-emblazoned leaves glittering upwards. We'd laughed about the old saying 'tails never fails' a few minutes before.

'Tails it is. Cambridge to choose.'

'Cambridge choose Surrey,' states Wooge flatly. It's good news, we'll have the big Surrey Bend in our favour, unlike last year.

Our allocated stations mean Cambridge's bowside will clash with the Oxford strokeside. Ben and I will duel with our brothers' oars. If there is a clash, which is likely, and one of us knocks the oar out of the other's hands, losing them the race, we are all well aware what that could mean for the family. I well remember Dave's humiliation and seething anger after Oxford's fixture with Leander.

A couple of minutes later we're in a new holding pen, the industrial greyness of the London Rowing Club's gym. Goldie's white hooded tops, with light blue lettering glittering on chests, seem all the brighter in the dim light. Busch is listening to his music, head moving to the beat, eyes staring at the concrete floor, oversized earphones covering oversized ears. Wayne sits at one side, arm in a sling. In one corner, Andrew Shannon and Nate perform their own bizarre warm-up routine to placate their old back injuries. This time as they rotate, twist and dip like dervishes, no one takes the mickey.

I'm in another corner, bouncing on the balls of my feet, facing the wall. I was already stretching before the toss and after this morning's outing – it was as good a way of killing time as any. I'm already loose. Now I start punching and jabbing at the air, lightly, quickly shifting my weight from foot to foot. 'Killing in the Name' by Rage Against the Machine is on repeat in my headphones.

I mouth the words, 'Fuck you, I won't do what you tell me. Fuck you, I won't do what you tell me,' silently as I continue shaking my legs out and easing the shoulders off. The base, animal fear is under control now, but still bubbling away in the background. Excitement and adrenalin have taken over.

Goldie, who are due to race half an hour before us, are called to boat up by a grave-faced Donald, who wishes us luck before turning to leave. There are hurried embraces and quiet words between the crews, all CUBC brothers.

'See you on the other side, man. Good luck.'

'Let's go do this thing.'

'A few hours from now we'll be drinking champagne together.'

As the crews exchange words I catch Ellie's eye, give her a thumbs-up and nod. I think of us this time last year.

She nods back. Her eyes are wide and white. She knows Goldie have the toughest job of any boat out there. Her desperate dream of winning the race looks bleak now we've taken Ben. But she'll go down fighting.

After they leave I walk into the erg room with Tom and Ben, sit on one of the accursed machines and pull a few casual strokes. My splits are superb for what feels like no effort at all; adrenalin has done its work. I watch my technique in the mirror as I push up to race pace, driving the legs, levering the back.

To my right, Tom and Ben complete a few strokes on the rowing tank, checking their technique and finding no flaws. I feel ready and at peace. All doubts have been worried over a thousand times and are dismissed by the logical antidotes I've developed for them. Walking back into the gym, I notice that even Wooge, not normally a man for warming up, is jumping up and down, loosening up his massive legs and getting ready to race.

First Robin reminds us of the strengths and drawbacks of our Surrey station, and what each bend is worth, before taking us through our key technical focuses and our race plan.

He finishes, 'Jim will call our big move between Fulham and the Mile Post. That's where we stamp our authority on this race. Oxford look scared today. There is no life in their eyes. I've seen them race and they'll bash it along with you for a while but they don't have your horsepower and over the four miles that will tell.'

The gruff Irish voice of Martin picks up where Robin stops. 'Take the race by the scruff of the neck; don't let them harry you.' It is comforting to think that he must have said similar words, in a similar pre-race brief, to the British Olympic eight before they took to the water in Sydney to win gold.

David:

Sunday 6 April 15:52, Westminster School Boathouse, Putney

'Ten minutes till hands on,' says Acer. Sean stands up from his chair and begins to shake the crew's hands, whispering a few quiet personal words to each of us in turn. This simple gesture signifies that Sean's job as a coach is done; he cannot do anything more for us now.

I shake his wiry hand firmly.

'Have a good one, Dave. Follow stern pair and set it up for the guys behind you. You can win this.'

'Thanks, Sean, I will.' My old distrust of Sean has finally given way to respect, even admiration. He's helped me prepare for this great opportunity.

He leaves Matt to the end. Together they have led and shaped this team.

'Final piss,' says Acer,

Once everyone has made a precautionary visit to the toilet, we meet downstairs in the ominously quiet boat bay.

'Bring it together,' BT says crisply and we huddle. Bas grips my left shoulder tightly, John the right.

'Here it is,' BT states, 'finally the day we've been waiting for. We've got a job to do today, boys. People think we are going to get destroyed. We're more than a stone a man lighter, we're younger, less experienced, weaker. I don't give a shit!' He's nearly shouting now. 'You saw Cambridge at the coin toss; they think they are in for a fucking easy ride. Well, they're in for a big surprise when they see just how fast we are. There is no way they are going to take this race from us.' I believe utterly in BT's call to arms.

'Look into each other's eyes,' he continues.

I look around at my friends. They look back. I see excitement, fear, adrenalin and aggression. Most of all I see eight others willing to sacrifice everything to win this race.

'Let's get out there and win this for each other,' he finishes.

The huddle breaks and we give each other a quick hug and a word of encouragement. This bond that has developed between us is so strong, and I cannot and will not let these guys down, like I did against Leander.

Daylight pours back into the boathouse as the wooden doors are pulled open, revealing our inner sanctum to the outside world. 'It's time to go,' says Sean gently, not wanting to intrude on the private moment.

'Let's get hands on, guys,' says Acer. I take hold of the gunwale of the pristine yellow boat and lift it on to my shoulder in synchrony with the others. We walk out of the darkness and into the light.

Crunch! The boat comes to an abrupt halt as carbon fibre hits wood. Unbelievably we've rammed a rigger of our precious boat into the door. Acer and Sean scurry to inspect it, looking absolutely petrified. Luckily no damage is done. The crowd noise explodes as we come into full view, stepping on to the dark blue carpet that stretches down to the river. I stare straight ahead. The sheer number of people is overwhelming. We gingerly place the boat on the water and with Sean holding on to it, we stride back into the boat bay to be individually introduced for the BBC coverage. Inside, we just have time for a few words with each other before we go out in seat order.

'John, have a good one,' I say patting him on the back as he picks up his carbon-fibre oar.

'You too, Dave. You too.' Enough has been said already. After all, we've practised each stroke thousands of times, hours of training for each one.

Steve Rider's familiar voice booms out of the loudspeakers outside. 'At bow, from University College, John Adams.' John strides out confidently and the crowd go wild. I close my eyes and take some deep breaths.

My turn quickly arrives. I pick up the number six oar, my trusty weapon that I will take into this battle. 'At six, from Christ Church, David Livingston!' I walk out into the mayhem of cheers and yelling. This whole circus is just a distraction from my job today. Through the general noise I hear Dad. 'Good luck, Dave,' he says and I hear it clear as a bell.

James:

In the KCS boat bay the dark metallic cyclops eye of the BBC camera strapped on to our boat's stern stares at us. We exchange a few quiet words, particularly between those guys at opposite ends of the boat who won't get a chance to communicate before the start. I put my hand on Matze's shoulder and grin at him, and he grins back. I know he'll never, ever give up, rib injury or otherwise. One of the toughest rowers I've met and one of the most modest. I'd only found out two weeks ago that he was among the select few who had beaten Steve Redgrave in international competition.

Rob snaps up the steel roller shutters and the entire world stares back at us. As in every other outing, Jim calls the boat up and we carry it down to the water, but this time it's to the whooping of a madly cheering throng. Sam has got to the front of the packed crowd, and my eyes are drawn to her. I wink at her and smile. It's great to have her here.

While we return for our oars, Rob and Wayne hold the boat steady in a couple of feet of water, the latter one-handed and stern-faced. A man from the BBC shepherds us out of the boathouse one by one, Ben first. Lining up behind each other, before walking out into the daylight, it feels as if we're waiting to go over the top. One by one out we go, oar in hand, Barry Davies giving mini biographies of each of us to those watching live on TV. My turn comes. I'm carrying two water bottles with me, one empty, and this draws a couple of knowing guffaws from the experienced oarsmen in the crowd. It doesn't do to be caught short during the warm-up.

I pass Sam again; another huge smile. Dad is buzzing around with his cameras, having waved some sort of press pass. Oars are snapped in and locked into their gates; we chuck our wellies to the bank, and, relieved to be on the water, push off into the stream. We're free of land and that feels good, back in our element. After a few strokes from stern four, Jim calls us to easy. He's leaning way out of the boat, looking around the vast silhouette of Wooge.

'I need that boat moved now!' he screams at a stationary boat blocking the normal route under Putney Bridge. Our warm-up is timed to the minute, and as the race start time is set in stone for TV, any disruption will be very detrimental to performance. The rowers remain silent. A debate isn't the answer, it's Jim's call.

He manoeuvres us precisely between two parked boats, out across the river, and we row in front of Isis and Goldie sitting on their stakeboats, ready to race before us. Cutting in front of them is a bold decision. Jim could so easily have lost his nerve after the crash.

'OK, guys,' Jim's voice comes calmly through the cox box as we row under Putney Railway Bridge. 'Just tune into my voice and the sound of the boat. Fade everything else out. We're on our way, boys.'

It's a sublime experience to row and be able to do something about making the boat go faster. At each stroke my internal coach is commenting, 'That's it, draw the finish. Lift the hands earlier coming into the front end. Squeeze the legs. Good.' I lose myself in the rowing and the race seems an eternity away.

David:
Sunday 6 April 16:23, The start

The noise at the start is deafening and intrusive. Cambridge sit to my right. The TV helicopter thunders above us, engine straining to hover on the spot. Behind, Putney Bridge is packed with people with a great grandstand view of the start. Close to the stakeboats, moored boats full of hospitality guests peer out of tinted windows. A river-wide flotilla of launches, inflatable ribs, cruisers, with their complements of coaches, journalists, press photographers, Old Blues, relatives and girlfriends, are bobbing around, all in their pre-allocated positions. The boats are constantly revving up, getting ready for the off. They too had a practice start yesterday, to avoid lane-changing or clashes in their eagerness to get a good view.

Needing to get the boat aligned correctly, Acer joins in the cacophony, 'Bas, hold water. That's enough.'

His microphone crackles on seconds later, 'John, hold water. Stop. That's fine. Race kit, guys.' We each pass water bottles, T-shirts and leggings down the boat to the stakeboat boy. We want no excess weight.

I take a look around and see Bas staring back at himself on the huge outdoor television screen on the north bank. Then I look over at James.

One of us will win this race. I will do absolutely everything to make sure it is me.

Acer interrupts my thoughts. 'Bas, hold water. One minute till the start.'

BT, in the seat behind me, grabs my tense shoulders. 'Yeah, Dave, let's go for this one,' he says. I turn slightly and grab his legs in acknowledgement. I know he will be there, pulling as hard as he can, for every single stroke of this race.

Henry in front turns around and we link hands, a gesture of solidarity. We all have our individual motivations. I could not be more proud to represent my college, my university, but above all I am thinking of these eight other guys. I could not face seeing them destroyed by a defeat.

James:

Sunday 6 April 16:27, The start

I snatch a quick look across to Oxford and see Dave's blond mop. He is focussed on his boat so our eyes don't meet. I'm glad.

On the Cambridge launch behind, Robin cups his hands and shouts over the din of the crowd, 'Goldie are going to do it! Leading Isis by four lengths at the Bandstand!' He's over the moon and my heart lifts. I manage a smile. They've done it! God knows how, but they've done it! It's reassuring that they've beaten Isis despite their loss of Ben. I think of Ellie's eyes this morning and I'm happy for her, JA, Nate, Andy Smith, Shannon, Buschbacher and the rest of them. They'd lost all hope and clawed back to victory despite everything. Surely this is a good omen for us.

The umpire stands up in his launch and the world stands still.

'Oxford, Cambridge,' he says slowly and clearly through his mega-phone, addressing each boat solemnly in turn. 'Get ready, please.'

This is it. I turn to young Tom behind me and tap his feet.

'Let's go, mate.' I smile at the nineteen-year-old, trying to generate an air of confidence, as he returns my glance and nods. Looking past Tom I catch Groves's eye and nod to him. He nods darkly back.

I turn to face the stern and Tim rotates to give me his oversized hand. I squeeze it hard and tell him, 'Let's go, mate. I'll back you up all the way.'

I don't want him to feel isolated in the stroke seat. He needs to know we'll follow him to hell and back before breaking.

We sit forward, arms outstretched, ready to go. Both coxes' hands are up, signalling to the umpire that the crews are not ready. We have got to get the perfect line out of Putney.

'Square it up, Matze.' The bow pulls round towards Oxford as Matze squares his blade and braces himself against the streaming water. 'OK, relax. My hand is still up. Ben, tap it.' The bows slew back towards the line of boats on Putney bank.

Wooge sits still, projecting an aura of complete relaxation. His inside hand is loose on his oar, occasionally scratching his face or realigning his sunglasses. I make a conscious effort to follow his lead and exude a similar level of calm.

I now feel ready. I remind myself I can only perform to my maximum potential, no one else's. First stroke. Just think about the first stoke. Not too long. First stroke. No ripping, just take up the pressure and press long.

The TV helicopter's rotors whir above us. I hate that noise. Bad associations.

'OK, Ben, hold it.' Ben squares up his blade and the boat swings again. 'OK, we're straight. My hand is coming down. My hand is down. Oxford's hand is up. Relax. OK, boys this is it. We're ready.' First stroke. Just the first stroke. Squeeze it off.

'My hand is up.' Jim calls breathlessly, his hand rocketing upwards.

'Matze. Hold it just a little. OK. My hand is down. His hand is down. We're ready.'

David:
Sunday 6 April 16:29, The start

I have visualised this moment for years. Just concentrate on the first stroke. Long and patient, don't rip it.

Acer's hand shoots into the air to warn the umpire that we're not ready. 'My hand is up. Bas, hold water.' The boat straightens. 'OK, hand coming down, now.'

The wind pushes us round again. 'Bas, hold water.' Every second seems like an hour. 'OK, hand down.' We listen for starter's orders.

'ATTENTION . . . GO!' the megaphone booms.

'DRRAAWWWW!' screams Acer as I squeeze my blade into the water. The crowd erupts. Engines roar from the flotilla behind. Someone has just twisted the volume knob from one to ten and beyond.

'Build . . . NOW!' Acer calls. We're away quick and clean. Cameras flash on all sides.

'Full length. Go!' he shouts, but he's barely audible. The boat is really flying. Out of the corner of my eye I notice we're level with Cambridge.

'Forty-seven, we're on the rate, boys, that's good!' He's quiet for two strokes. 'Length, ready, go!' I compress my legs further to get a longer reach. So far, so good.

'That's it, boys, we're on our rhythm.' My breathing is short and fast. The pain builds.

The umpire waves his flag. 'Oxford! Cambridge! Move apart!' he shouts. Acer puts on his rudder slightly, steering us apart very gradually but keeping us in the main line of the stream.

'That's good, boys. Lever the backs into the headwind,' he calls. I open my back out more forcefully against the push of my legs. My whole being is assaulted by noise, movement and pain.

Cambridge veer towards us.

'Blades close,' screams Acer as he fights for the best water. I glance at my blade. Cambridge oars scissor past a foot away from mine. I flashback to the Leander fixture.

Fuck, I'm not going to lose it this time.

'Acer, Jim, move apart!' Boris shouts again from the umpire's launch, gesticulating with his flag.

Lactate sears through my veins from the sprint start. Neither crew has taken a lead. We're punching through the headwind as well as them so far.

'One minute 15 seconds. Rhythm, ready . . . GO!' calls Acer. Matt drops the rating down a gear and we glide further between each stroke. It's a marginally more sustainable pace. The black buoy flashes past. Now we've left the crowds at Putney behind us. We're edging ahead.

'Yeah, boys, 38 on the rate. That's good. Two seats up on Cambridge.' I'm deep in pain territory. Normal crews would settle much lower, 38 would be considered insane, but we need to harry them, put them under pressure.

I can hear their cox spurring his guys on. This is a crucial point for us; we must seize our early advantage on the inside of the Fulham bend.

James:
Sunday 6 April, Black buoy, boats level

'Hands up! Hands up! Hands up!' Jim calls in rhythm as we reach the front of the stroke. We lift our hands as one, spearing the oars into the water.

The noise of the crowd, the screaming of the coxes, the bawling of the umpire and the rhythmic but frantic thunking of the oars all overload our senses. Usually, two minutes after the start the pain hits, as the body desperately tries to deal with the initial sprint, but adrenalin has flooded all our systems and we are running on that magical fuel. We got off to a clean, fast start, big Tim leading us with an agility of movement belying his size. I could sense Oxford scrambling to grab an initiative, but we've taken back their initial two-seat advantage. We're level.

'Yeah, Cambridge, we're on our rhythm. Backs for ten. Go. Backs BACK, backs BACK, backs BACK,' Jim barks in time with each stroke. The grey hulk of Fulham Football Ground hovers on the edge of my vision to my left. We've come into a great rhythm.

'Defend the bend. Push, ready, go! Now! Thirty-seven. Sit Up. Sit Up. And LEGS. Legs. Legs. That's it,' Jim barks as we squeeze on, upping our effort into the Fulham bend. 'Here we come. Yeah, that's it.' The rough water drags at the boats and blades, and sprays across us. Oxford, on the inside, start to creep up and Jim turns the rudder to cut into them.

'Cambridge to Surrey! Cambridge to Surrey!' the umpire bellows through his megaphone over the roar of the crowd.

'Yeah, they're off their line, boys,' Jim screams proudly, happily ignoring the umpire's warning to him. Our blades clash. I grip my oar and duel with Matt, at stroke. They're a few feet up. My lungs already feel as though they're beginning to fill with battery acid and I can taste metal in my mouth.

'Good. Good solid rhythm here. Staying right on it. Staying right on it. And spring off, spring off.'

David:
Fulham Bend, boats level

We come to the the apex of the Fulham bend. We're out of the start phase and into the second round.

'Smell the fear, boys, in two,' a stroke passes, 'in one,' another stroke, 'GO!!' Another wave of adrenalin floods my system. I'll give it 20 to hurt that arrogant German.

'I'm taking the turn. And we're moving on them.' The first advantage in the course is ours. We're going to use it to put them on the ropes.

I lean even more weight on to the oar, and push my legs even harder. I have to go beyond the limit. Henry's back in front of me is flexing and straining with every stroke. To take my mind off the pain, I count the strokes of our push in my head: 'One, two, three, four, five . . .'

We are starting to creep away from the massive Cambridge crew. I hear a grunt of encouragement from Bas in the bows. It is only inches per stroke but we are definitely going faster than them. Our extra effort is taking its toll, though; my legs surge with lactate, my lungs sear with a massive oxygen debt. Whatever we are feeling, Cambridge must be feeling it worse, I tell myself.

James:
Fulham Bend, Oxford two men up

Out of the bend and on to the straight heading towards Hammersmith. I sense Oxford pushing, straining to keep on top of us. Their boat is inching ahead.

'They're pushing, boys, spending their chips. Hold! Hold!' Jim screams. 'On our rhythm.' Oxford are moving faster now, but there is a sense of control in our boat; we're waiting to spring the trap.

Now they have their nose ahead, Acer pulls to his left to push us off our line. Jim doesn't give an inch and again our blades overlap. Acer is feet away from me, screaming at the top of his lungs. The blades rip into the water at the catch and thump after the finish, drumming along the carbon fibre hulls.

'Oxford, move!! Oxford to Middlesex. Acer, move!' the umpire screams, 'OXFORD, move to Middlesex, NOW!' Acer grudgingly pulls away.

The moment Acer touches his rudder, Jim barks, 'Atomic push in two strokes.' We brace ourselves on the recovery up to the next stroke. 'Ready, NOW!' Together we unleash ten huge power strokes that Jims counts down. 'Give me that length!' he calls and we start moving.

David:

Mile post, Oxford three men up

'Three men up. Rate is 36½. Keep moving into the headwind.' If we can win this round up to Hammersmith, we might be able to deliver a knockout.

'Cambridge are pushing. Hold their push.' Cambridge have begun, slowly but steadily, to move back on us, without respect for the third of a length lead we worked so hard to obtain. I'm level with Kris Coventry in the four seat. Cambridge sense the advantage of their station looming into view. The inside of the mighty Surrey Bend will be worth at least half a boat length to them.

Acer's microphone crackles on. 'Coming up to Harrods Repository. Boys, we are going to have to defend round the Surrey Bend.' Our chances of winning the race early are over. Now we need to hold on for grim death on the outside of the long bend. To minimise our disadvantage, Acer steers closer to the Cambridge crew.

'Blades in close!' he shouts, warning us of possible clashing. I tighten my grip on my oar, ready for whatever they have to throw at us.

'Clash ten,' screams Acer. Both boats close up and interlock oars. At the finish of my stroke my oar hits McGarel-Groves's. It doesn't interrupt their rhythm.

Fuck off, Cambridge!

Boris is going mental, yelling and flag-waving. 'Oxford, Cambridge, move apart. Acer, MOVE!' He shouts again. The crews move apart. Cambridge are still coming through us, slowly but surely. I'm now level with Tom James, my opposite man. Each stroke we fight for every inch.

'YEAH!' screams Scott behind me to steel our nerve.

Six minutes in. Most races are decided by now.

'Every stroke, that's it,' Acer steadies us. 'Crisp, sharp.' I concentrate on being precise at the the catch. 'They're not moving, Oxford. They've got nothing left! Lever the backs off as one, ready.' He gives us a stroke to prepare. 'GO! Backs through. Backs through,' he calls in rhythm. We're fighting tooth and nail but we start losing ground again.

I imagine myself watching our race on Heather's dusty TV. The helicopter shot showing the long meander of the Surrey Bend. The bigger Cambridge crew on the inside punching out their lead. The younger Oxford crew digging in. The commentator remarking, 'Eighty per cent of the crews ahead at Hammersmith Bridge win the race.'

James:

Hammersmith Bridge, Cambridge four men up

My heart lifts with each stroke. Our big moves have worked. We inch further ahead every second. We can do this!

'Coming up on Hammersmith Bridge. I'm on my line,' Jim calls. Two strokes later the steel arches fly overhead. Ten strokes through the bridge we have them on the ropes. Surely now they will crumble. They can't keep up with us.

Now I'm up level with my old GB junior crewmate, Bas Dixon, in the Oxford bows. The green of the bridge recedes, and St Paul's School slipway appears on my right. We prepare to land the killer blow. As if sensing our imminent move, Acer pulls to his left and their bows cut towards our stern, and again the blades overlap.

'Clash ten,' Jim calls. I grip tighter as stroke after stroke my blade cuts past Bas's and chops into the water. On the next recovery our blades collide with a crack. His oar goes skyward while I dig mine into the water. Disappointingly, he recovers quickly enough to remain just about in time with his crew. If only his blade had caught in the water we could have moved to a comfortable lead.

David:

St Paul's, Cambridge six men up

Cambridge are ahead and out of my peripheral vision. I resist the temptation to look round. A wave of dread comes over me.

Are we going to lose this?

No sooner has the thought flashed into my mind, than I refocus on my technique. I will not give in.

'Boys, 35 on the rate. Keep it moving, Oxford.'

'Come on!' Henry breathlessly calls.

'Boys, Cambridge are using their advantage. Defend the bend. Don't give them one fucking inch.' Acer has to think for us now.

We're three quarters of a length down on the outside of the huge Surrey Bend. The situation is critical; we might lose the race in the next minute. Cambridge are trying to deliver the knockout blow.

Acer goes quiet for a few strokes, analysing the situation. Is he going to use our call of last resort?

'Boys, we need to move. 1963 in two . . . in one . . . GO!!' Acer bellows.

This is it, our last chance. I will not let my friends down.

Clamping my eyes shut, I go for broke. It's suicidal – there are still eleven minutes left and we're sprinting to save the race. The next 250 metres are all that matters to us now; we've put the next two miles out of our minds. I send down all I have for the sake of friendship. Everyone is putting in a similarly huge effort and our oars tear the water into lumps of foam. Matt feels our surge and raises the rate. We will not give up!

'YEAH! Thirty-six and a half and we're back on it,' Acer shouts. The rhythm of the boat has come alive. 'Now we're holding them!'

John lets out an encouraging scream, lifting my spirits and concentration. We're not giving up on our dream.

James:

Chiswick Eyot, Cambridge four men up

'Guys, we need to finish it now. Take our advantage. Finish them!' Jim barks.

Our bend has almost run its course.

'Go now,' I hear Tim say.

'Two-man move . . . ready.' Jim preps us for our breakaway move. 'Now!!'

'Yeah!' screams Matze. Again I steel myself and push as if these are the only ten strokes in the race, counting them off in my head.

On the fifth stroke I realise to my horror we are not moving away from Oxford. If anything, they are creeping up on us. I grit my teeth and give another huge five. Still they come.

'Oxford to Middlesex. Oxford to Middlesex,' the umpire calls, sounding exhausted and desperate. Oxford are leaning tightly on us as the last part of the bend unfolds.

The green island of Chiswick Eyot appears on our left and Oxford keep coming. We just can't shake them. I can feel an unspoken horror seeping through our crew. They're coming back. We've just had our best chance at victory. Now our bend is over. We have no more favours from the river. They're almost level.

My body is screaming at me to stop. I wish they'd just lie down and die. Some part of my subconscious even thinks Oxford suddenly being five lengths up wouldn't be such a bad thing. Anything so that the pain could be over. It doesn't stop, though. And they don't stop. They push into the lead.

David:

Chiswick Steps, Oxford one man up

'YEAH, BOYS, and we're still moving on them!' shouts Acer, hoarse and excited as we pull ahead. I feel another adrenalin surge in my muscles. 'We are back on it . . . thirty-seven, that's good.'

The Cambridge stern is in my view. I can't believe it!

'That's it, and we're still moving, their bend has run out, Oxford!

Oxford's year . . .. Oxford's year . . . Oxford, you're going to win this!'
A flash of belief runs through me.

The momentum is with us. The oars spear into the water faster and
easier. It's our best rowing so far – we're flying!

My body hurts desperately but the advantage is coming our way. The
Barnes bend will give us half a length if we use it well.

'Eyes wide open!' Acer's voice penetrates my subconscious. I open
my eyes, which were half closing. It is like I have been woken from a
deep sleep. I refocus and remind myself: rebound the hands around the
finish, lever the oar.

'And we're moving. Thirty-seven, YEAH!'

Don't take an easy stroke, I tell myself. Make them hurt.

I can tell Cambridge are feeling tired: the rhythmic thump of their
finishes is less pronounced, and fewer calls come from inside their
boat. We continue to move up, bit by bit. The possibility of winning
the race flashes into my mind like a magnificent vision but passes just
as quickly as it appeared. Cambridge are tough racers. We could still
lose.

The Bandstand flies past on our left-hand side. Four minutes left.

James:

Bandstand, Oxford five men up

The rising ecstasy at Hammersmith has plummeted to a growing
darkness as Oxford have built a lead. The cruelly sharp advantage of
their last bend is yet to come. Still, we fight to stay in the light. Our hope
has not been extinguished.

We pass the Bandstand and Jim calls desperately, 'OK. We're going to
have to do something special now, boys. How do we want to be
remembered?' He gives us two strokes to consider our legacy. 'For
Cambridge. For each other. Sprint, ready, now!!'

He is demanding our final sprint into the finish line, but we're still
four minutes from home.

My inner demons tell me I can't sprint now, I'll never make it. All our
bodies are racked with pain. Much of me wishes it were over. Together
we suppress the inner voices and push the rate up.

Oxford are now clear of me; I can only just see their stern in my peripheral vision. We are going to have to do what Oxford did to us last year. Row round the outside of Barnes bend, done only three times in the last century. It's a huge mountain to climb. Here we go.

David:
Barnes Bridge, Oxford five men up

'That's it, 35½. Legs spring, ready, GO! Eight of us on one of them. Eight of us on one of them,' shouts Acer. Our band of eight brothers will never give in. It only needs one of them to crack like last year and it's ours.

'Move the hands at the finish . . . eyes wide open, focus. Focus. Eyes wide open.' I force open my eyes, they'd begun to close again with the pain.

'Ready to take the bend . . . Clash ten, go.' I hit Ben's oar with mine, the vibrations shoot up my arms. I wish he would give up and let us win.

'They are trying to cheat by crashing into us, boys, just like Leander. Let's teach them a lesson.' The familiar profile of Barnes Bridge looms overhead. We have two-thirds of a boat length.

'Ready, steady, GO!' This is our call for home. 'Ready, STEADY, GO!'

I can't row another stroke, I want the pain to end. I just want it to be over. But I have to do it for the boys. The finish is coming. We can win this.

James:
Barnes Bridge, Oxford five men up

We're in the nightmare scenario, almost a boat length down on the outside of Barnes bend. I remember our guest Aussie coach, Tim McLaren, outlining this exact scenario and telling us, 'That's the hardest position you can find yourselves in and still be in the race. To win, that's what you've got to be prepared to do.' We'd looked at each other and winced at the impossibility of it. Now we're in that nightmare.

As the bridge recedes I can feel Oxford's puddles closer to our hull as both eights have been squeezed together through the middle arch. Both coxes fight for the best stream. The umpire is having none of it. 'Oxford to Middlesex! Cambridge to Surrey!'

Somehow Wooge has moved the stroke rate up again and I've gone with him, as I pledged to do at the start. His shoulders are stooped in pain. 'Yeah!' I manage to call breathlessly to remind him we're right there with him. A few strokes later, through it all, I notice Oxford have stopped moving further ahead; Acer's voice is at a constant volume and not drifting away any more.

We go again. Despite being flat out for at least fifteen minutes, the rate and power come up again. Desperation has hit the crew, a collective feeling of 'If not now, when?'

'We're moving! We're moving! You're doing it, boys.' Jim calls, hope startlingly back in his voice.

Slowly it gets through to my oxygen-starved brain that we have started coming back, but we're still half a boat length behind.

Acer's screams are sounding closer second by second, stroke by stroke. 'Crisp, sharp, Crisp, sharp,' he calls, but the tone in his voice has changed; there's a twinge of fear now.

Jim keeps calling us up and we keep responding. Where we find it from I don't know but somehow there is a response. 'Last 60 strokes of your lives!' I start to count down from ten in my head but it's too far and I almost break and give in. I don't think I can do another stroke. Then I see the green of the Mortlake brewery and I know we're almost there.

'Cambridge, everything you've got! Now!' Jim shouts himself hoarse.

'Let it be over!' my body screams.

'One minute!' Jim calls desperately, willing us on.

We are doing it, we're moving back on the outside of the bend! We crank like fury. This is superhuman. Impossible.

David:

Barnes Bend, Oxford three men up

'Forty strokes left in the race of your lives!' screams Acer. 'Hold, hold, hold.' I'm sending down all I have. How can they be coming back?

'We have to go again. Ready, go!' Acer sounds increasingly desperate. 'Ready, steady . . .' With gritted teeth I resolve myself to one last effort. 'GO!'

Matt and Henry launch again.

'Crisp. Rate 42,' screams Acer.

They shall not pass us.

I search but there is nothing left in the tank, I have nothing left.

I must find more.

Fuck, Cambridge are still coming back!

'Hold . . . Hold . . . HOLD!'

Twenty strokes left, I can do this. I can win this race. I summon up the very last bit of energy.

'Last ten. Keep moving.' I'm on the verge of passing out.

The crowd on the finish line has erupted.

Keep it going. Hold on. Fuck. Where's the finish?

James:

The Finish, Oxford two men up

Somehow, I'm level with Acer now. A stroke later it's Matt. God, we're going to do it. Up, harder, go. Sprinting and screams. My body and brain are shutting down. My hearing suddenly switches off and the cacophony of noise, coxes and roaring crowd vanishes.

Sight begins to go. Darkness envelops me until I can only vaguely sense the dark hulk next to us.

The finish line comes.

Then there is nothing. Inky blackness. My eyes have rolled back into my head. My chest heaves, frantically pulling oxygen into my gaping mouth, but I am out of it, collapsed and aware of nothing.

David:

Chiswick Bridge

I slump over my oar. It is over. The agony of the race is so deep, my breathing so hurried and lactate so prevalent that I don't know what's happened. I cannot think of anything apart from getting oxygen into my lungs.

Then, after a few moments my thoughts turn to the outcome.

I still don't know who won.

Looking up from my slumped state I see Acer, his head in his hands. We must have lost the race. Has this all been for nothing?

We sit silently, recovering from what has been the most physically destroying experience of our lives. No one knows what to do. Have we won or lost? The last nine months of training and the years before that: the sacrifices, early mornings, physical exhaustion, all day and every weekend in all weathers, even the torn relationship with my brother. Has it all been worth it? Have I beaten him?

James:
Chiswick Bridge

Light and noise come flooding back together. I push myself upright. Tim is slumped on his rigger, gasping. My eyes focus on the launch behind and the fraught umpire on the radio to the finish judge.

'Jim?' is all I muster. I see our cox is aghast, mouth pouting, his features wrung into an anguished mask. 'I think they got it,' he says quietly, with a flicking motion of his chin in Oxford's direction. Immediately, it feels like I've taken a body blow. Some hope still lingers though – Jim isn't certain.

The umpire is silent. Everything seems silent. Our boats drift together under Chiswick Bridge. We could reach out and touch each other. If we wanted to.

'THE VERDICT,' booms out the umpire's megaphone. He has everyone's attention. We are all roused from semi-consciousness.

'Oxford.'

Cambridge heads fall and hang limp on necks, sagging under the awful weight.

'One foot.'

Eyes widen and bulge in horror. Our desolation is total.

Part V

'Pain? Yes, of course. Racing without pain is not racing. But the pleasure of being ahead outweighed the pain a million times over. To hell with the pain. What's minutes of pain compared to the pain they're going to feel for the next six months or six decades. You never forget your wins and losses in this sport. YOU NEVER FORGET.'

From *Assault on Lake Casitas* by Brad Alan Lewis

Chapter 12
Nothing Else Matters

James:

Sunday 6th April, Chiswick Bridge

There is some half-hearted cheering from the other boat. One or two of them weakly punch the air in recognition of victory. Both sides are totally exhausted; some vomiting, some almost unconscious. Tim lies flat in front of me, gasping for breath, a giant slain. Oxford complete a breathless three cheers for Cambridge and our returning three cheers is even more rag-tag, and barely audible over the applause from the supporters lining Chiswick Bridge.

Slowly Oxford turn their boat and row to the bank to be greeted by their jubilant Isis colleagues. We drift on, deep in our own despair. 'One foot. One foot,' I realise I'm muttering under my breath.

One of the old wooden launches brimming with old Cambridge heavies idles past. There is clapping and a muffled, 'Well done, Cambridge.' Another voice, 'We're proud of you, Cambridge.' Amid the blazers and blue caps their sad, rubicund faces clearly read, 'You poor bastards.'

There's a deathly silence hanging over us. It already feels like an age since we crossed the line. The noise of the Oxford celebrations drifts over the water.

That was my last chance.

KC bravely breaks the quiet. 'Let's get in, Jim, no use sitting here.' The boat turns slowly and we pull a few mournful, and still shockingly painful, strokes. Muscle fibres are torn. Levels of lactic acid in the blood will still be rising as it works its way free of tortured muscle. As we reach the bank there is pitying applause. Goldie start to pull our boat into the bank by the oars but I can't sit any longer and just get out. The Tideway soup is up to my waist but I'm oblivious to the cold and the sharp stone river bed. Fresh blood glistens on the white shoulder of my lycra shirt; I don't know where it came from.

Goldie come down the shingle to meet us. They look aghast, shell-shocked, even though they just won a famous victory. As I congratulate Ellie on her win my breathing starts coming in gasps and I tug at the neck of my shirt, which suddenly feels tight round my throat. I stumble off and collapse as my airways constrict.

It's all over.

Visions and feelings flash before me. Me as a toddler sitting on my father's shoulders on the river bank, feeling safe and enjoying the cheering and the boats passing by. Cycling alongside the race as school kids with Dave. The last three years of struggle at uni. The Cherokee war cries of victory from Oxford last year.

The dream is over. Extinguished.

When I come to, I realise our physio and a medic are giving me oxygen. After a few moments I can breathe again but remain sitting on the shingle alone, quiet. Then a hand on my shoulder. It's Dave. I stand to meet him. He has a look of horror at what he's done. Somewhere his crewmates are whooping. I pull him to me and embrace him. It is too painful to let him see my face.

David:

Mortlake, Anglian and Alpha Boathouse

'I'm so proud of you,' he says, his tears dropping on to my shoulder. He holds his head in clenched white hands.

'I'm so sorry,' I reply gently. His tears only confirm my profound sense of guilt. How could I have done this to him? I hug him tightly, but I don't know what to say. I know there is nothing that will help take the pain away. He is my brother and it is awful to see him like this. The cuts are deep, open and raw. We could be ten years old again. Will he ever forgive me?

His last chance of winning is gone. It was all he'd wanted, trained for and thought about for years and I've taken that dream from him.

I admire and look up to him. Yes, I'd wanted to beat him to prove something to myself but now it seems too real and too hurtful to have been worth the pain it's caused.

If I hadn't pulled quite so hard and had thought of him, even for one stroke, he would have won. But then again I know I could never have done that: there is no way that I'd have ever let my Oxford crewmates down.

'I'm so sorry,' I say again. I feel the deepest sense of remorse, yet I know it cannot be undone.

How can he ever consider me his brother again? Tears well and roll down my cheeks.

He composes himself with a few deep breaths and takes his head off my shoulder. Then he brings his bowed head in close to mine. 'Enjoy it,' he whispers. It is such a massive gesture from my brother, especially when the wound is so raw. He still can't look me in the eye.

A reporter intrudes on the moment and after a few words to him we stumble back along the shore to rejoin our crewmates. My discomfort at seeing James doesn't leave me feeling celebratory, but then I see my happy crewmates and my mood starts to lighten.

'Right, everyone here? Ready?' Smithy says.

We grab Acer. I reach down and seize his right leg. Soon he's horizontal, held by the eight guys at either end like some human tug of war.

'One . . .' We swing him towards the shore and then back towards the water. 'Two . . .' God, he's light, all those bamboo shoots must have worked. 'Three . . .' We let go. Acer flies six feet into the air before splashing into the murky Thames.

He resurfaces drenched and stands up in the waist-deep water. 'YEAH!' he shouts, jubilantly punching the air, 'Woohoo!' Bottles of champagne apear from nowhere; suddenly we are surrounded by friends and relatives. I overhear John talking to his father about our response to the '1963' call. I can't help but smile at how we'd refused to lose. The party has begun.

James:

Mortlake, Anglian and Alpha Boathouse

There are some difficult interviews. I can't explain in words what this meant to me and how it feels to have it snatched away by my own brother. Dad finds me and gives me a huge hug. In his arms I can briefly be a child again, seven years old; he can shield me from it. The expression on his face is similar to Wayne's. Stoical; the pain caused by watching people you care very much for get hurt.

I overhear Wooge giving an interview. He is totally honourable and congratulates Oxford on what they have done today. I want to scream, 'If we hadn't crashed and lost Wayne we would have won! We were faster all year! It was ours!'

Our crew is corralled into a waiting area for the prizegiving by some TV girls. We would all love to click our fingers and get away from here. At one end of the tent a TV is showing the replay of the last moments of the race and we gather around it, horribly fascinated. We watch the bow of our boat ebbing and surging up, up and up on the Oxford bows. We're moving so fast, we must win. The boats get closer and closer. We're struck silent. We're going to do it!

Then the line comes. The Oxford bow crosses inches ahead. There's a collective gasp of dismay; we've all unconsciously been holding our breath. The TV switches to a slow motion replay of the last metres. One foot behind when the Oxford bow touched the digitally imposed line, we watch, frame by frame, as our bows come precisely level twelve inches after the line. Two feet past it and our boat is ahead. It's like watching a train wreck.

David:

Mortlake, Anglian and Alpha Boathouse

'Good afternoon, ladies and gentlemen,' says Steve Rider, interrupting our party. 'I am here to announce the winners of the 149th University Boat Race. By one foot. Oxford University!' The crowd erupts with claps and cheers and Matt leads us through the assembled mass of people up on to the stage. We are each handed a bottle of champagne and line up behind 'little' Steve, who is dwarfed by the five-time Olympic gold medalist, Steve Redgrave. I catch Sean's eye in the crowd in front of the stage; there's no trace of his usual cold exterior, he looks absolutely overjoyed. We'd executed the race of our lives and he's obviously proud to be our coach.

'I can't believe this, John, I just can't believe it,' I mutter to John Adams in front of me. It feels unreal; all those years of watching the race and now I am here, a winning Oxford Blue!

All the sacrifices: the early mornings, missed birthdays, unhappy tutors, relentless physical pain and exhaustion are worth it for this moment. It is an overpowering feeling of relief and joy; of completeness.

'Here to present the trophy to the winning president is Sir Steve Redgrave,' Rider finishes, passing Redgrave the microphone. Henry meanwhile stumbles to the floor, his legs giving out beneath him. I'm barely able to stand myself; we've rowed ourselves into the ground. I hold out my hand and help him back up. In the crowd I notice Bill and Vickers, who'd raced for Isis. The redness underneath their eyes tells of their savage disappointment. I wonder what went wrong.

Redgrave lifts the microphone, 'On behalf of the sponsors I would like to present the Boat Race trophy to Oxford University.' He steps back and lifts the massive silverware from its plinth and passes it to Matt, who thrusts it skyward. The crowd and our Isis crewmates cheer. We've done it!

Champagne sprays everywhere. Even Sir Steve, dressed in his finest, can't avoid it, to his obvious dismay. I pull Henry, upright once again, in close. 'Henry, we did it, we won.' He smiles breathlessly back.

The trophy is handed around, each of us savouring it for a few moments. Finally I have it in my hands. Just last week I'd been frowning over it for the cameras with James, and now it has been already been engraved:

'2003   Oxford   1 foot.'

I stare at the lettering. I still can't believe it. It feels as if I am going to be woken any moment by my alarm to go down to the gym for another ergo. After I've marvelled at it long enough, and given the trophy a sloppy kiss, I pass it on to a soaked Acer.

The revelries continue for a while but I decide to go and see James again. This time I find Matt and Ben talking amidst the miserable, desolate Cambridge camp. I give Ben a hug. 'I'm sorry, mate, it was a great race,' is all I can muster. He puts on a brave face. Four brothers, school mates, old friends and it has come to this.

The minibus is packed with girlfriends, family and all the crew too; Henry's girlfriend, Kath, sits on his lap so I can take a seat. As our chauffeur, Heather's son Chris, drives us out through the crowds, back towards his house, where the remaining friends and family are assembling, an extreme lethargy comes over me, as the adrenalin of winning begins to evaporate. I close my eyes and picture the final few strokes before crossing the line – hold on, hold on and then it is over.

Henry looks worse than I feel. After the race I'd helped him to the ambulance to get oxygen. As he lay there prostrate, Ben Smith, the Cambridge bowman, was helped on to the stretcher next to him. With oxygen masks clamped to their faces they leaned across and clasped hands, an acknowledgment of the experience we'd all just gone through. A shared bond had been created between them.

The minibus flies along the road towards Hammersmith. Stopping at the lights by a pub, I decide to rouse us from our stupor. I lean out of the window.

'Excuse me,' I shout to a couple of guys outside the pub, grabbing the attention of the bus, 'Do you know who won the Boat Race today?'

Taken aback slightly, one of them replies, 'Yeah, Oxford.' There's a chorus of cheers from inside the bus as the lights turn green and we screech off. I can just make out the laughter of the bystanders when they spot the OUBC insignia on the back of the bus.

All I can think about is seeing Maria and enjoying the party tonight. My phone shows tons of text messages, missed calls and answerphone messages. I see a text from Maria received a few minutes ago.

'WELL DONE DAVE!!! Such an amazing race. I am so proud of you!!! I can't wait to see you tonight! I love you. xxx'

'Henry, tonight is going to be awesome.' I turn and realise he's asleep.

The van turns into Heather's driveway. Applause breaks out as Matt enters the basement. Walking in, I see so many friendly faces: Jonny, Sally, and even Mum and Dad are here too. I break into a smile.

James:

Sunday 6 April 18:56, The Royal Overseas League, Piccadilly

As we enter the room reluctantly, heads bowed, hundreds of Old Blues and Goldies of all vintages turn from their conversations and clap our entry to the Royal Overseas League. The legends I grew up admiring are there. Today's racers wear the Blues and Goldie blazers while the vintage oarsmen wear black tie as a mark of respect. I wish I could be wearing the anonymous penguin suit tonight. Small gaggles of the old boys take each current oarsman aside, pat him on the back and start administering medicinal gin and tonics. Wayne, his white wrist-strapping poking glaringly out from the sleeve of his black dinner jacket, is taken in by one of the old Canadians.

In the grand dining room Tim, Robin and Wayne sit on the head table, alongside the most luminary or ancient Blues. The rest of the crew are dispersed, sitting morosely while old boys reminisce about old times and Goldie get steadily drunker. Robin looks absolutely broken, shell-shocked, at the centre of the head table. Nate, in contrast, is particularly happy. I wonder whether he's now glad that selection went the way it did? Andy Smith, the Moth, is over the moon; it's about the first time I've seen him smile in three months. He still can't quite believe his last-minute call-up from spare pair to Goldie to victory. Ellie is the toast of the dinner, not only because she's one of only three ladies present, but because she's radiating joy. A weight has come off her shoulders; I'm glad to see the ghosts of 2002 have left her.

Huge ornate honours boards line the walls and I distract myself by studying the names of old viceroys and lords of the subcontinent who were once members here. But I can't escape what is going round my head. What if we'd pulled that fraction harder for one single stroke? What if we hadn't crashed? What if we'd had Wayne on board? What if we'd pushed earlier and broken them at Hammersmith? What if we'd lost another hundred grams of fat each in the weeks up to the race? What if, what if, what if? Why not, why not, why not? It was so horribly within our grasp.

After the dessert is cleared, one of the greyer men on the head table stands and the chatter dies away. 'Members of the CUBC. Pray silence for your president.'

Tim stands, looking serious, brow furrowed.

'In sport we all take risks,' he begins. 'A Boat Race campaign is particularly unique. You may for example miss out on the boat you were aiming for. If you do make it then you risk losing the race itself. This experience, this offering oneself up, is shared throughout the room and connects us all.

'I would like to say another well done to Goldie. They really came together and showed true spirit.' He leads a round of applause. When that peters out he thanks the coaching team and Robin in particular. There is more applause. 'I would also like to recognise those from the 1943 crew who are here. They beat Oxford by four lengths.' Four of the oldest men sit creakingly to attention; one looks exactly like Charles Darwin. 'Their race took place at Ely, as London was under attack from my countrymen. My apologies.' It's good to hear some laughter.

The master of proceedings stands again. 'Thank you, Tim. I would now like to invite our head coach Robin to say a few words.' Robin gets to his feet, unable to hide his devastation with a polite smile.

'I'm at a bit of a loss as to what to say. Up to today we had a really good year. I'm not sure what I'd have changed. I'd like to thank Tim for leading us this year; we had a great working relationship. I would also like to recognise Jim, who really held it together after a potentially lethal crash. Rarely has a better course been steered on the Tideway than today's. Again, well done to Goldie for a very well-deserved victory.' There is more applause. Watching Robin is painful as it is obvious how much it all means to him. To prevent tears I stare at the mahogany board behind his head, listing donors who gave £30 towards the refurbishment of the Hall of India and Pakistan in time for Coronation Day 1937. His Exalted Highness, the Nizam of Hyderabad, Nawab Lutfuddowuh Bahadur, His Highness the Maharaja of Bikaner. What fantastic names.

Robin continues, 'Tim's right about risk. Sport always carries a risk, a risk of loss, of not performing, of not winning. But that's why it's so worthwhile.' I catch TJ's eye a couple of seats down. He has barely said a word all evening and looks bereft. I feel a brotherly pang. I should have looked after him. 'I would like to recognise two people in particular. Ben Smith; he took the last-minute call up in his stride and did a great job today.' There's a hearty round of applause. 'And also Wayne, for his stoicism in the face of his injury and for remaining truly part of the crew throughout. You didn't row today but we are as proud of you today as any in here.' The applause in the hall is deafening and TJ, Hugo, Matze, Jim and each of our crew stand to applaud him, with the rest of the room following us to their feet – even if some do have to use their walking sticks.

James:
Sunday 6 April 22:46, The Royal Overseas Lague, Piccadilly

After dinner the new and recent CUBC members filter out to board the bus to take us to the Boat Race Ball, where we will meet with girlfriends and friends, and get a fresh round of, 'I'm sorry it turned out like that,' and 'you did your best'. As the bus pulls away I find myself staring out of the window into the darkness, wondering why we never quite found the great rhythm we had against Croatia, when it felt like you were locked into the boat with the other guys and it couldn't be broken and you could just add to it and add to it.

'In the park she wheels a perambulator,' sing Goldie and some recent Blues behind me.

'She wheels it in the spring time and the merry month of May, hey, hey, hey.

'And if you ask her why the hell she wheels it, she wheels it for the Cambridge uni oarsman far, far away.'

'Far away,' sings Lukas.

'FAR AWAY,' sings the crowd.

'Far away.'

'FAR AWAY.'

'She wheels it for her uni oarsman far, far away.

'In the cupboard her father keeps a shotgun,

'He keeps it in the spring time and the merry month of May, hey, hey, hey,

'And if you ask him why the hell he keeps it, he keeps it for the uni oarsman far, far away . . .'

I think of seeing my Mum after the race. She couldn't face watching from a launch and so she watched with Sam, her parents, my old headmaster and other Cambridge friends and family at our boathouse in Putney. I'd just about got myself together, but when I saw Sam and then Mum, their tear-stained cheeks, I just broke down again. An outpouring of disappointment. Matze was the same when he saw his girlfriend.

At the Ball I meet up with Sam and a large contingent of old Hampton school mates waiting for Matt, Ben, Dave and me. It's like being back in the sixth form. I can see they're treading on eggshells around me, with concerned looks in their eyes. We continue drinking. I haven't had a private moment with Sam since the race, but the way she squeezes my hand says it all. Thankfully Oxford haven't arrived yet, obviously too caught up in their celebrations.

When I stumble to the loo I meet JA on his way back out to the bar. He drunkenly hugs me. 'I've got so much respect for you, ever since we were fifteen,' he slurs. 'You're the best, Bungle. You really are.' He is virtually hanging off me and I'm not particularly stable, but somehow we stay upright. In the toilet I find myself in a cubicle just repeating, 'Fuck, fuck, fuck.' That was my last chance. Their will conquered ours. My brother's will conquered mine. We were not physically beaten. We were mentally beaten. That it was by the slimmest of margins made it worse.

I go to wash my hands and in the cubicle next door I discover Jim passed out on the floor, being tended by Hugo and Wayne.

David:

Sunday 6 April 23:56, Notting Hill, London

I stumble out of the coach. My world is spinning thanks to the bottle of champagne I drank at the Blues dinner. It was a great event. Acer, sitting next to me, reiterated just what a superhuman effort we'd made in response to the 1963 call. We'd been true to our charter and to one another.

The dinner had also given us time for reflection and celebration. Matt revealed to us that he'd been ill with the flu for the last week in the run up to the race. Matt had not wanted to burden us with the news given there was nothing we could do about it. If anything this reaffirmed what a legend he had been. Whatever ups and downs we'd been through, the

Boat Race was all about one day and one performance. It was all about getting our bows across the line in front of Cambridge's. Who knew what challenges we'd face today – that's the nature of the Boat Race – but together we were the kind of crew that was prepared to do whatever it took to cross the line first.

At the entrance to the ball Jim the Martian, as we've been calling the Cambridge cox all year, is helped out of the door by Hugo and Matthias, his feet dragging on the pavement. He's unconscious. I sidestep the queue and walk straight in, flashing my blazer as currency.

In the hallway I see a number of familiar Cambridge faces and I feel a wave of anxiety at the prospect of seeing James again. Bas walks off ahead, probably searching for Ellie – now they can be seen together publicly.

Then I see her.

'Dave!' Maria exclaims excitedly, running up and kissing me. She looks absolutely stunning in her long ball gown. The night just got even better.

'It's so fantastic you won, baby, you were amazing.' Her voice sounds husky from screaming support. 'I'm so proud of you.'

'You're sweet,' I say, searching for words. 'Let's get some drinks!' I take her hand and lead her into the main room. Some Goldie oarsmen and their girlfriends dance to one side. James and Sam are drinking at one of the tables in the corner.

'Maria, I'm just going to say hi to James.' I approach him sheepishly. Outwardly he seems more composed than earlier. He looks up as I reach his table.

'Hi James.'

'Hey, would you like to join Sam and I for some champers?' he asks generously, but when I see his face up close the guilt rushes back. I turn and beckon Maria over.

Sam smiles politely at me as she pours a glass, 'Well done, Dave,' she says, handing it to me. It's nice of her after what I've done to the person she loves. Maria brings another bottle to replenish the ice bucket. A few glasses later we're all dancing around together. Win or lose we are at least acting like brothers again.

James:
Monday 7 April 11:28, London

Consciousness dawns. The defeat hits me and I wish I could have stayed asleep. I wrestle my eyes open from the glue that seems to have been poured on them in the night. I tear my tongue from the roof of my mouth. I remember Sammy's old saying for this stage of a hangover, 'a tongue like Gandhi's flip-flop'.

I don't recognise the room. It's rather smartly decorated. I look to the sleeping figure on my right. Sam's still asleep. I slump back and try to take in my surroundings again with as little movement as possible. Just moving my eyes in their sockets results in unpleasant shooting pains across the surface of the eyeballs.

Sam rolls over and smiles at me, bleary-eyed. This sparks off a flashback of last night, more a feeling than an actual memory. A stabbing pain in the shoulder as I fall badly into a taxi. Dave and Sam squeezing in next to me. Maria in the front giving directions to her family's house in Belgravia. I look around the room again with new-found recognition.

I cuddle Sam and we are both sighing about how hideous we feel when the phone on the bedside table rings, an odd electric buzz. Sam picks up, guessing correctly it's an intercom meant for us.

'Yes, pretty bad too. Yes. Yes, we'll be down in ten minutes,' she says in a faux chirpy voice.

'Breakfast,' she says to me. I look at my watch. Almost half eleven. Sitting up results in something horrible turning in my stomach and an immediate return to the horizontal. The phone rings again and Sam picks it up to prevent the ringing drilling further into our heads. This time it's not Maria. Sam frowns and hands me the phone, the look on her face telling me to sit up.

'Hello, is Mr Wright there?' says a formal, American-accented male voice. Shit. Maria's dad doesn't even know we're staying and now we're answering his business calls. 'Er, I'll just get him,' I reply hoarsely. Shit!

I race out of the room to find Maria, realising as I stand on the landing that there are many rooms in the large town house and I have no idea which she'll be in. Then a door opens in front of me and a blond GCSE-aged schoolboy walks out. He looks me up and down, utterly bemused. I glance down to my bare chest and purple-checked Calvin Klein boxers.

'Er,' I say, which doesn't improve matters. 'There's a phone call for your f-father.' I try to adopt a stance that doesn't suggest near-nudity. 'A business call, I think,' for what it's worth.

The boy's expression asks, who is this nearly nude, battered-looking bloke standing on the landing and answering Dad's business calls?

'I'll get him,' he says finally, keeping his eyes on me until I retreat gratefully back inside the room.

I describe the scene to a giggling Sam as we dress quickly to prevent further embarrassment. Sam's ball dress and my dress shirt look rather the worse for wear and there are a variety of new stains added to my already patchwork Blues blazer, none of which I remember adding. I try to vomit in the beautifully appointed marble bathroom in an attempt to clear the nausea but can't. Then we make our way downstairs.

After a perfunctory 'breakfast' of tea, Mum arrives and drives us home. We have to stop the car a couple of times for me to be sick. When we get home I head up to the bathroom to throw up again, passing piles of newspaper sports pages with headlines proclaiming the closest Boat Race of all time and Oxford's triumphant giant-killing. When I look up from the bathroom sink I see a TV crew setting up in our garden to interview Mum and Dad. As the numbness of the hangover wears away, the reality of the defeat dawns in its full horror. That was my chance. There will never be another. I can't rerun it.

David:
Thursday 10 April 17:58, Strawberry Hill, Twickenham

Days have passed since the race. I keep replaying it in my head, over and over, elated – momentary diversions from revision at home for my end of year exams. Looking back, it seems as if our win was meant to happen. Against the odds, my Oxford brothers and I had done it – we'd won.

Finally I feel free; no longer trapped by my desire to win, to beat James, and no longer caged in by training and preparation. But if I thought that winning the Boat Race would bring me unbridled joy, I was wrong. For the few days that James and I were both home together before he went back to Cambridge, I avoided him: each time I saw him I was hit by a disturbing and conflicting wave of emotions, the most powerful of which was guilt. Despite his forced smile for me, I could see the real story of disappointment in his lifeless eyes. There was no room in the Boat Race campaign for split loyalties. On race day I thought I hated him, that I wanted to crush him and his dream in order to achieve mine. But he is still my brother and I love him; I realise that now more than ever.

I must speak to him, must tell him how much I admire and look up to him, but I cannot yet manage it face-to-face. Without waiting another moment I grab the nearest pencil and begin to write.

James:

Saturday 12 April 11:54, St Catz, Cambridge

Silence blankets the library. Theories of organisational design stare back at me from the page. Management studies had allowed me one last attempt to realise my dream and now I have to pay back all it has given me, with interest. The St Catz management students have selected the older, more classic Sherlock library to swot in this year. Smaller and less easy to get to, it is almost crypt-like after dark with its intricate wood panelling. It lacks the Formica and vending machines of the college's other booky den we used last year.

It is difficult to focus though I know I must. Part of me is liberated, a huge commitment lifted. I can choose when and how I live my life, even though it is mostly revision right now. Another part of me is empty. Lost. I absentmindedly start fiddling with the red leaves of the pot plant, christened 'the love fern', which Sam bought me to brighten my desk.

In the first few days after the race I withdrew into myself, plagued by a new set of 'what ifs'. What if we hadn't crashed? If we could move so much faster than them on the final bend, why could we not have done that at Hammersmith Bridge and broken away from them when they were on the ropes? How could the finishing judge be sure of one foot difference? After all, he was standing on the roof of an un-anchored boat that gets buffeted by the tide. Sure, the driver tries to keep the judge aligned with the line between the Post and the Stone but surely he's not inch perfect?

Was the BBC television camera actually right on the finish line? There was no photo finish machine but I'd heard they're now putting one in for next year. Were we perfectly level at the start? I doubted it. One more stroke and we would have won. I'd scribbled some calculations on my manufacturing throughput notes: one foot was a 0.0043 per cent difference between the boats after four and a quarter miles.

Everyone I knew said what a great race it was and offered their condolences, but I could not escape a sense of resentment. Surely by rights it should have been the elder brother's turn, on his last attempt, his bowing out? Dave had more years before him.

Now the accusations have settled down to be replaced by a persistent doubting of everything about myself. All the little neuroses that sit in the dark recesses of the mind, waiting for a quiet moment to haunt, have been fleshed out, become paralysingly real. Clearly I just don't have it in me to win.

I've done a lot of reading. A couple of lines in *Catch-22* seem poignant.

'To Yossarian, the idea of pennants as prizes was absurd. No money went with them, no class privileges. Like Olympic medals and tennis trophies, all they signified was that the owner had done something of no benefit to anyone more capably than everyone else.'

Well, I'd done something of no benefit to anyone infinitesimally worse than my younger brother and his crewmates. Why did it matter? Because we cared about it so much. Why did we care? Because of how much we put into it and how, in the end, his band of brothers had beaten mine. His belief in the Oxford way was founded and mine in Cambridge flawed.

I couldn't choose not to care. If you stop caring where does it end? A smile becomes just teeth. Children? – a biological inevitability. Love? – a release of hormones in the brain. Death? – the balancing of the equation.

In some ways more hurtful than the race outcome is the fact that our crew has split to the four winds, each of us turning to salvaging our degrees and dissertations. It's more than no longer being together for six hours a day and on a shared mission. We are avoiding one another. Privately, some are blaming others for the result. At least if our easy fraternity had remained intact those friendships would be one tangible result to our efforts. Instead we've all retreated to our libraries and labs.

The shadow of a bird flits across the sunny green court below and I realise I've been staring out the window for the last ten minutes. I need to distract myself from my distraction. I head down and across the main court, past the in-bloom flower boxes. The new Master of the college is a botanist by background and appears to have inspired the gardeners. The red-brick porters' lodge glows in the late spring sunshine and I head in, down the stairs to the pigeonholes. I rifle through my post and an odd letter catches my eye as I re-emerge into the sun. A blue slip, carefully folded and glued. No stamp.

Back at my desk I push operations management, marketing and accountancy to one side and quietly tear along the perforations, trying not to disturb the hard-working hush of the library.

When it's opened I scan to the bottom. Joe. Recollection takes a few seconds. I got to know him a couple of years ago; we both ended up looking after a mutual friend after his 21st birthday and a timed yard of ale. Joe was at Corpus Christi College and boxed for the university. I remember going for a curry with him and our friend. I remarked that he 'was a marine' for tucking into his Phal with such aplomb, one forkful having reduced me to tears. He replied, 'I am actually', grinning from ear to ear. And now he was in Basra, a million miles away from Cambridge, the May Bumps and curries on Castle Mound. People are getting killed over there, in that desert hell, for a war that most Brits don't believe in.

Dear James,

This must come slightly out of the blue but I listened to your race on the BBC World Service while on a rooftop in Basra and I just had to write to you. I am so sorry about the result, but remember, you must be rightfully proud of what you've done, what you've been part of. Out here you appreciate England and its traditions.

I'm doing OK. We've seen a bit of action here, contacts with small arms fire and some mortars. My section are staked out on the same roof tonight and we're expecting a hit on this place later. Remember, keep your head up and be proud. I know you gave everything you could and in life that is what matters. Must sign off now, just got some intel over the radio that a crowd is developing and heading towards our position.

Let's go for a curry with Bottomley when I'm back.

Joe

I read it and reread it. Then I read it again. Then I pass the letter over to Belita, the Moth's girlfriend and a fellow MST student, who's been watching my reaction to the odd-looking letter. It is odd. A guy I met a few times, and who, to be honest, I really didn't know that well, had written to me, whilst in mortal danger, to say bad luck about the Boat Race. I should be writing to him, not him to me. I can't help laughing out loud at the madness of it. 'Don't worry about me, Joe, sounds like you've got enough to worry about yourself!'

Unwilling to return to accounting just yet, I flick through the remaining post. Something from the bank, something from Orange, and then an envelope with my brother's handwriting. I rip it open. We haven't really been able to talk since the race. It's written in pencil.

James,

I just thought that I have to write this note to you explaining how sorry I am that one of us had to win on that Sunday. You are so much the better man; just look how well you have taken it. You have been great about it. Rowing is a big part of our lives but it is NOT our lives.

Yes, it must feel very difficult to lose and have me around but whether you lose or win a race does not dictate who you are. You are a great brother and it is awesome, a privilege, to be your bro. You also have a lovely girlfriend and a great set of friends. They are not there because you are a good rower.

Your brother,

Dave

Postscript

2008

James:

It's now five years since that fateful day in April 2003 when my brother tasted victory by the slimmest of margins. The evening after getting his letter I gave Dave a call to thank him and we actually talked about what was going on for each of us, which we hadn't done in months. On reading his letter I realised we'd never actually spoken about our relationship as brothers before, we'd just got on with it, doing what brothers do, growing up together, fighting, playing, competing, obsessing about the same things. Eventually, though, our shared obsession had come between us. People say you don't know what you've got till it's gone. They're right. It took the race and almost losing what we had to make me think about life from the perspective of a younger brother. Things between us didn't heal overnight; it's taken years, and distance from our respective universities and the race. In fact, writing this book together has been the best form of therapy. We managed not to have any fist fights, which must be a good sign.

A couple of weeks after receiving those letters I asked TJ to row with me in a pair at senior GB trials. This meant TJ was bypassing the normal route of several years of under-23 trials, trying to skip directly from junior to senior ranks in twelve months; almost unheard of. We raced with utter abandon, driven by the anger of our recent defeat and without any shackles of pressure. We surprised the selectors and ourselves by making the final, beating the two Oxford Blue Boat pairs along the way, which was, it must be said, extremely satisfying. Every other pair in the final had a world or Olympic gold medallist on board. We went for it, leading everyone to the 250-metre mark before being overhauled and coming sixth in Great Britain, which booked us slots in the national team. It came just at the right time, persuading me that I was fundamentally good enough to win the Boat Race but the dice just didn't roll our way.

After some more trials TJ was selected to stroke the British eight while I took up the bow seat of our coxed four. After my four almost broke the world record in training we knew we were moving rapidly. Unbeaten, we lined up for the final of the World Championships in Milan, on a lake built by Mussolini for his Second World War flying boats, alongside the also-unbeaten US coxed four. They led from the start and we had to throw everything into the chase, sprinting for home from a long way out. It was just us and them; the rest of the field fighting for bronze. As we reached the grandstand with 200 metres to go and slipped past them. I even managed a rictus smile. Then, with 100 metres to go, they went up another gear and with 50 metres to go they passed us and took the gold. They were stroked by an Oxford man from the 2002 crew, back to haunt me.

While we must have looked gutted on the medal podium, just a few hours later we were reflecting happily. We'd raced as hard as we could and done a good job. At the athletes' party that evening, by the side of the course, it felt to me like Cambridge had just won the Boat Race. Josh, Rick, Stu Welsh, and Tom Stallard from the 2002 Blue Boat had all done well in the GB coxless four, Aussie coxless four and GB coxed four respectively. TJ had stroked the British eight to a surprise bronze medal. Wayne, rowing with Scott Frandsen, made the final of the pairs. Sam flew out and we spent a few great days in Milan afterwards.

Two weeks later TJ and I started training with the national team full-time in the run-up to the Olympics, funded by National Lottery grants, which have had a hugely beneficial effect on UK sport. I wrote a nice letter to my future employer, asking to defer my start date for another year, and I got a nice letter back telling me OK and good luck. TJ managed to put his second year at university on hold. The training was back-breaking. Two, three or four sessions a day. One day off a month – after all, your body doesn't know when it's a weekend or a bank holiday. A simple life. Train your body to total exhaustion during the day, gorge between sessions, then pass out on the sofa until bed.

Winter faded into spring and it was Boat Race time again. Wayne had turned down the opportunity to remain in Canada and try for the

Olympics and had been voted in as president for the 2004 campaign. He was joined in the Blue Boat by Hugo and Kris Coventry again, plus Nate, Andrew Shannon, Buschbacher and Chris Le Neve Foster, who graduated up from Goldie. Sebastian Mayer, of my 2002 crew, made a brave comeback and was vital to pushing the crew onwards in training. Unfortunately Ben Smith had suffered with illness over the winter and had missed out; 2003 was his only Boat Race.

The honour of dropping the finishing flag fell to me as one of the previous year's crew. Sam, Ellie and big Josh from the 2002 crew joined me on the finish judges' launch and we were glued to my father's minute portable television with a screen four inches square to watch the initial stages of the race. Oxford, with Dave at six once again, surged into the lead off the start and I found myself screaming at the tiny screen for Cambridge.

After a couple more minutes Cambridge inched back level and there was a major clash of oars. The Oxford bow man was knocked clear of his seat and Cambridge shot into the lead. With the bowman struggling to fix his seat, it became clear that Oxford would suffer a momentous defeat. I felt the strangest emotions as I waved Cambridge home, cheering at Wayne's and the other boys' victory. Oxford, Sean Bowden and the whole dark blue attitude had lost. Cambridge was victorious again. Then I turned to see Oxford struggling home. I dropped the flag for the second time and my heart broke for Dave as I saw his blond mop sink. It was the darkest moment of his life. I felt his pain; I knew exactly what he was going through, and he was my little brother.

While I was very happy for the guys – Seb in particular – the Cambridge dinner that night was bitter-sweet for me and probably for all those that had lost in that room as well. Listening to the celebrations, I knew that if I'd found another course, and done another year at Cambridge, I too could have enjoyed a victory. During Wayne's superb presidential speech I toyed with the idea of coming back, standing for president, and leading the most committed and burning squad. I could do a PhD – I was sure I could find a good subject. After that I could move on with my life.

But first I would focus on trying to make the Olympics. I trained 110 per cent every session to try to make my mark, got injured a few times, and ended being close to but fairly missing out on the British eight by a couple of seconds. I went to the World Championships again and then straight on to the Athens Olympics in the spare pair. It was fantastic but I never once felt nearly as nervous as Boat Race day.

A week after the Olympic closing ceremony I started work at a strategy consultancy in London, having decided it was time to get on with life and get over the Boat Race. I retired from the sport at my peak, knowing I was unlikely ever to win an Olympic gold. In the national team there was extensive scientific testing, even more than at Oxford or Cambridge – lung capacity, VO2 max, lactate tolerance, peak power, haematocrit count – the list goes on and on. Most Olympic gold medallists had at least one freakish, innate physical quality: maybe ten-litre lungs, maybe a heart so big they have a resting pulse of 28. All were mentally as hard as iron, of course. I was bigger and stronger than average but not off the chart in any respect.

My consultancy job was interesting and different, and it was great to meet new people. Being back at the bottom of the ladder, however, having risen to almost the top of my little sporting world, was tough. And not knowing everything, or indeed much at all, was disconcerting. For three months I sat at a desk and happily took no exercise at all. Then I read the Trial Eights' report in the paper and the lure of the Boat Race started to work on me. I reconsidered going back to do that PhD – returning to the environment I knew and was at the top of, back to the freedom that university allows. It was extremely tempting. Plus of course there was the appeal of escaping office politics, mortgages, fighting with builders and the other trappings of adulthood. Most of all I missed spending half my day with twenty of my best friends. But to go back would have been to live in the past. Time moves on and people should too.

Sam and I braved it together. As Sam came to London for a pupillage at the Bar and her first hard years as a family law barrister, we were there for one another, ready to laugh together or listen to one another's troubles. Lots of our friends set up lives and careers in London. Bas and Ellie put their university allegiances behind them, moved in together round the corner from Sam and I, both now lawyers. Groves became something in property. Wooge went into banking. KC returned to the sunshine of Oz and Jim to the USA. Dave joined us in London after a couple of years. It was great to have him back.

Wayne moved in with girlfriend Morgan. They soon married, with Matze and Hugo as groomsmen and the rest of the crew present as guests. Wayne and Morgan had been long-time friends at Harvard and in her wedding speech she said the seeds of something more were sown around the 2003 Boat Race, seeing the way Wayne dealt with his injury. Matze recently got engaged to Laura, one of Morgan's bridesmaids, whom he had met at Wayne's wedding. Perhaps the crash had been for the best after all.

Each March, Matze, Wayne, Hugo, Groves, Wooge and I got together to cheer on young TJ, who raced in three further Boat Races. He lost two more but then, on his last attempt and as president, he won, which was richly deserved. The next year the quiet, thoughtful TJ went on to win a gold medal for Great Britain at the Beijing Olympics in the coxless four, with me, Sam, Dave and others screaming from the stands. Months later TJ says it still hasn't sunk in. Robin, who had been headhunted in 2006 to coach the GB lightweight team after eleven years at Cambridge, guided his squad to their best ever set of Olympic results.

The week after Beijing, Sam and I got engaged, on a beach in Borneo. We're going to get married next year in our Cambridge college chapel. Dave is going to be Best Man.

While the result of our Boat Race can never change, our relationship has. It took our shared obsession and opposing factions to reveal our innate competitiveness and push us so far apart that we could see what we meant to each other. We are all the closer now we understand what drives us both.

Still, I know I'll always be down by the river on Boat Race day, willing Cambridge to victory. If they lose I will be depressed, unhappy that the dark blue view of life reigns supreme for another year. If Cambridge win I'll be happy but also envious as they cross the line and hands go up in triumph. That will be my curse and I'll be sullen until the Blues dinner later that evening, when I'll sit with those of my era and talk of the old days and remember that while we may not have achieved the victory I so longed for, we are blessed with the deepest of friendships and respect for one another – far more important than any three-letter or four-letter word.

David

After I wrote the letter, life somehow became easier. I left my angst and competition with James behind. I had walked my own path. I'd been successful. If I hadn't won I might never have escaped his shadow. But seeing him upset, because of me, also made me realise how much I appreciated him.

Some two years after racing James, my life at Oxford University and my love affair with the Boat Race terminated with my graduation. Being a Blues rower and studying at Oxford had been a sacred experience which had forged lifelong friendships and helped me learn a great deal. But it was time to move on.

That summer I rowed for Oxford for the last time at Henley and very narrowly lost in the prestigious Grand Challenge Cup, against the German national eight. Three weeks later I represented Great Britain at the World Under-23 Championships in Amsterdam. After that I moved all my belongings home and went travelling with Maria to Malaysia.

When I returned my identity was gone. I was no longer part of Oxford University Boat Club. No longer 'Big Dave, the Blues rower'.

I didn't expect the change to bother me. I was still rowing. Living at home, I had started training full-time at Molesey Boat Club, just upriver from Hampton Court. Like James, my aim was to try to win World Championship medals and perhaps one day make the Olympics.

It was an odd training group, but one that seemed to work. Clive, ex-marine hard man from the north, would tell us stories from his various tours of duty, always beginning with, 'No word of a lie, right, Dave'. Rob the East End waterman, who referred to his face as his 'Boat Race'. Then there was Ocky, a single-minded single sculler who managed a farm somewhere nearby. On the odd occasion we would even see Stevo, who turned his house into a Christmas pudding factory to support his rowing training.

This strange team went through a punishing seven-day-a-week, three-sessions-a-day regime. Sure, I was getting stronger and fitter but life was certainly a little less interesting. I still had no money or time to do fun things or see Maria, and now I'd lost my university status. In early November I wangled a precious weekend off and drove up to visit Maria. It was a good weekend, but little did I know that it was the start of the end of our almost four-year-long relationship. In the following weeks we began to talk less, and instead of her normal, happy and carefree self, she sounded upset. I knew something was up. Then she announced suddenly that she would come to see me on Friday afternoon. When I asked her what was wrong, she said she'd tell me then, before breaking down in tears.

I went rowing as usual the next morning. The coach shouted at me to make technical changes but I barely even heard him, I was so deep in thought. Had I sacrificed my relationship with Maria for this stupid sport? I cycled home, showered and changed. I walked down to the local parade of shops and bought a dozen red roses. She was to arrive at one-thirty that afternoon. I stood in the street, flowers in hand, card written, stomach churning, waiting for her. I hoped this wasn't the end. I still loved her. She had been there through it all with me: the wins, the losses, the good times and the bad.

Through tears, she did finish it. Her reasons were understandable: she wanted some time apart, to be independent while she was young. I understood but it made it no easier to swallow. I felt crushed. I got straight on the train up to central London and went out with some of my closest friends: Henry, Bas and the OUBC boys. James changed his plans to come and console me. And over the course of a drunken evening I decided that it was over between me and rowing too. I didn't know what I wanted but I knew that it wasn't to train endlessly. I blamed the sport for what had happened between Maria and me. Now I wanted to enjoy the life that I had missed out on before.

But I was at sea. After all, you construct your identity from the people you have around you and the things you do, and this construction, I was now discovering, was much more transient that I'd ever imagined. The inevitable party question of 'What do you do?' – I hated it. It seemed to fix your place in the social hierarchy and define you as a person. I was now an unemployed ex-rower, living with his parents. A nobody. Would I ever find anything that meant as much to me as the Boat Race? Would my fifteen minutes of fame mean the rest of my life was doomed to pale into insignificance? For a while I drank to help numb the pain. To forget.

Outwardly I soon seemed fine. I found myself a job at a finance firm in Battersea fairly quickly. I was going out most nights, meeting people, dating new girls, having a good time. But on the inside I was still deeply confused. I wondered if all the past rowing Blues had gone through this emotional void after their time at Oxford, having to redefine themselves as new people with new goals and passions. Of my 2003 crew, those that weren't still rowing with Olympics aspirations had thrown themselves into new challenges at high-powered investment banks or law firms. All except John Adams who, impervious as ever to worldly pressure and true to his own internal direction, had settled down with his wife Emily and become a teacher.

Time passed, though, and things improved. I saw lots of Mum, Dad and James, whose view of me never wavered, even while my view of myself did. I moved in with Reevo, Henry Morris, Nick Tuppen and other OUBC guys, and while we reminisce about the old days a bit, we're all absorbed in new challenges. This summer we all went out to Beijing together to cheer on Acer, BT and Scott. James and Sam came out too to support old Cambridge crewmates. It was nice to finally cheer the same flag. Scott determinedly raced his way to a silver medal – Canada's first medal of the Games. Acer coxed the GB eight with James's old crewmates Josh West and Tom Stallard, to an amazing silver medal. Sally was there too to cheer on her new boyfriend, and my ex-pairs partner, Peter Reed, who along with Tom James won gold in the GB coxless four.

The Olympics reminded me of our eternal bond and although we're now scattered – with Scott living with his beautiful fiancée back in Canada and BT serving his country as an army officer – our pride will never leave.

I'd found an exciting job and a great new girlfriend. I'd gained perspective – I didn't have to benchmark myself against my latest rowing race, or my brother. London was a fantastic city to be young in. Life had changed and I embraced it.

2009

David:

The Kings Road is busy with mid-morning shoppers. The crisp, cool air of early summer rushes through my hair as I cycle through the traffic. Reaching Edith Grove I pull right on to the pavement and park my bike against the railings. I buzz the intercom – what a great new place this. Nicer than my tired Clapham digs.

James buzzes me in and into the shared hallway.

Their door swings open to reveal James in cycling shorts and Athens Olympics T-shirt. 'Hi, bro! Hold on, I'll just grab my stuff.' Their cat Charlie sprints past in a scared blur.

'There's the Best Man!' says Sam, appearing in the doorway, immaculately presented as always.

'Hey, Sam. Congratulations again.' I bend down to give her a hug and a kiss on the cheek. Over her shoulder I notice a multitude of cards along the mantelpiece. James fumbles out of the spare room with his racing bike.

'See you later,' he says, kissing her.

'Bye, Sam,' I say, retreating down the steps.

We cycle off slowly to Putney together, laughing about the plans for the stag party, hotly touted to be in Las Vegas.

At the boathouse the Thames is calm; the sun shining. Climbing the spiral staircase into Crabtree, we find the door is already open. Matt sits inside, ready to go rowing. 'Hey, guys.'

'What's up, Smithy,' James says as they high-five.

'Where's Ben?' I say.

Matt raises an eyebrow. 'Some party last night.' Nothing changes.

We head downstairs to prepare the boat. A few minutes later Ben screeches in. 'Wowwwee, last night was full on!' He runs upstairs to change. Matt and James exchange the knowing look of older brothers. I guess Ben and I will never escape it.

Soon we're out on the water. James sits in front of me in his light blue lycra. Matt, in front of him, leads us. He left Oxford as one of the most acclaimed strokemen in the history of the Boat Race – even 'office fit' he sets a great rhythm.

The boat flows gloriously over the water. Out here we are free; no thoughts of jobs or house-buying or anything else. Just open air, flat water and the Zen of exercise. We're not rowing for any particular reason or race. Just fun, like in the old days before it all got complicated.

We stop under Hammersmith Bridge for Ben to take his top off so he can work on his tan. Looking up at the bridge, I think of April 2003 and how I hated the man now in front of me. My own flesh and blood and near constant companion since birth, and now best friend. I'm thankful for what the race taught us but I'm glad we've moved on. We row off again. I catch myself instinctively eyeing the puddle left by his oar and comparing it with my own. A smile goes across my face – I realise I'll never quite let go of my competition with James. But whatever comes between us we'll always be brothers.

Crew Lists

	Cambridge	Oxford
Cox	Jim O'Martian (23) 5'6" American (Harvard & St Catharine's)	Acer Nethercott (25) 5'8" British (Mark Hall & University)
Stroke	Tim Wooge (30) 6'7" German (Northeastern & Peterhouse)	Matt Smith (21) 6'1" British (Hampton & St Anne's)
7	James Livingston (22) 6'5" British (Hampton & St Catharine's)	Henry Morris (20) 6'0" British (Radley & Magdalen)
6	Thomas James (19) 6'3" British (King's Chester & Trinity Hall)	David Livingston (19) 6'7" British (Hampton & Christ Church)
5	Alexander McGarel-Groves (22) 6'6" British (Eton & Peterhouse)	Robin Bourne-Taylor (21) 6'3" British (Abingdon & Christ Church)
4	Kristopher Coventry (25) 6'5" Australian (Melbourne & Queens')	Scott Frandsen (22) 6'1" Canadian (University of California & St Edmund's Hall)
3	Hugo Mallinson (23) 6'5" American (Harvard & St Catharine's)	Samuel McLennan (23) 6'2" Australian (University of Wisconsin & Corpus Christi)
2	Matthias Kleinz (27) 6'2" German (Tilemannschule Limberg & Gonville and Caius)	Basil Dixon (21) 6'2" British (Bedford & Pembroke)
Bow	injured: Wayne Pommen (23) 6'1" Canadian (Mt Douglas & Pembroke) replacement: Ben Smith (19) 6'3" British (Hampton & Trinity Hall)	John Adams (20) 6'4" British (Eton & University)
Coach	Robin Williams	Sean Bowden

Acknowledgements

We would like to thank our mother and father, and those friends who read drafts of this book, whose feedback helped immensely. Thanks also to crewmates for permission to quote from personal correspondence. For their vibrant photos, many thanks to Wayne Pommen, Matthias Kleinz, Mark Hall, Sam McLennan, Scott Frandsen, Henry Morris and, of course, Dad. *The Oxford and Cambridge Boat Race 1829–1953* by R. D. Burnell (OUP, 1954) provided useful information on the early history of the Boat Race.

James would like to thank fiancée Sam in particular, for putting up with the demands of the other love of his life (rowing, in case anyone's wondering) and then being so supportive when the demands of rowing lowered only to be replaced by the demands of writing a book about rowing.

David would like to thank his older brother for helping him find purpose and his friends for always being there. James would like to show his appreciation for Dave – his best friend, Best Man and little brother all rolled into one.

Thanks to our literary agent David Luxton of Luxton Harris for his friendship and support, and also to Andrew Longmore for the introduction.

At Bloomsbury our thanks go to Michael Fishwick, Colin Midson, Alexa von Hirschberg, Kate Tindal, Sarah Morris, Ruth Logan and Trâm-Anh Doan. We are grateful to Mike Jones for banging the table for this book to be published. And especially huge thanks to Victoria Millar and Anna Simpson for their advice, gentle editorial nudging and saint-like patience.

Finally, we are indebted to all those in the coaching teams and squads of the 2002/2003 Oxford and Cambridge University Boat Clubs.

Index

A Note on the Type

The text of this book is set in Bembo. This type was first used in 1495 by the Venetian printer Aldus Manutius for Cardinal Bembo's *De Aetna*, and was cut for Manutius by Francesco Griffo. It was one of the types used by Claude Garamond (1480–1561) as a model for his Romain de L'Université, and so it was the forerunner of what became standard European type for the following two centuries. Its modern form follows the original types and was designed for Monotype in 1929.